WHAT DO YOU SEE WHEN YOU LOOK IN THE MIRROR?

WHAT DO YOU SEE WHEN YOU LOOK IN THE MIRROR?

Helping Yourself to a Positive Body Image

THOMAS F. CASH, PH.D.

BANTAM BOOKS

NEW YORK   TORONTO   LONDON   SYDNEY   AUCKLAND

WHAT DO YOU SEE WHEN YOU LOOK IN THE MIRROR?
A Bantam Book/February 1995

Library of Congress Cataloging-in-Publication Data

Cash, Thomas F.
What do you see when you look in the mirror? : the new body-image
therapy for women and men / Thomas F. Cash.
p.   cm.
Includes bibliographical references.
ISBN 0-553-37450-8
1. Body image.   2. Self-acceptance.   I. Title.
BF697.5.B63C37   1995
158'.1—dc20   94-15548
                                                            CIP

Published simultaneously in the United States and Canada

PRINTED IN THE UNITED STATES OF AMERICA

FFG   0 9 8 7 6 5 4 3 2 1

CONTENTS

ACKNOWLEDGMENTS

WRITING A BOOK IS ultimately an experience of solitude. Alone, a writer must find the ideas, the words, the motivation, and the time to communicate—sometimes in the middle of the night. The roots and evolution of a book, however, are always the product of collaborative experiences. Many wonderful people are responsible for this book's fruition:

Nellie Sabin is the wizard behind my words. She is an exceptionally talented writer and editor who consistently made my best efforts even better. With intelligence and sensitivity, she always knew what I wanted to say and helped me to express it. Over the course of the project, Nellie became a valued friend. We should all be so lucky!

For over twenty years, I have been a faculty member in the Department of Psychology at Old Dominion University. I am grateful to my colleagues and students, who have provided a workplace stimulating my intellectual and professional growth.

I wish to give special thanks to Tom Pruzinsky, Tim Brown, Jill Grant, James Rosen, Kevin Thompson, Rita Freedman, Jon Butters, and Peter Mikulka. Their ideas and interest have contributed to the essence of this book.

My literary agents, Linda Chester and Laurie Fox, believed in me and in the value of this book from its inception. I am fortunate that they have been in my corner. I am grateful for their expertise and support.

The talented people at Bantam, especially Linda Gross and Maria Mack, have been encouraging, patient, and constructive in their feedback. I am pleased to have a publisher so devoted to its authors.

I am forever indebted to my family. My sons Thomas and Benjamin, each in his own terrific way, have contributed to the pleasure and productivity of my work. My wife Diane has given me immeasurable tolerance and support. I am deeply appreciative of her generosity.

The task of writing, hour after hour, is possible only by having intermittent moments to step back and refuel. In addition to the people who have energized me, I am obliged to the beauty of the Chesapeake Bay. Whenever I needed to sort out my thoughts, the calm and vitality of the Chesapeake would always instill clarity of mind and renewal of purpose.

Finally, I wish to thank the many clients and research participants who have helped me understand "body image" and the importance of overcoming a negative body image. Through their struggles, insights, and accomplishments, these people are truly the inspiration of this book.

WHAT DO YOU SEE WHEN YOU LOOK IN THE MIRROR?

INTRODUCTION

Creating a New Body Image
One Step at a Time

DO YOU EVER WISH you could change your looks? Are there parts of your body that you really dislike?

Do you spend more time thinking and worrying about your appearance than you think you should? Do self-critical thoughts about your looks run through your head?

Do your feelings about your physical appearance interfere with your enjoyment of everyday situations? Do you avoid some situations or activities because of how you look?

Are you sometimes so bothered by your appearance that you spend a lot of time and effort trying to improve your looks? Do you try to conceal those physical characteristics that you believe are unattractive? Do your attempts at damage control produce results that don't last or actually make you feel worse?

What *do* you see when you look in the mirror?

WHAT'S THE PROBLEM?

All these questions are about your *body image*—your relationship with your looks. Your physical appearance is an undeniable part of who you are. If you are having trouble accepting your appearance, your negative body image makes it hard to accept yourself. This problem guarantees to bring you some degree of unhappiness, because self-acceptance is the only route to real happiness.

As a psychologist, I have dedicated most of my career to understanding the psychology of physical appearance. I have conducted over one hundred scientific studies on various aspects of human appearance, ranging from "appearance discrimination" in the workplace to the psychological effects of dieting and cosmetic surgery. In recent years, I've devoted my efforts to helping people who are unhappy with their physical appearance.

The help I offer differs from the tried-but-failed alternatives that may be familiar to many of you. I do not run a weight-control clinic, teaching people how to gain confidence by losing "ugly fat." I am not an "image consultant," giving advice on color coordination and how to "dress for success." I am not a plastic surgeon, nipping here and tucking there to sculpt the perfect body. I am not an exercise trainer, promoting happiness through "pumping up." I am a psychologist. I believe that dissatisfaction with one's looks is not a problem with the "exterior self," but a problem that exists in the "interior self." Your relationship with your body is less about what you *actually* look like than it is about how you *perceive* your looks.

A negative body image can cast a pall over all of life's experiences. Minor discontent with your appearance can cause you to feel a gnawing self-consciousness that interferes with your enjoyment of everyday situations. Extreme body dissatisfaction can lead to a state of almost constant anxiety and unhappiness. Whether it results in mild annoyance or chronic self-loathing, a negative body image produces needless suffering.

Fortunately, a negative body image can be overcome, and

this book provides step-by-step guidance in transforming your view of your body from a self-defeating outlook to one of self-respect. After over twenty years of studying this fascinating subject, I have gleaned insights that can empower people to develop a brand-new body image—one that is positive, satisfying, and enhances the quality of life.

In this era of self-help, there are many informative books that can truly aid people in finding solutions to various problems in living. In fact, psychologists at the University of Alabama recently scrutinized the results of forty scientific studies of self-help therapies and concluded that self-help really can be effective. Of course, all self-help books are not equally therapeutic. Some of these books remind me of the joke about the fellow who goes to the doctor and complains that his neck hurts whenever he turns his head to the right. The doctor runs a series of diagnostic tests and pinpoints the problem. In detailed medical terms, the doctor helps the patient understand the cause of his pain. Pleased with the information he's been given, the man then asks what can be done to remedy the condition. "It's simple," the doctor replies. "Just stop turning your head to the right."

Self-help books that tell you what your problems are without teaching you how to overcome them offer empty insights. Knowing that you come from a dysfunctional family or have too much codependency may shed some light on your difficulties, but popular labels alone cannot change much. On the other hand, insights that translate specifically into positive steps for change are powerful self-discoveries. Step-by-step, this book provides the prescription for overcoming a negative body image.

A SCIENTIFIC APPROACH TO
BODY-IMAGE CHANGE

Not all of us therapists fit the common public perception of our profession—a bearded guy who says, in a thick Viennese accent (while you lie on a couch), "Tell me about your mother . . . for the next twelve years!" The practitioners of modern therapies are committed to offering help that is grounded in our knowledge from psychological science. They strive to discover and provide solution-focused therapies that really work.

This describes my approach to psychotherapy. This eight-step program for body-image change is not something I conjured up on a rainy Sunday afternoon. It is firmly rooted in scientific psychology, and its effectiveness has been tested and verified in controlled studies. In 1987, Dr. Jon Butters and I pioneered this new approach to body-image therapy using the first version of the program to treat thirty-one people who were very unhappy with their appearance. After only a few weeks, our clients learned to gain more satisfaction from their looks and to feel improvements in their self-esteem. We refined the program over the next several years, during which Dr. James Rosen at the University of Vermont conducted several independent tests of its effectiveness. His research not only confirms that the program works, but also that it is significantly more beneficial than a more traditional "talk therapy" approach.

In 1991, I published an audiocassette version of my updated program—*Body-Image Therapy: A Program for Self-Directed Change* (Guilford Publications)—to assist other professionals in helping clients overcome body-image distress. I was pleased to make this contribution, but I still wished to help people who were not in professional therapy.

Most recently, psychologist Jill Grant and I conducted another test of my body-image therapy program at Old Dominion University. In this study, half of our subjects suffering from a negative body image completed the program administered by professionals in weekly group therapy, and the other half completed the program on their own with little professional assistance. Clients became less preoccupied, dissatisfied, and self-conscious about their appearance. As a result of their body-image improvements, they also began to feel less socially anxious, less depressed, and more self-esteem. Furthermore, we discovered that success could be achieved *without extensive direction by a therapist*. By following the program in a largely self-help format, people really learned to like their looks better and successfully improved the quality of their lives. Our research also taught us how to make the program even more helpful. These advances are reflected in the program that I now offer to you.

This Book's for You! . . . or Is It?

I have written this book for the millions of people who are unhappy with their looks and wish they weren't. This book is for both sexes, because a negative body image affects men as well as women. This book is for the young, the old, and people in between. It is for people who are average looking and for people who look different—whether tall or short, fat or thin, physically disfigured or "flawless."

So is this program for *anyone* who's dissatisfied with his or her appearance? Almost, but not quite. Certain people experience intense body-image difficulties as one aspect of a much more complicated problem. These problems include "body dysmorphic disorder," certain eating disorders, and severe depression. These bigger problems require more help—

professional help. If you recognize yourself in the descriptions that follow, I urge you to seek the advice of a trained therapist.

In a culture as appearance-conscious as ours, preoccupation with one's looks has almost become a national pastime. For some, however, this preoccupation becomes obsession. Practically all they can think about is their appearance. Their excessive concern is known as *body dysmorphic disorder*—the disorder of "imagined ugliness." What they see when they look in the mirror is a grossly distorted view of what they actually look like. Others look at them and either see nothing wrong or regard the "defect" as relatively minor. People with this problem may spend hour after hour in front of the mirror, inspecting their "hideous flaw" and trying to conceal or fix it. Going out in public is extremely difficult. They avoid social situations or endure them with excruciatingly painful self-consciousness. These people have an intense desire to have their appearance "repaired," which may send them on an endless and unsatisfactory search for remedies from plastic surgery.

Body dysmorphic disorder reflects the greatest extreme of a negative body image. Dr. James Rosen's research has shown that the program in this book can help people with such intense body-image discontent, but the expert assistance of a professional is needed if the program is to provide its optimal benefits.

Negative body image is also a driving force behind various eating disorders. There are three eating disorders that call for professional assistance. *Anorexia nervosa* is a life-threatening disorder of relentless self-starvation in pursuit of thinness. It mostly affects young women, who refuse to eat practically anything and therefore become increasingly emaciated. Their fear of gaining weight is overwhelmingly intense, and they continue to feel fat even after they have become dangerously thin.

Another eating disorder in which sufferers loathe their appearance is *bulimia nervosa,* a binge-purge syndrome that is even more common than anorexia nervosa. The bulimic pattern involves recurrent binge-eating episodes—the rapid consumption of very large amounts of food in a relatively short time. I'm not talking about an occasional "pigging out" by having an unusually big dinner or eating that second piece of pie. The binges of bulimia may consist of the entire pie, plus a gallon of ice cream, plus a large bowl of popcorn, plus a bag of potato chips, plus . . . all consumed rapidly within a half hour or so. Often these binges are carried out in solitude and secrecy. Following the binge is the purge, which is an effort to "undo" the binge. Purging is frequently accomplished by self-induced vomiting, but it may also involve the use of laxatives, diuretics, dietary fasts, or vigorous physical exercise. Bulimia nervosa takes people beyond a preoccupied dissatisfaction with body shape or weight. It traps them in a dangerous, self-destructive pattern over which they lose any sense of control. Ultimately, their hatred of their body and themselves continues to worsen.

A third eating disorder involves binges without efforts to purge. This *binge-eating disorder,* sometimes called "compulsive overeating," also entails a loss of control and an erosion of self-esteem. Obviously, it will usually lead to weight gain and an even more negative body image.

A variety of studies have indicated that patients treated for eating disorders must also learn to have a realistic, satisfying view of their looks. If not, they are at risk of relapse, eventually returning to self-starvation or binge-purge episodes. Nevertheless, body-image therapy should not be the sole remedy for an eating disorder.

The final problem that needs more help than I can provide in the pages of this book is *major depression*. This severe, often recurrent disturbance of mood is frequently accompanied by a negative body image. In a study that my colleagues and I conducted in 1985, we found that depressed people have a distorted view of their appearance—seeing themselves as less attractive than they really are. Their feeling ugly, however, is only a symptom of a far greater problem: self-hatred. Depressed people feel worthless or terribly guilty. They are unable to derive much pleasure from life. Their minds are filled with negative thoughts and with hopelessness. They may even have thoughts of suicide. Normal day-to-day activities are a chore, which leads to a sense of helplessness and incompetence.

Overcoming major depression requires more than improving one's body image. Of course, as I explained earlier, my research does reveal that developing a more positive body image can help reduce less-severe depression. The key question you must ask yourself is whether intense depression colors your view of your looks (and your life), or does your negative body image itself lead to experiences of despondency and dejection?

In recent years, mental-health professionals have developed excellent therapies for eating disorders, for body dysmorphic disorder, and for depression. If you recognize yourself in any of these descriptions, please seek professional help immediately. Contact your local mental-health association or mental-health center. Describe your problems and ask for an appropriate referral. You can also get referral information from the Association for Advancement of Behavior Therapy by phoning (212) 647-1890. With these resources, you can find a therapist to help you start to reclaim your life. Because a negative body image is an important part of your difficulties, together you and your therapist can use this book to achieve the maximum benefits of a more positive body image.

What If I Want to Change My Body, Not My Body Image?

Understandably, most people who are unhappy with their looks fantasize about being rid of whatever physical characteristic they loathe. Rather than wishing that they could change their body-image feelings, they wish for a different body—a slimmer physique, a more youthful complexion, bigger breasts, a fuller head of hair, or other physical "improvements." Annually, millions of people opt for diets to alter their weight, cosmetic potions to "hide the flaws," and surgical procedures to transform some disliked feature. The truth is that the basic psychological goal of all these remedies is body-image change—to feel better about your appearance.

If you're thinking about going on a diet or about changing your looks with cosmetic surgery, I recommend that you first do all you can to improve your body image. After completing this program, you may not want to change your looks. But if you still do, you will be much better equipped to reap the benefits you seek. In the final chapter, I'll have lots more to say about dieting, plastic surgery, and other approaches to "exterior remodeling." Until then, let's focus on the underlying, interior problem—your body image.

BUILDING A BETTER BODY IMAGE

Developing a positive body image is a building process. This book contains an eight-step program to construct lasting, satisfying changes in your body image. The diagram on page 13 identifies the specific building blocks of my program. Briefly, I'll describe each step so that you can see what's in store for you.

Step 1: First, we must lay the foundation. There are numerous myths and misunderstandings about physical appearance that interfere with self-acceptance. Psychologists have acquired valuable knowledge about how our physical appearance shapes our lives, in both positive and negative ways. We understand a great deal about the causes and the consequences of a negative body image, and I will present the latest information so that you can begin your program for change on solid ground.

Step 2: Body image is as distinctive as a fingerprint. Each of us has our own unique appearance. Also unique are our experiences of our own appearance. In this second step, you will take several self-evaluation tests, each scientifically designed to enable you to discover the many facets of your body image. Then, based on your test results, you will translate your self-discoveries into specific goals for body-image change. You will learn how to keep a special diary of your body-image experiences in daily life, so that you can identify your difficulties and track your success in reaching your personal goals.

Step 3: Dissatisfaction with your appearance produces emotional distress. Feeling anxious, self-conscious, or ashamed about your looks interferes with your being in control of your life. I will share with you two therapeutic tools that will enable you to feel more comfortable with your looks. With "Body-and-Mind Relaxation" and "Body-Image Desensitization," you will start being more in charge of your body-image emotions.

Step 4: Our feelings about our appearance are strongly affected by the perceptions, beliefs, and thoughts that we hold in the privacy of our own minds. Most of us harbor assumptions about our looks that set us up for disappointment. In this step, I will help you first discover what faulty assumptions you've been making and then show you how to begin to "change your mind" about them.

Step 5: When we think about what we look like, we engage in a type of inner conversation that I call "Private Body Talk." People with a negative body image have Private Body Talk that reflects certain mental mistakes that create lots of problems. In this step, you will learn to eavesdrop on your Private Body Talk, identify your own faulty thought patterns, and develop a whole new way of conversing with yourself about your looks.

Step 6: In addition to changing your old, self-defeating thought patterns, you can also take direct action to stop feeling unhappy with your looks. People with a negative body image are preoccupied with and worried about the physical characteristics they dislike. Feeling defensive about their appearance makes them act defensively. Unfortunately, many of the actions they take to try to prevent discomfort exacerbate and become part of the problem. If your defensive maneuvers make your body image even worse, you will come to feel defenseless. This important step of the program will help you identify and eliminate your own self-defeating behavior patterns.

Step 7: In prior steps, you will have made major progress overcoming the negatives of your body image. Now you will develop the positives, by creating a more pleasurable, affirming relationship with your appearance. In this step, you will expand your horizons and forge ahead with a new body-image lifestyle.

Step 8: You will want to ensure that the new body image you've achieved lasts forever. By being aware of your vulnerabilities and planning now for your future, you can protect your new body image and prevent the old one from sneaking back into your life. This final step is your insurance policy.

Change Depends on You

The success of my program relies on your *active* involvement. This book is *not* for reading—it's for *doing*. Understanding the program is only the beginning. To effect change, you will need to put what you learn into action. In each of the program's eight steps, I will show you how to create certain experiences necessary for body-image improvement. These therapeutic experiences require that you think, plan, and *act*. They require that you try out new ways of approaching your problems.

Throughout the program, I'll be giving you special "Helpsheets" to use in the creation of your new body image. These Helpsheets are not "optional assignments." They are an essential path for your achievement of satisfying changes in your body image.

At the end of each Step, I've included a special summary, "Progress Check: How Am I Helping Myself?" to review the therapeutic activities that you should be involved in at that stage in the program. One step at a time, you will be building your skills and improving your body image as you progress through the program.

You won't achieve the desired results from this program if you are just a bedtime reader, perusing a chapter or two each night until you reach the final page. Each chapter contains a step that takes as much as a week or two to carry out and internalize completely. If you'd like, you may first read through the entire book to appreciate the overall structure of

YOUR EIGHT-STEP PROGRAM
FOR BUILDING A POSITIVE BODY IMAGE

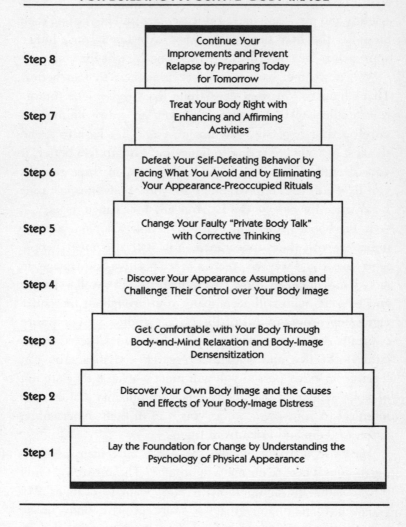

Step 8 — Continue Your Improvements and Prevent Relapse by Preparing Today for Tomorrow

Step 7 — Treat Your Body Right with Enhancing and Affirming Activities

Step 6 — Defeat Your Self-Defeating Behavior by Facing What You Avoid and by Eliminating Your Appearance-Preoccupied Rituals

Step 5 — Change Your Faulty "Private Body Talk" with Corrective Thinking

Step 4 — Discover Your Appearance Assumptions and Challenge Their Control over Your Body Image

Step 3 — Get Comfortable with Your Body Through Body-and-Mind Relaxation and Body-Image Densensitization

Step 2 — Discover Your Own Body Image and the Causes and Effects of Your Body-Image Distress

Step 1 — Lay the Foundation for Change by Understanding the Psychology of Physical Appearance

the program. Afterward, go back and complete the steps one at a time. If you prefer, you may skip the initial cover-to-cover reading and just jump in. In this case, you will be reading each Step for the first time as you are carrying it out. Either approach is fine. Just decide which one is right for you.

When we feel bad, we all are impatient to feel better. That's human. We want everything fixed today—or tomorrow at the latest! Although it's taken an entire lifetime to develop your negative body image, you don't have to spend the rest of your life trying to figure out how to feel better. If you carefully follow my eight basic Steps, in three months you'll see a vast improvement in your body image. Your impatience for change can be your ally for change.

In this book, you will meet lots of people who, like you, are unhappy with their appearance. You will also meet people who have found ways to create a more positive body image. In fact, you will get to know two individuals very well—Laurie and Everett, who will accompany you throughout the entire eight-step program. All of these case studies are composite portraits drawn from real people I have encountered in my clinical practice and scientific research activities. You can learn from every person you will meet—even if they are not of your gender or have body-image complaints that are not identical to your own. So, as you read of their experiences, listen to them and learn from them.

Have you heard the old joke that asks, "How many psychologists does it take to change a lightbulb?" The answer is "Only one . . . but the lightbulb *really* must want to change." My program to help you create a more positive body image assumes that you *really* want to change. It assumes that you are motivated to *do* something about feeling unhappy with your looks. In this program, I am merely your guide—a "catalyst" for your changes. Because I truly want to help you, I've done my part by carefully developing an effective program, re-searching ways to make it the best, and presenting it to you clearly, step-by-step.

So, now it's your turn, and your turn of the page promises a new beginning for your body image.

In the Eye of the Beholder

Understanding the Psychology
of Physical Appearance

ASHLEY HESITATED BEFORE STEPPING in front of the full-length mirror in my office. "Do I *have* to?" she asked nervously. I replied as I always do: "I know you feel uncomfortable. It'll be okay. Just look at yourself a while and tell me what you see."

She stared at her reflection for a few seconds. Then, in a cracking voice, she said, "I see somebody who's short and fat. I see how big her hips are—really huge. I feel sick to my stomach just looking at them. I see her face, and it looks mostly plain. I'd like it better if it didn't have such a stupid nose. That nose sort of takes over her face, and pretty much destroys everything else. Her eyes are nice. People say they like those eyes. Too bad the compliments stop there. I can't look at myself anymore. I hate being put down."

Michael stood in front of the mirror. Though he tried to appear nonchalant, he couldn't conceal his self-consciousness. "So what do I see?" Michael repeated. "Well, I don't see

Robert Redford. The guy in the mirror looks more like Woody Allen. I see a skinny body that needs to work out more. There are bird legs hidden in those jeans, so he'd better keep his pants on. I see a face with acne scars that'll never go away. I see a mediocre beard that hides only some of his bad complexion. Oh yeah, look at the thinning hair on his head—give it a few more years. I see a guy who hasn't got a chance at being nice-looking. I think I've frightened your mirror enough for now."

From womb to tomb, each of us exists within the physical reality of a human body. Unless we have an identical twin, each of us is unique in our physical appearance. What we look like can shape our lives in ways that are both subtle and profound. Our relationship with our appearance—how we think, feel, and react to our own looks—forms an essential aspect of our personality, an aspect called "body image." What Ashley and Michael see as they stand in front of the mirror has little to do with what they actually look like. What each sees is a highly subjective view—one that reflects his or her own body image.

PHYSICAL APPEARANCE: A VIEW FROM THE OUTSIDE

Some years ago, as a psychology graduate student, I was searching for ideas for that ultimate academic hurdle, my doctoral dissertation. I had decided I wanted to study the factors that influence the formation of social relationships. To my amazement, one of my professors suggested that I consider the influence of "physical attractiveness" on people's social interactions. I remember thinking that his suggestion was silly. After all, "beauty is only skin deep" and is "in the eye of the beholder." Surely, people don't "judge books by their covers." Such a superficial topic hardly seemed to be a worthy subject for scientific inquiry—especially for *my* dissertation. Eventually, he convinced me otherwise, and I went on to discover that people's perceptions of a stranger's physical appearance as well as their perceptions of their own looks influenced what they were willing to disclose in their first encounters with the stranger. These findings whetted my scientific appetite and launched my career-long interest in the psychology of physical appearance.

Many behavioral scientists who have studied physical appearance have researched what I call the "outside view." This perspective considers how our actual appearance—our height, weight, hair color, or other physical attributes—influences our lives. It poses questions about whether people's physical characteristics affect how others think about them and treat them. Most often studied has been the influence of *physical attractiveness*, defined simply as how good-looking people are judged to be on a scale from 1 to 10. Although beauty is partly in the eye of the beholder, there is still considerable social consensus about how physically attractive people are. After all, every culture conveys strong messages about the criteria of good looks, and we judge appearances through our common cultural lens.

This outside view essentially regards people as "social objects" and asks: Does physical appearance play a role in first impressions? Are people misjudged based on their physical appearance? Are good-looking people really more popular than plainer folks? Are there prejudices against less physically attractive people that cause social discrimination? If attractive people are treated better, does this treatment produce real differences in their personalities? How about differences in their ultimate happiness?

The answers to such questions are complex. Keats's memorable ode asserting that "Beauty is truth, truth beauty" is not the truth about beauty. Let me summarize what we know from psychological research on this "outside view." (And if you are interested in further reading about the psychology of physical appearance, take a look at the resources I've listed for you in the appendix of the book.)

Physical Attractiveness: At First Glance

Physical appearance often provides the most readily available information about a person. It conveys the person's gender, race, approximate age, and possibly even economic status or occupation. We all hold assumptions and attitudes about physical attributes and, often unconsciously, sort people into a variety of mental categories based on their appearance. Can you picture a "dizzy blonde?" How about a "fat slob?" A "nerd?" A "handsome hunk?" A "dumb jock?"

Because of our need to feel that we understand people, we all rely initially on such handy categories. Though it's a lazy way to think that often leads to an inaccurate understanding of others, we do it anyway. It makes things simpler. Unless we are stubbornly close-minded, we usually modify our perceptions as our interactions with people give us new information about what they are really like.

What I am describing here is social stereotyping based on physical appearance. The lion's share of the research on this topic concerns our cultural belief that what is beautiful is good (and conversely, what is ugly is bad). The strongest aspect of this belief is the presumption that good-looking children and adults of either sex are socially confident (i.e., socially skillful, outgoing, popular) and well-adjusted (i.e., happy, with loads of self-acceptance).

If we take a good look at good looks, do we find any truth to this stereotype? In 1992, Dr. Alan Feingold, an experienced researcher of physical appearance, examined nearly one hundred published studies that compared the personalities of physically attractive and unattractive people. He found that very few real differences exist and that the perceptible differences are "trivial."

Objectively good-looking people, Dr. Feingold discovered, are slightly less likely to be lonely, somewhat more comfortable in social situations, and a bit more sexually experienced. But for most measures of personality and mental ability, physical attractiveness was irrelevant. Though beautiful people are not necessarily happier than plainer people, they do seem to feel somewhat better about their social worth. If cute babies become cute kids, nice-looking teenagers, and attractive adults, they will have spent their lives in a more accepting social world. To the extent that physically unattractive people encounter more social indifference or outright hostility in their lives, they are going to have a tougher time feeling confident around others.

Stereotypes can foster self-fulfilling prophecies, giving the good-looking certain social advantages. For example, we might forgive an attractive person the same faux pas for which we would indict a less attractive individual. As a result, the latter worries about appearing foolish and becomes more socially anxious and awkward. Research by Dr. Mark Snyder at the University of Minnesota confirmed the phenomenon of self-fulfilling prophecies. He conducted an experiment in which men had telephone conversations with women whom the men had been led to believe were either physically attractive or unattractive. The women whom the men *thought* to be homely (though they really weren't) ended up acting less socially likable than those *thought* to be attractive. The interactions were judged by people who listened to the conversations but were given *no* preconceptions about the women's looks. What happened was that the men treated the women differently based on assumptions about their looks. Those women who were treated more favorably reacted more sociably, in ways that created more favorable social impressions. Conversely, the women who were treated less positively behaved less positively.

This provocative experiment shows that our looks can affect how we are treated, which, in turn, can influence how we act. However, before you rush to see a plastic surgeon, remember Dr. Feingold's conclusion: Looks affect our lives, but if looks are everything, then physically attractive and unattractive people should be psychologically very different from one another. The fact is that they aren't. The realities about the power of appearance are seldom as pronounced as our stereotypes.

Why Looks Aren't Everything

Our societal worship of physical attractiveness and the lengths to which people will go to pursue good looks reinforce the belief that being physically attractive pays bigger benefits than it actually does. There are numerous reasons why good looks, while undeniably helpful sometimes, don't fully deliver on their promise. There are also plenty of reasons why being average looking or less don't end opportunities for happiness. To help you develop a more realistic perspective on appearance, here are some reasons why looks aren't everything.

"BEAUTY IS AS BEAUTY DOES"

What we *do* speaks with a stronger voice than what we *look like*. Friendliness, intelligence, honesty, a sense of humor, and sensitivity to others are valued human traits, no matter what physical package they arrive in. As James Ellis once said,

"Better an ugly face than an ugly mind." Think about the people who have impressed you or touched your life in a very special way. I'll bet they aren't all "10s" on the appearance scale. In fact, I'll bet their looks are largely irrelevant to how you feel about them.

Our initial perceptions of a person's appearance are not frozen forever in our minds. We come to see likable people as increasingly nice looking, as if their inner attractiveness were radiating outward and enhancing their physical presence. Have you ever met someone whose looks weren't especially striking at first, but who turned out to be a really nice, interesting person? As your enjoyable relationship evolved, did the person's appearance seem more and more attractive? Good looks *are* more than skin deep!

"BIRDS OF A FEATHER . . ."

Have you ever noticed that people form relationships based on shared similarities? This is called the *principle of homogamy*. People are attracted to others who are like themselves in various respects—for example, those with common interests, religious and political values, ethnic backgrounds, and educational levels. Researchers have found that this "likes attract" phenomenon works for appearance as well. Friends, dates, and mates are frequently matched in their physical attractiveness. On the occasions when you've seen a couple in which one partner appeared much more attractive than the other, you probably did a double take and wondered about their relationship. Although homogamy means that beautiful people tend to stick together, it also means that nobody gets left out. As folk wisdom proclaims, "There's a cover for every pot."

THE UGLY FACES OF BEAUTY

There is a downside to physical attractiveness that actually results from the positive stereotype. First, we assume that good-looking people possess interesting personalities and have social advantages not afforded to plainer persons. From there, we figure that attractive people must be well aware of their good looks and their social advantages. This, in turn, suggests that they must be vain and self-centered. In effect, we are blaming the victims of our own stereotype.

Imagine for a moment that you initiate conversation with a stranger at a party. Suppose this person offers little eye contact, seldom nods or smiles at you, fails to respond to your friendliness, and exits abruptly. If he or she were strikingly good-looking, you would likely decide that the stranger is "stuck up." However, if the person were somewhat homely, you might be more sympathetic and assume that he or she is simply shy.

Once we start making harsh judgments about attractive people, the list is endless. Even Shakespeare warned, "The Devil hath power to assume a pleasing shape." If we see good-looking folks as "sold on themselves" or opportunistic, we may assume they are less dutiful in the mundane chores of parenthood, for example, or less faithful as romantic partners. This negative stereotype of attractive people erodes some of the benefits of their looks.

SUPERMEN, SUPERWOMEN

Another stereotype that frequently causes the physical beauty of men and women to backfire is the "sex-typing stereotype" of appearance. Attractive men are sometimes presumed to have "masculine" personalities, with such traits as dominance and unemotionality. Attractive women are sometimes presumed to have "feminine" personalities, with characteristics like unassertiveness and emotionality. These stereotypes are incorrect. However, my research and that of other psychologists shows that attractiveness can lead to narrow, sexist assumptions about women and men. When this happens, attractiveness loses some of its positive power.

LOOKS GOOD ENOUGH TO HATE

Have you ever heard anyone express loathing for people simply based on their attractiveness? "They are so good-looking (or thin, or well-built)—I hate them!" Not surprisingly, beauty breeds envy. As I'll explain further later on, we often compare ourselves to attractive people who have what we desire. As a result, we feel worse about our looks and therefore dislike attractive people for "making us feel ugly." As the eighteenth-century English historian Edward Gibbon observed, "Beauty is an outward gift which is seldom despised, except by those to whom it has been refused." Most of us fall into the latter category.

WOULD YOU STILL LOVE ME IF . . . ?

I remember a conversation I once had with a woman who had been my friend for years. Nancy was strikingly beautiful. I'd never commented to her about her looks until one day when, for some reason I cannot recall, I told her how pretty I thought she was. To my surprise, my compliment brought her to tears. "I thought you liked me for who I am," she explained. "Now I'll never be sure that it's not just because of what I happen to look like."

Nancy's point reveals another disadvantage of good looks: wondering whether people really like who you are *inside* and wondering whether you've really earned the good things that come your way. Wouldn't you rather know that the social attention you get comes from your being a terrific person and not a physical commodity? Wouldn't you rather be certain that the praise you receive is genuine and not an attempt to butter you up because you look like a good catch?

HEY, BABY . . .

Most of us want to feel that our romantic partners find us sexy. Few of us want to be seen solely as a sex object by everybody we meet. Compliments are nice; meat-market treatment isn't very fulfilling. Many attractive people, especially women, are subjected to unwanted remarks that focus on their looks and ignore their other assets. This experience becomes tiresome and demeaning, possibly constituting sexual harassment. Who would want to go through life as *only* a pretty face or a great body?

BEYOND STEREOTYPES

We all know people who are "nearsighted" in their perception of others. All they can see is what is in front of their face. They talk nonstop about appearances and judge others solely by their body, hairstyle, or outfit. As poet Robert Southey wrote, "How little do they see what is, who frame their hasty judgments upon that which seems." Thank goodness, some people are blind to such superficial things and see beneath the outer shell of human appearance. Whether we are fat or skinny, tall or short, dressed up or wearing our grungy clothes, bald or having a really "bad hair day," these people can see past the surface. They see us and accept us for who we are. They are great equalizers in our otherwise appearance-preoccupied society. We should all aspire to be more like these terrific human beings.

Overcoming a negative body image requires that you keep appearances in perspective—both your own appearance and that of others. Beauty is a mixed blessing, and its pursuit takes us along narrow paths that restrict our lives and lead to unfulfilled promises. Better than the glorification of beauty is the celebration of our physical diversity. Letting go of stereotypes frees us to embrace all kinds of possibilities for appreciating our human worth.

PHYSICAL APPEARANCE: THE INSIDE VIEW

Several years ago, I appeared on ABC-TV's *20/20* news program to talk about my research on the causes and consequences of having a negative body image. In that program, reporter John Stossel interviewed professional models, both men and women, about how they felt about their looks. Despite the fact that all were "knockouts" and epitomized what many of us wished we looked like, they were self-critical of their bodies. They pointed to specific physical features that really bothered them—"too much" of this or "too little" of that. Their candid comments support exactly what the scientific evidence makes clear: Negative body image has little to do with outward appearance; it's a state of mind. Being truly handsome or beautiful does not of itself guarantee a positive body image, nor does homeliness decree a lifetime of loathing one's looks.

Body Images: Who Hates What?

You are not alone in your experience of a negative body image and your desire to do something about it. In 1985, my colleagues and I conducted a national research survey on body image in *Psychology Today* magazine. Over 30,000 people answered our questionnaire (great for us, but not a happy time for the folks in the university's mailroom). From our survey, we discovered that about two of every five women and about one in three men are dissatisfied with their overall looks. This certainly disproves the myth that only women have body-image problems. One reason many people incorrectly assume that women hate their appearance much more than men do is that women are more vocal about their body-image complaints. By talking openly about their dissatisfactions, women seek reassurance and receive support from other women. Their misery finds company. Guys are more likely to suffer in silence, feeling that "real men" are not supposed to be concerned about such things. Still, the fact is that a sizable percentage of both sexes have trouble accepting their appearance.

What do people with a negative body image complain about? I have summarized our survey results for you in Table 1. Weight was the most disliked physical attribute—55 percent of women and 41 percent of men are dissatisfied with their weight. The Duchess of Windsor is alleged to have said, "No woman can be too rich or too thin," and she obviously wasn't speaking about men. While women are mostly worried about being too fat, men are as concerned about being skinny as they are about being fat. We found that among people who were *really* at a healthy weight (based on the Metropolitan Life Insurance standards), about one-half of the women and one-fourth of the men *believed* they were overweight. Regarding these "weighty matters," we made an interesting discovery. We included a measure of self-esteem in our survey and found that overall body image and self-esteem are much more strongly related to what people *believe* about their weight than how much they actually weigh. Being overweight or underweight is often as much a state of mind as it is a state of the body.

TABLE 1
The Sources of Our Discontent

Disliked Physical Attributes	1972 Survey		1985 Survey	
	Men	**Women**	**Men**	**Women**
Height	13%	13%	20%	17%
Weight	35%	48%	41%	55%
Muscle Tone	25%	30%	32%	45%
Face	8%	11%	20%	20%
Upper Torso	18%	27%	28%	32%
Mid Torso	36%	50%	50%	57%
Lower Torso	12%	49%	21%	50%
Overall Appearance	15%	23%	34%	38%

Adapted from Cash, Winstead, and Janda (1986).

Our survey also revealed that 57 percent of women and 50 percent of men are dissatisfied with the size of their stomachs. A slimmer waist is something most people wish for. Furthermore, though rounded hips are the biologically natural expression of womanhood, half of the women (yet only 21 percent of the men) dislike their lower torso—their hips, thighs, and buttocks. Being too flabby is a common concern, evidenced by the fact that muscle tone is a focus of dissatisfaction for 45 percent of the women and 32 percent of the men. About 30 percent of both sexes dislike their chest or breast area. The two physical attributes with which people are most satisfied are their face and height. Roughly 20 percent of men and women are not content with these characteristics.

The bottom line is that the vast majority of people are dissatisfied with at least one aspect of their appearance. In our survey, we found that only 28 percent of men and 15 percent of women expressed satisfaction with *all* body areas listed in the survey. Thus, total contentment is more the exception than the rule.

Table 1 also includes the results of an identical *Psychology Today* survey done thirteen years earlier. You can compare the percentages of dissatisfaction between the two surveys to determine how things have changed over time. The evidence is pretty clear. Our body images aren't getting any better. In most respects, both men and women are reporting even more dissatisfaction in recent years than in the past.

REFLECTIONS IN THE MIRROR

At the beginning of this chapter, Ashley and Michael described what they saw as they stood in front of my mirror. To each, it was not a pretty picture. Last year, I conducted a research project in which I asked a random sample of people—just regular, ordinary people—the question posed by the title of this book: What do you see when you look in the mirror? I also asked them to describe their thoughts as they viewed their reflections. Before asking you the same question, I want to share with you some of the answers I was given:

"What I see I really hate. I hate my thighs. I hate my butt. My mouth is too big. My eyes are too big. My hair is too straight. I wish I didn't have to spend so much time on my looks. Tomorrow, I'll start working out." (White woman, age 25)

"I see a body that needs toning. I see those sad eyes. Even though I'm not sad, my drooping eyes look it. I don't like them." (African-American man, age 50)

"I see a short, fat, balding man. What a bozo! How did I get this way? I remember when I was in high school and liked what I saw in the mirror. I really have to work on my appearance more. At least I know my girlfriend loves me even though I look this way." (White man, age 29)

"I see a slim, healthy-looking woman, until I look into her eyes. What am I going to do about these growing bags under my eyes? I look pretty good for 32. But what will I see when I'm 50 or 60? Perish the thought!" (White woman, age 32)

"I see a person struggling with her weight. I'm scared I can't control it. Then I'll become my big, fat mother, except I'll have the ugly birthmark on my face." (White woman, age 22)

"I see a nice-looking guy with a warm smile and friendly eyes. I like his haircut too. He looks healthy and happy. Not bad. I'm glad he's me!" (Hispanic man, age 34)

"I see a person who's not short and not tall. She's not thin and not fat. She's not pretty yet not ugly. Everything I see is average—boringly average." (White woman, age 21)

"I see a woman whose face I've grown to love and accept. I look at the nose I hated when I was a teenager. It's the exact same nose, but I don't see it the same way. My past worries about the size of my nose were really misguided worries about my worth as a black person." (African-American woman, age 21)

"What I see has looked worse. And it'll probably look worse again." (Asian-American woman, age 39)

"I see a pear. I see crooked teeth. This is not a pleasant sight. Thank God I don't have a boyfriend right now.

He would definitely be grossed out." (White woman, age 30)

"I don't see perfection, but I see nothing I want to change. I see *me*—135 pounds of love." (African-American woman, age 61)

"All I see is an aging woman, with no muscle tone. What a flab!" (Native-American woman, age 41)

"I see a woman who looks like a girl. If it weren't for my big nipples, I'd have no breasts at all." (White woman, age 31)

"I see a tall, well-built young man, who has a crippling injury of his right hand. If it weren't for my deformity, I'd be the happiest person in the world." (White man, age 19)

"What I try to see (but can't) is what I dream about being: Rich! Rich enough to afford to have plastic surgery on my nose and to have my teeth fixed, plus a chin implant. Rich enough to have my makeup and hair done professionally. Then, there are the fashionable clothes. Dream on! I'm always going to be a plain Jane." (White woman, age 33)

"What do I see? Are those spots in front of my eyes? Nope, just freckles everywhere. So get out your pencil and let's play 'connect the dots'—on my body." (White woman, age 27)

"I see a guy with curly hair and glasses. I see several scars on his knees, hands, chin, and forehead. I see his well-developed legs, but he's got a flabby stomach with 'love handles.' Why can't he grow a decent mustache?

Oh well, at least he's not real short." (White man, age 22)

"I see a medium-size person, with a little chest and a big rear. I see Chinese eyes. But mostly I see boat feet that look like they have fingers for toes." (Asian-American woman, age 20)

"I see a *fairly* attractive young lady who cannot stop thinking about the things that keep her from being a *very* attractive young lady." (White woman, age 28)

"I see a tall young man with skinny arms and legs and a large, fat torso. I see a rapidly receding hairline. What a dork! What did I do to deserve this? What can I do to change it?" (White man, age 37)

"All I can see when I look in the mirror are wishes—wishes that everything looked better." (Hispanic woman, age 18)

"I see a short girl with an hourglass figure, but the sand stays settled in the bottom. Maybe I'll dye my hair blond, get green contacts, and go get a perfect tan." (White woman, age 19)

"I see an average-looking dude. I wish I was bigger. I wish my hair was fuller. I wish I was a couple of inches taller. Why am I kidding myself? I'm less than an average-looking dude. I'd settle for average." (African-American man, age 26)

"I see a gal who looks pretty good. Just don't ask her to take her clothes off. Then, you'll get another story. (I'll spare you the ugly details)." (Hispanic woman, age 41)

"I see a girl who needs to lose weight. I look disgusting in whatever I wear. My arms are covered with dark hair that I'm always hiding or bleaching. I don't look feminine enough. Why can't I look as pretty as the other girls?" (White woman, age 22)

"I'm looking at someone who looks old. Too many wrinkles on her face. Arms and legs that are too fat. I'm going to have to diet some more." (White woman, age 54)

"What I see when I look in the mirror is always changing. Not because I'm really different, but because of my mood. I try to remind myself that it doesn't matter how I really look, it matters how I think." (White woman, age 63)

"When I look in the mirror, I see nothing. That's because I'm too scared to open my eyes. Sorry." (Pacific Islander woman, age 19)

"I see a tall, thin girl with bad posture and a worn-out expression on her face. I feel like she's not really me. Before I leave the mirror, I fluff my hair and adjust my clothes (as I always do). After a few seconds, she begins to look more attractive; she begins to look like me." (White woman, age 23)

"All I see is a guy in a wheelchair with skinny legs. Unfortunately, I know that's all everybody else sees too." (Asian-American man, age 48)

"Mirror, mirror on the wall, who's the fairest of them all? It ain't me, babe!" (Hispanic woman, age 38)

You can see that most of these reflections don't reflect a very favorable body image. Now, on the Self-Discovery Helpsheet on page 36, I'd like you to answer the same question they did. What do you see when you look in the mirror?

What Difference Does Your Body Image Make?

Your body image is central to how you feel about yourself. Psychological studies reveal that as much as one-fourth of your self-esteem is the result of how positive or negative your body image is. If you don't like your body, it's certainly hard to like the person inside it—you!

People with a negative body image are susceptible to a variety of unhappy experiences. I'd like to describe some of the most prevalent ones. See if any apply to you:

• As I mentioned in the Introduction, depression can cause people to hate their looks, but the dynamic can also work in the opposite direction. To the extent that you feel hopeless and helpless about what you look like, your negative body image can make you depressed.

• A negative body image can also lead to shyness and social anxiety. If you cannot accept your appearance, you probably also assume others think less of you because of what you look like. This can cause you to feel self-conscious, uncomfortable, and inadequate in your social interactions. As a result, you may avoid certain social situations and miss out on many of the joys of human relations.

• If you feel physically self-conscious in your intimate relationships, this can interfere with your ability to derive either emotional or sexual fulfillment. Sharing your naked body with another person can be extremely difficult if you believe your body to be ugly or unacceptable. Famous sex therapists Masters and Johnson established two key causes of

We don't just wake up one morning with the realization that we cannot stand our looks. Our body image forms gradually over time, beginning in early childhood.

Our fundamental sense of self has its roots in our experience of being embodied. Our body is the boundary that separates us from everything that is not us—the outside world. We humans, like certain other higher primates, have the capacity of self-awareness. By the age of two years, most of us are able to recognize ourselves in the mirror. Increasingly, our physical reality comes to represent who we are—in our own eyes as well as in our perceptions of how others view us.

As preschoolers, boys and girls have already learned the lessons about physical appearance that our society teaches. They know what's valued and what's not. They know that lovely Cinderella gets the prince; her ugly and mean stepsisters do not. They know that the prince is handsome (and gets Cinderella). Developmental psychologists have discovered that body image takes shape as children internalize the messages and physical standards of society and then judge themselves against them. In this way, children develop conceptions of what is good (how one *should* look) and what is bad (how one should *not* look) with respect to height, weight, muscularity, hair color, or even the style or brand name of clothing.

From childhood on, we evaluate our bodily appearance in terms of how well it matches the "shoulds." Likewise, we judge our self-worth by the physical standards we've absorbed. These judgments lead us to develop expectations of what is in store for us in life. Will we attract a prince or princess? Will we be a sports hero? Will we be popular? Will we be a success? Or none of the above?

Cultural Messages: The Mirrors of Society

Our body image does not develop in a vacuum. We experience and relate to our bodies against the backdrop of the culture in which we grow up. Culture is an ever-present teacher of social norms and values, schooling us in the meanings of human appearance. For example, in Western society, we learn that thinness for women and muscularity for men are desirable. Let's take a closer look at these lessons—first the messages for women and then those for men.

THE FEMININE MYSTIQUE

During certain periods of our cultural history, a full-figured physique was heralded as the feminine beauty standard. The rounded hips and thighs of prehistoric goddesses epitomized fertility as a symbol of femininity. Between the fifteenth and eighteenth centuries, full-bodied women were viewed as beautiful, as reflected in much of the art of the period. In the past several decades of this century, however, a thinner, not-so-curvaceous body type has been increasingly promoted as the standard of feminine attractiveness. Fashion models, film stars, and beauty pageant contestants have become thinner, even as the female population has gotten heavier. Recent social pressures require not only that women be slender but also that they have a well-toned slimness. The message is that thin is feminine, but the "liberated" woman needs to look strong as well. The continued cultural emphasis on thinness is evident in the mid-1990s. In addition to the thin-but-toned image of beauty, emaciated "waif models" like Kate Moss increasingly appear on magazine covers and in television ads.

The worship of thinness hasn't been as evident in other cultures as it is in contemporary Western society. In the ancient Orient, a fat wife was a symbol of honor for her husband, to the degree that some men force-fed their wives to glorify their own social status. In societies in which food is scarce, corpulence is a sign of success and survival. In our society even today, the term "fat cats" refers to the wealthy.

The power of culture to ingrain body-image standards is evident from an interesting study in England by Drs. Furnham and Alibhai. They compared the attitudes of native Kenyans, Kenyans living in Great Britain, and British women. Native Kenyans had the most positive view of a heavy body type; native British women had the least-favorable attitude. Kenyans who had immigrated to Britain held an intermediate view, a compromise between the values of their culture of origin and their culture of residence.

Even within a given culture, there's considerable diversity of standards. Some subcultures are more forgiving than others. For example, in one study, my student Cliff Rucker and I compared the body-image attitudes of African-American and white-American women. African-Americans had a more positive evaluation of their looks and were less fat-phobic than were the whites. We showed the women pictures of a range of female body types and asked them to rate how fat they thought each body was. White women rated the same bodies as fatter than black women did.

Another example of diversity among subgroups of society comes from a study in which one of my students, Charles Finch, and I found that lesbians have a significantly more positive body image than heterosexual women. (And, by the way, the opposite is true for gay versus straight men.)

In the name of beauty, women in our society are asked to shave or wax their legs and armpits, pluck their eyebrows, dye and either curl or straighten their hair, pierce their ears, paint their faces and all twenty nails (including the fake ones), and walk around in uncomfortable high heels. Even the "natural look" demands lots of effort and alterations to achieve. Women are further told that they should worry about "unsightly age spots," the emergence of a single gray hair, a chipped nail, and (God forbid) a visible panty line.

TALL, DARK, AND HANDSOME

What are the appearance expectations for men in our society? Though less demanding than the standards for women, they definitely do exist. Men are "supposed" to be tall, have broad shoulders, a muscular chest and biceps, a small rear, strong facial features, and a full head of hair. Charles Atlas, Robert Redford, Arnold Schwarzenegger, Kevin Costner, Richard Gere, and the Marlboro Man are certainly no ninety-eight-pound weaklings. Our manly heroes are big and strong. John "the Duke" Wayne protected his masculine, stand-tall image by refusing to appear in public without his hairpiece. Burt Reynolds also keeps his hair on in public. When actor Sean Connery said he wanted to appear without his hairpiece, the movie makers refused to let James Bond be a bald guy.

Growing up male in our society means encountering pressures to look tough and be tough. During my early teen years, I attended an all-boys prep school in which "winners" were the brute athletes and "losers" were the little guys who made good grades. I spent hours each week hoisting barbells in the hope of attaining the well-defined body I saw in the sports magazines. I remember that during one period, I ate high-protein food supplements and doubled up on my consumption of meat and potatoes. I was going to make sure nobody kicked sand in my face.

Many of these pressures persist in today's society. They lead some boys and men to compromise their health with steroid abuse and excessive exercise. In record numbers, men now seek cosmetic surgery—including hair transplants, pectoral implants, face-lifts, and liposuction. Men who used to seek a "competitive edge" through hard work are now hard at work on their looks in the belief that appearance is a prerequisite for getting ahead.

FROM SOCIAL IMAGES TO BODY IMAGES

At various times in different cultures, attractiveness has required tattoos covering the entire body, decorative scars on the face, a shaved head, jewelry inserted in holes drilled in the teeth, large disks placed in the lips, stacked brass rings to elongate the neck, and the crippling binding of women's feet. All these things have been done for the sake of good looks, as seen through the eyes of a particular culture.

Just as you may find these foreign beauty practices to be quite outrageous, I urge you to begin to question the standards of our own culture. In later steps of your program, I'll help you defend yourself against these unhealthy messages. Right now, I want you to consider two very important facts about these cultural standards or "ideals:"

First, *societal standards cannot hurt you unless you buy into them.* By adopting these ideals as your own and pressuring yourself to live up to them, you will allow your sense of self-worth to be determined by forces beyond your control. Substantial research by Dr. E. Tory Higgins at Columbia University shows that if you think you should possess certain traits that you believe you lack, you will experience agitation or dejection in situations that remind you of your "shortcomings."

My own psychological studies reveal that this is true of body image as well. I have found that people with extreme standards for how they should look are vulnerable to a wide range of disturbing emotions like shame, anxiety, and depression, which lead to self-defeating behaviors such as avoiding certain situations, dieting excessively, or spending considerable time and money trying to look right. Events that remind you of your physical ideals and your relative imperfections will trigger self-conscious thoughts, feelings of inadequacy, and attempts to defend yourself against distress. On the other hand, if you hold ideals that are more moderate and reasonable, your more favorable body image will promote self-acceptance.

The second fact you should realize is that *others do not hold you up to the same extreme and demanding standards.* In research by Dr. April Fallon at the University of Pennsylvania, as well as in studies I've conducted, men and women were asked to indicate their physical ideals for themselves and for the other sex. In addition, they were asked what they believed the other sex is most attracted to. These studies reveal that we are too hard on ourselves. For most aspects of appearance, we expect more physical "perfection" of ourselves than we *think* others expect of us, even more than others *actually* expect. For example, men are often more appreciative of a heavier female body type than women *believe* men are. Nor do men idealize blonde beauty to the degree women think. Similarly, women don't necessarily hold the same narrow standards of macho male attractiveness that men assume women hold. One of the goals of this program is to help you adjust your ideals so that you can stop making inaccurate and unfair judgments of your worth.

Teasing Looks . . . Displeasing Looks

This process of socialization about the meaning of the body goes beyond the television commercials and magazine ads that convey to us that we must look a certain way to succeed and be happy, or that we should desperately fear being fat, or that we should do all we can to disguise the natural wrinkles of aging. These messages are also conveyed, sometimes quite painfully, in our interactions with peers, parents, and other loved ones.

We grow up in families that teach us how to value our own physical characteristics. Early on, we may be told, "Eat everything on your plate if you want to grow up to be big and strong." Later, we hear that "If you eat all that food, you'll get big and fat, and nobody will like you." When I was a child, my older brother called me "Little Lizard" to make fun of my being skinny. The irony (and explanation) was that he too was skinny, for which he was teased relentlessly by classmates.

Families also communicate subtle messages by what psychologists call *modeling*. For example, if you grow up in a household in which a parent or sibling constantly frets about his or her appearance, you learn that looks are something to worry about. If you have a sibling doted on for being exceptionally attractive, you may come to feel cheated by your looks and feel resentful and envious. The parent who spends considerable time, effort, and money trying to make the kids look perfect is modeling the attitude that good looks are crucial to acceptance in the "outside world." This message is also apparent in the familiar parental question, "You're not *really* going to leave the house looking like that, are you?"

According to Dr. Kevin Thompson at the University of South Florida, being taunted or teased about appearance during childhood can have a lasting negative effect on body image. Many people with a strong dislike for their adult appearance can recall instances in which they were teased or criticized as children because of their looks. Etched in their memories are childhood episodes of ridicule for being too skinny or too plump, too tall or too short, for having ears or a nose or a mouth that was too large, or for how they were dressed.

When I recently surveyed college students about whether they had been recurrently criticized or teased about some aspect of their appearance earlier in their lives, 72 percent revealed that they had. Of those who were teased, half said the teasing occurred moderately to very often, especially during the mid-childhood to early teen years. The "big teasers" were their peers in general, followed by a particular peer or friend, then by a brother or sister. Almost half reported having had an unappealing nickname—Bubble Butt, Butterball, Beanpole, Four-Eyes, Freckles, Crater Face, Carrot-Top. They felt that their appearance had impeded their social acceptance. Of those who were teased, 70 percent said they still think about these experiences sometimes or more often, and 71 percent said the teasing had permanently marred their body image.

Puberty brings dramatic changes in appearance. It can also bring an intense preoccupation with these changes and with how they will be perceived by others. Girls whose breasts and hips develop earlier than those of their peers often receive unwanted attention and become self-conscious. Moreover, rather than welcoming their new shape as a sign of emergent womanhood, many girls view it as unappealing fat. Boys whose growth in stature and muscularity lags behind that of their friends often experience concern about their body and whether it will ever "grow up." Thus, the timing of physical maturation can be pivotal in the emotional meaning that teenagers attach to their changing bodies. To some, the metamorphosis they've undergone has not resulted in a butterfly, and they only wish they could return to the cocoon.

The interpersonal experiences of adolescence strongly influence body-image development. Teenagers' sense of acceptability—whether they expect to be popular and successful, especially in the dating game—revolves in part around how they *believe* their looks are regarded by their peers. This period in one's life is a pivotal time in the formation of identity and self-concept. Having the "right look"—the cool clothes or the "in" hairstyle—becomes of paramount importance. Fear of rejection grows, and doesn't necessarily recede once adulthood is reached.

As you can see, our body image develops as we learn what our body means to the society in which we live. Body image is very much the result of cultural and interpersonal conditioning. Sometimes the source of our discontent—the zits, the knobby knees, or too much of this and too little of that—vanishes with time, but the "afterimage" still burns in our private perception of ourselves. There are skeletons in our mental closet, so to speak, that continue to haunt us. We feel our emotional scars and see them as physical scars.

For example, some people who were overweight during their youth but are now average weight experience a phenomenon I call "phantom fat." In 1990, I compared the body images of three groups of women: average-weight women who had never been overweight, average-weight women who were formerly overweight, and currently overweight women. I discovered that the currently and formerly overweight groups had a similar body image. Although they'd subsequently lost weight, the formerly overweight women hadn't lost the feeling that their bodies were unacceptable; somehow they still *felt* fat, even though they weren't. "Phantom fat" is similar to the experience of the amputee who still has painful sensations of the *presence* of the lost limb.

Changes in how we look are a natural part of aging and development. Some changes we like; others we dread. If you are strongly invested in your looks, you are at great risk for eventual disappointment. If, on the other hand, you can accept bodily changes with equanimity, your future body image will be much more satisfying.

We have control over some elements of our appearance and can make choices—like a new haircut or style—that either can enhance our body image *or* can lead to the gnawing concern that we've ruined our looks. Other elements are beyond our control; they are thrust upon us by heredity or by life's misfortunes. For example, many men and women have *androgenetic alopecia,* or hereditary pattern hair loss. I have published several scientific studies of the psychological effects of hair loss. I've found that some people feel helplessly unhappy about their progressively thinning locks, while others just take it in stride. People also may struggle with their altered appearance following severe facial burns or following a mastectomy for breast cancer. Many of these individuals do come to accept even such drastic changes and to incorporate them in a healthy body image.

My point here is that how your body appears on the outside does not have to determine how you feel on the inside. Among people born with a disfiguring condition, some agonize that they don't look "normal," yet many others have little difficulty "looking different." Your looks don't mandate how you must feel. If you are faced with unwelcome changes in your appearance, it is important that you know that it is possible to accept and accommodate them. In this program, I'll help you learn how.

Different Paths for Different People

A final factor that is pivotal in body-image development pertains to the presence or absence of certain personality traits. The "slings and arrows" of adversity aimed at us by our culture, family, or peers do not have the same impact on everyone. Some of us who have grown up with the dictates of our appearance-obsessed culture have somehow remained impervious to them. Some of us have been able to transcend any ill effects of our peers' teasing on our evolving body image. Moreover, as I indicated above, disfiguring conditions do not inexorably damage one's emotional well-being. So, who are the fortunate people who are resilient to the forces that urge them to loathe their looks? Conversely, who is at risk for the development of a negative body image?

Self-esteem is a powerful buffer against many of life's misfortunes. The child, adolescent, or adult who has acquired a positive sense of self—as someone who is lovable, competent, and invested in living—doesn't succumb to societal "shoulds" or assaults on his or her physical acceptability. On the other hand, people whose nature and nurture have given them a basic sense that "I'm not okay" are predisposed to find fault with themselves. Insecurity about how others regard them readily becomes insecurity about how others view their physical appearance. Given a modicum of provocation from the powers that be, people with poor self-esteem will generalize their discontent to their looks, moving mentally from the "inner me" to the "outer me."

Self-consciousness is another personality characteristic that contributes to the foundation for a negative body image. Human beings (and other primates) focus their attention in two directions—an outward focus on events in the environment and an inward focus on aspects of the self. The latter focus of consciousness may be directed toward private experiences, such as thoughts, feelings, and sensations, or it may concern publicly observable matters, such as one's overt actions and one's physical appearance. Psychologist Arnold Buss at the University of Texas has verified that people differ considerably in their degree of private and public self-awareness. Those with publicly self-conscious personalities are inclined to view themselves as an audience might; they scrutinize how they might appear to others. Such self-consciousness potentiates preoccupation with one's physical appearance and with how others evaluate one's looks.

Psychological research reveals that body image develops differently in different personalities, which operate as either strengths or vulnerabilities in determining the effects of the events that life thrusts upon us. Poor self-esteem and public self-consciousness pave the pathway for the development of a negative body image. These traits are predispositions, not predestinations. Overcoming the distress of a negative body image is possible for everyone.

YOUR BODY IMAGE: FROM THEN TO NOW

Before I shift from the forces of the past to the here-and-now causes of your negative body image, I want you to take a few minutes to get in touch with your personal body-image history. When Ashley, whom you met at the beginning of this chapter, did this exercise, she remembered two seminal experiences in her body-image development. One occurred when she was seven years old and her parents were getting a divorce. She overheard her father ridiculing her mother's "flat chest" and "fat ass." Ashley began to worry about her own looks, fearing that something about her appearance might disappoint her dad and cause him to stop loving her. The second crucial event happened when Ashley was sixteen and ran for president of her sophomore class. She printed campaign fliers with her photograph on them and posted them on the walls of the school. Some mischievous boys altered her posters with graffiti that said "Pig Face," "Out with Snout," and "Oink for President." Ashley was humiliated, and when she lost the election, her classmates kidded her for weeks that she'd "lost by a nose." Even today, Ashley refuses to allow anyone to take her photograph.

On page 51 is a special Helpsheet called "My Body and Body Experiences: From Then to Now." Write down your description of your body as you recall it appearing during various periods in your life. What were the most influential events and experiences that have shaped your body image? Try to capture how your present body image came to be.

THE POWER OF THE PRESENT: THE EYES OF THE BEHOLDER ARE YOURS

Past cultural and social conditioning contribute to a negative body image, but they aren't the whole story. Even more important, as you will see, are the current causes—the ongoing forces and factors that affect how we experience our body *now,* in our everyday lives. Our current experiences can work either for or against us. They can create, intensify, and reinforce our personal body-image problems, or they can counteract negative lessons from the past. As you learned earlier, research shows that, while body-image problems are by no means rare, *most* people are satisfied with their looks. They accept their physical imperfections and have a reasonably favorable attitude toward their overall appearance. If past conditioning were everything, a positive body image would be practically impossible.

Human beings are "explainers." We explain to ourselves why we do what we do and why we feel what we feel. Nothing is more upsetting than to be upset and not know why. So we might attribute our unhappiness to the mean-spirited, mindless, or misguided actions of others. We think, "I'm upset because *they* made me upset." We blame our incompetent

SELF-DISCOVERY HELPSHEET

My Body and Body Experiences: From Then to Now

At each period of your life listed below, what did you look like? What events and experiences were key influences on how you felt about your looks? Be sure to mention important cultural and interpersonal influences.

Early Childhood (up to age 8)
    My body: _____
    Influences: _____

    _____

Later Childhood (age 8 to puberty)
    My body: _____
    Influences: _____

    _____

Early Adolescence (during puberty)
    My body: _____
    Influences: _____

    _____

Later Adolescence (up to age 21)
    My body: _____
    Influences: _____

    _____

Adulthood (age 21 to last year)
    My body: _____
    Influences: _____

    _____

The Past Year of My Life
    My body: _____
    Influences: _____

    _____

parents, our insensitive spouse, our overly critical coworkers, or our tactless friends. If we attribute our troubles to poor genes, hormonal fluctuations, bad luck, or our astrological sign, we are saying that factors beyond our personal control are responsible for our miseries. So we throw up our hands and try to change nothing. Blaming our past or forces outside of our control helps us justify having the problem, but it doesn't help us solve it.

Certainly our emotions, including our feelings about our looks, result from multiple causes. What people seldom realize, however, is that *we feel what we think*. Our *perceptions* and *interpretations* of events, rather than the events themselves, determine our emotional reactions.

For example, imagine that as you shuffle through your mail one day you see a letter from the Internal Revenue Service. Your name and social security number are typed boldly on the envelope, which is marked: "IMPORTANT! IMMEDIATE RESPONSE REQUIRED!" Now tell me, how do you feel as you imagine this scenario? Your emotional reaction will probably depend on what you believe the envelope contains. A tax rebate? A request to verify your address? Or a notification that you are going to be audited? If you *assume* the latter, then you might have the following private conversation in your head: "Oh no, I knew I shouldn't have claimed my vacation as a business expense!" Even before you open the envelope, you're worried and anxious. Others may interpret the same event quite differently and, consequently, react with different emotions. We *do* feel what we think!

Our body-image emotions also are caused in this way. The often subtle and unspoken messages we give ourselves—our assumptions, perceptions, and interpretations—are decisive determinants of our feelings about our looks. To a great extent, we create our own conditioning. We relate to and interact with *ourselves* in ways that produce a negative body image. Body-image distress may have its roots in our cultural and interpersonal history, but its existence and growth are in the present.

To help you understand the power of the present, I want you to think about the aspect of your appearance you like least. Picture it now in your mind's eye. I want you to think the following thoughts about this physical attribute: "It's ugly. It's really ugly. It's awful to look at. I hate it. I really hate it. Everybody hates it. People think I'm ugly. People hate looking at me. I'm *really, really* ugly." Spend one full minute saying these things to yourself, over and over.

How do you feel now? This exercise leads many people to have unhappy feelings about themselves in general. After a few moments of self-critical thinking, you graduate to feeling hopeless and unlovable. I suspect many of you found the exercise quite familiar. In fact, this may be exactly what you did earlier when you completed the Helpsheet that asked you to record your perceptions and thoughts while looking at yourself in the mirror.

Scientific research confirms that when we believe we have some unattractive physical feature, this belief colors the way we perceive ourselves and outside events. About ten years ago at Dartmouth University, Drs. Kleck and Strenta conducted an intriguing experiment. Using theatrical makeup, the researchers constructed a facial scar on a subject prior to his or her interaction with a "stranger." The stranger was actually working for the researchers and was told to act in a standard way with each subject. Unbeknownst to the subjects, however, the scar actually had been removed before their face-to-face conversation with the stranger. Compared to a control group, the subjects who *believed* they had an unappealing facial scar reported witnessing more discomfort in the stranger's behavior (like staring or avoiding looking at them). They experienced the self-conscious and adverse effects of a serious scar even though none was present! Obviously, since there was no actual scar, subjects were creating their *own* reality based on what they believed about their appearance, not based on the facts of the situation.

This experiment illustrates that among the most potent forces behind negative body-image feelings are your own habitual ways of perceiving and thinking about your body. Many of your self-defeating thoughts may have become so automatic that you're not even aware of them. A variety of situations might trigger these thoughts, but once they begin, they do their emotional damage. This, in turn, leads to more self-critical thoughts and then even more body dissatisfaction. These "messages from your mind" may cause you to attempt to control your discontent, but the self-defensive actions you take will most likely offer only temporary relief and may even make matters ultimately worse. For example, you may avoid those people or situations that activate your negative body-image feelings. Or, you may engage in time-consuming rituals in attempts to "fix" or hide what you perceive to be wrong with your appearance. These short-term defensive measures obviously don't help correct your longstanding body-image problem.

The diagram on page 55 summarizes the historical factors that can predispose negative body-image development and the current influences on our day-to-day body-image experiences. The latter—a vicious cycle of self-defeating thoughts, emotions, and behavior—is what a negative body image is all about. Overcoming a negative body image is accomplished by breaking the cycle. It's too late to alter the events of your childhood or adolescence. History is history! It's unlikely that you will single-handedly halt the messages of your culture. It's

THE DEVELOPMENT OF A NEGATIVE BODY IMAGE

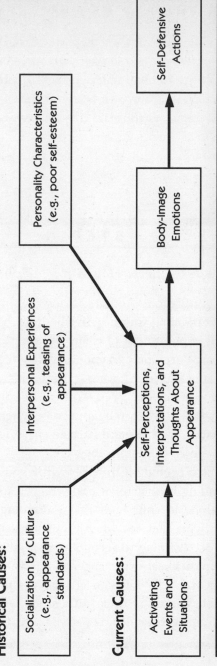

Historical Causes:

Socialization by Culture (e.g., appearance standards)

Interpersonal Experiences (e.g., teasing of appearance)

Personality Characteristics (e.g., poor self-esteem)

Current Causes:

Activating Events and Situations

Self-Perceptions, Interpretations, and Thoughts About Appearance

Body-Image Emotions

Self-Defensive Actions

bigger than you are! You *can,* however, learn to think, act, and feel differently now and in the future—and this program will help you do it. You will unlearn the self-defeating patterns in which you create your own body-image misery and discover new, satisfying ways to relate to your physical self.

STEP 1

Progress Check: How Am I Helping Myself?

• Congratulations! You are taking the important first step toward overcoming your negative body image. You are making a personal commitment to change—one step at a time.

• You are developing an understanding of the psychology of physical appearance—how our outer looks and our inner body image affect our lives. You can see from the research evidence that, despite our appearance stereotypes and our preoccupation with physical attractiveness, looks aren't everything they're cracked up to be.

• You are beginning to apply what you've learned to an understanding of your own body image. You know that you are not alone in your body-image discontent; many people don't like what they see when they look in the mirror.

• You are learning to recognize how cultural conditioning and your past social experiences have left their mark.

• Soon you will begin to change the most powerful yet controllable causes of your difficulties—the ways that *you* currently create your own negative body image.

Where Does It Hurt?

Discovering Your Personal
Body Image

Laurie

Laurie is a 23-year-old woman who recently started her new job as a medical technologist. Most people, including her husband Dave, would say she's nice looking. She is of average height and weight, and she dresses attractively. Laurie's greatest discontent concerns the size and shape of her hips and thighs. "My enormous butt and thighs totally destroy any chance I have to be pretty," she complains. Laurie also dislikes her teeth and is sure that their slight misalignment ruins her smile. Though she admits being pleased with the style and texture of her hair, she's neutral about most other areas of her body.

Several times each week, Laurie becomes especially despondent about her looks. Three specific situations never fail to trigger her body-image distress. Whenever she meets someone new at work or at a social gathering, she is struck by a wave of self-consciousness and feels as if her body is under a microscope. Another troublesome situation occurs whenever she weighs herself and sees that she weighs more than she'd like. Finally, Laurie gets upset about her appearance whenever she wears any snug clothing—for example, a bathing suit at the pool or beach, or a leotard in aerobics class.

A predictable pattern of thoughts runs through Laurie's mind in these situations: "Nobody could ever take me seriously. I'm the fattest, ugliest person here. I wish I could be invisible so nobody could see my stupid-looking rear end." She seldom has pleasant thoughts about her looks—not even about her hair, which she regards as her best feature. Laurie is so preoccupied with what others might be thinking about her appearance (like whether they notice her less-than-perfect teeth) that she has trouble keeping her mind on conversations that occur.

How does Laurie handle her body-image distress? How do her experiences affect her behavior? To avoid embarrassing encounters with people she doesn't know, Laurie stays away from parties and tries to avoid meeting new people. When she does meet someone new, she often cuts the interaction short to make a quick escape. Laurie weighs herself only if she feels confident that her latest of many diets has slimmed her by a few pounds. She seldom goes to the pool, especially if she thinks more than a few other people will be there. She'll go to her aerobics class only if she can sneak into the back after the class has begun.

Laurie knows she is a clothes horse. The only thing that seems to lessen her intense discomfort with her body shape is a new, loose-fitting outfit or the latest cosmetics. So she shops often and buys a lot of these items. Unfortunately, Laurie's three over-the-limit charge cards are the subject of frequent arguments with her husband. Dave thinks Laurie looks just fine and cannot understand "her insane obsession with her looks."

Everett

Now I'd like you to meet Everett. He is a thirty-nine-year-old divorced salesman. Everett hates his receding hairline and thinning scalp and despises the shape of his Roman nose. Everett is also dissatisfied with his stature of five feet, five inches. He feels cheated that his genetics did not give him a full head of hair, greater height, and more handsome facial features. He dreads turning forty. Everett often feels angry and disgusted about his looks. Once his thoughts focus on his appearance, he will usually be in a nasty mood for the rest of the day. Because Everett is convinced that no woman will ever find him attractive, he often feels resentful toward women.

Several situations can be counted on to trigger Everett's body-image distress. When he's with good-looking people or those taller than he is, Everett becomes consumed with bitterness. He also becomes distressed most mornings while shaving. With contempt, he stares at himself in the mirror, inspects his balding head, and examines his profile from every angle. For Everett, a third activator is certain memories that he relives in great detail—memories about teasing that he received as a child. Other kids dubbed him "Pee Wee Parrot." They chided him about his height and his nose until he cried. Painful recollections of this abuse haunt him still.

If we could record Everett's thoughts, they would sound something like: "I look like a scrawny, damned bird. It's not fair. I don't deserve to look like this." And he thinks, "I look worse every day. The more hair I lose, the weirder my nose looks. I can't win."

So what does Everett do to defend himself against his unhappy experiences? To avoid feeling short, he stays away from taller people as much as he can. At work, he prefers to sit at his desk or at the conference table; he seldom stands around chatting. Everett wears caps and hats, even indoors, to hide his hair loss from others. He parts his hair just above his ear and combs it over the top of his head to conceal his balding scalp. He's wasted hundreds of dollars on ineffective potions for hair growth. For at least two hours a day, Everett stands in front of a mirror, fretfully trying to figure out how to fix his flaws. Afterward, he usually feels worse instead of better. Everett avoids allowing others to see him in profile, and he has an unconscious habit of covering his nose with his hand when he speaks. Ironically, Everett's attempts to hide his nose and hair loss seem to call more attention to them. He nervously belittles himself to others with half-hearted jokes about "my beak" and "the bowling ball between my ears."

THE ESSENTIALS OF SELF-DISCOVERY

Both Laurie and Everett have a negative body image, yet the experience is unique to each: They focus on different physical features, are distressed by different triggering events, and have different thoughts and emotions. Though similarly futile, the behaviors that each uses to cope with body-image distress differ as well. What Laurie and Everett share is that, like you, they are tired of feeling trapped by their negative body image and have decided to do something about it.

In Step 1, you revisited your past to examine the seeds of your current discontent. Now it is time to pinpoint exactly how your body-image experiences unfold in your daily life. I will guide you along your personalized journey of self-discovery.

The Body-Image Tests

On the following pages, you will complete a series of six tests that probe your body-image experiences in great detail. These are the same diagnostic questionnaires I use with my clients in body-image therapy. Each test provides a fine-tuned, informative summary of one or more specific aspects of your body image.

Scoring Your Body-Image Tests

After you've taken each body-image test, I'll show you how to score it. For each test, compute your scores carefully—it's wise to use a calculator and to check your math for accuracy. For each test, I'll tell you what the lowest and highest possible scores are. If your score doesn't fall within this range, recalculate!

Charting Your Personal Body-Image Profile

Once you've calculated a test score, enter it on your Personal Body-Image Profile, located on pages 90–91. We will then compare your scores with norms that are based on responses of hundreds of people so you can gain some perspective on your body-image problems. Because the tests' norms sometimes differ for men and women, there is a separate Body-Image Profile form for each sex.

The Profile uses five categories to depict how your score on each test compares with the results for people of your gender: Very Low, Low, Average, High, and Very High. A *Very Low* score means that at least 80 percent of your peers scored higher than you did. A *Very High* score means that at least 80 percent scored lower than you. A *Low* score is one exceeded by 55 percent to 80 percent of your peers. A *High* score means you exceeded 55 percent to 80 percent of them. An *Average* score indicates that your answers were typical of your sex.

Interpreting Your Test Scores

What does each score say about you? Immediately after you chart each score in your Profile, I will guide you in its interpretation. But ultimately, the insights must come from you, not from me. Don't try to set a speed-reading record here. Pause to think about what I suggest. Try each statement on for size. Does it fit? In our discussion of your test results, I will *ask* you as much as I *tell* you.

MAXIMIZING YOUR SELF-DISCOVERIES

Before you take the tests, here are a few helpful tips:

Most people can complete, score, and interpret their body-image tests in about ninety minutes. Pick a time when you have privacy and won't be interrupted. Take the tests when you feel as you typically do, *not* when you are in a particularly rotten mood or are feeling unusually upbeat. Don't feel compelled to finish the tests all at once. If you wish, you may complete one or several tests at one sitting and take a break before resuming. However, it's best not to stop in the middle of a test.

The only way to fail these tests is by failing to be open and honest with yourself. Some people have a tendency to portray themselves in a flattering light. Others paint their experiences with a brush of negativity. Try to adopt an attitude of thoughtful introspection. Your answers will not be published in tomorrow's newspaper. No one will see them but you.

Some of the questions are deeply personal and may bring to mind unpleasant emotional experiences. If there were no anguish in your relationship with your body, you probably would not be reading this book in the first place. Try not to race through the painful questions. On the other hand, dwelling on them serves no purpose. It's best to answer such questions candidly and move on. Any feelings of distress you have while taking the tests should be momentary reminders of why you want to change.

Some of you may be tempted to skip the tests and move on to the next chapter. In a word, *don't!* I understand that you are eager to change your body image, and I applaud your zeal. This is a valuable opportunity to assess the strengths and vulnerabilities of your body image. What you learn from these tests is essential to achieving the changes you want.

1. THE BODY AREAS SATISFACTION TEST

On this first body-image test, you will use a rating scale of 1 to 5 to evaluate how satisfied (or dissatisfied) you are with eight areas or aspects of your body. If there are specific features you dislike that are not listed (e.g., your teeth, your knees, a scar, or a birthmark), simply write them in on lines 9 and 10 and rate your level of dissatisfaction.

Scoring Your Body Areas Satisfaction Test

To obtain your Body Areas Satisfaction score:

1. Add your ratings for items 1 through 8.
2. For now, ignore items 9 and 10.
3. Check to be sure your score is between 8 and 40.
4. Enter your score in the space provided on your Personal Body-Image Profile on page 90 or 91. Then mark an X in the appropriate box on the Profile grid.

THE BODY AREAS SATISFACTION TEST

How satisfied are you with each area of your body?

1 = Very Dissatisfied; 2 = Mostly Dissatisfied; 3 = Neither Satisfied Nor Dissatisfied; 4 = Mostly Satisfied; 5 = Very Satisfied

_____ 1. Face (facial features, complexion)

_____ 2. Hair (color, thickness, texture)

_____ 3. Lower torso (buttocks, hips, thighs, legs)

_____ 4. Mid torso (waist, stomach)

_____ 5. Upper torso (chest or breasts, shoulders, arms)

_____ 6. Muscle tone

_____ 7. Weight

_____ 8. Height

_____ 9. Any other area/aspect you dislike: _____

_____ 10. Any other area/aspect you dislike: _____

Self-Discovery: "What Am I Complaining About?"

People with Low or Very Low scores usually find plenty to dislike about their appearance and are less satisfied than the majority of persons of their sex. If you scored Low or Very Low, you have trouble accepting several aspects of your looks. There are three possible reasons for this:

First, there's the "spill-over factor." If you are unhappy

with your weight, for example, this complaint may spill over to any body area you think betrays your weight. You really have only one complaint, but it is manifested in several different features.

A second explanation for a Low or Very Low score may be that you have several distinct sources of dissatisfaction. Overly critical of your looks, you find a number of different physical characteristics that you cannot accept as they are. Your body is a "moving target" for your discontent.

Third, you may be "body neutral." You have no strong feelings about any aspect of your appearance. You find little to like or dislike. Research has found that men are especially prone to evaluate their looks this way. This pattern may prevent the pain of discontent, but it also eliminates opportunities to appreciate and enjoy your best features.

Because most people read this book to overcome a negative body image, most will score Low or Very Low on the Body Areas Satisfaction Test. Those of you with Average or higher scores are not miserable but probably feel there's room for improvement. You feel satisfied with much of your appearance, but there is something about your looks that troubles you. Remember, over 72 percent of men and 85 percent of women have at least one complaint about their appearance. For you, maybe it's your weight, or a facial feature, or your hair. Maybe it's your chest size that's difficult to accept. Maybe it's a scar. Maybe it's your big feet.

Whatever your score and whatever imperfections you focus on, your dissatisfaction is an unnecessary experience. Change is worth the effort.

2. THE MIRROR IMAGE TEST

Now I want you to find a mirror, preferably a full-length or dressing mirror, where you will have privacy. Wearing only your underclothes, spend exactly *two minutes* looking at your reflection in the mirror. Examine yourself from head to foot. Look at yourself sideways as well as face on. During this time, notice how you feel. Do this exercise now before reading any further. Immediately afterward, answer the questions on the following Mirror Image Test.

Scoring Your Mirror Image Test

You get two scores on this test. Your score on Part A is your Mirror Discomfort rating from 1 to 100. Record this Mirror Discomfort score on your Profile. Put an X in the proper box.

Score Part B as you scored the Body Areas Satisfaction Test:

1. Add items 1 through 8.
2. Do not score items 9 and 10.
3. This is your Mirror Image Satisfaction score and should fall somewhere between 8 and 40.
4. Enter it in the proper space on your Personal Body-Image Profile; then place an X in the appropriate grid space.

Self-Discovery: "What Do I Feel When I Look in the Mirror?"

On the Body Areas Satisfaction Test, you were *thinking about* what you like or dislike about your body. When you took the Mirror Image Test, you had just stopped *actually viewing* your body's reflection. For many people, looking at the real thing intensifies dissatisfaction. Was your Mirror Image Satisfaction

THE MIRROR IMAGE TEST

A. On a scale of 1 to 100, how did you feel while looking in the mirror?

1	25	50	75	100
Completely Comfortable	Somewhat Uncomfortable	Moderately Uncomfortable	Quite Uncomfortable	Extremely Uncomfortable

B. How satisfied were you with each area while looking in the mirror?

1	2	3	4	5
Very Dissatisfied	Mostly Dissatisfied	Neither Satisfied Nor Dissatisfied	Mostly Satisfied	Very Satisfied

_____ 1. Face (facial features, complexion)

_____ 2. Hair (color, thickness, texture)

_____ 3. Lower torso (buttocks, hips, thighs, legs)

_____ 4. Mid torso (waist, stomach)

_____ 5. Upper torso (chest or breasts, shoulders, arms)

_____ 6. Muscle tone

_____ 7. Weight

_____ 8. Height

_____ 9. Any other area/aspect you dislike: _____

_____ 10. Any other area/aspect you dislike: _____

C. What did you see when you looked in the mirror? Circle the 2 or 3 physical areas or aspects above that you focused on the *most* during your two minutes in front of the mirror.

score from Part B lower than your Body Areas Satisfaction score? If so, this suggests that your body-image discontent is especially upsetting.

Now review the individual items of each of these two tests. Though the items are identical, your responses on the two tests may, surprisingly, vary. Area by area, compare your answers to see if your satisfaction changed after you confronted yourself in the mirror. This will help you discover how much your feelings are magnified when you directly confront what you look like.

What was your Mirror Discomfort score from Part A? Higher ratings reveal that the "simple" task of looking at your body is not simple at all. It's unsettling. Your body image is anxiety laden—needless anxiety you can learn to eliminate.

Which items did you circle in Part C of the Mirror Image Test? These were the areas you gazed at the longest. Are these areas the same ones with which you are dissatisfied? If so, you may be prone to dwell more on your disliked features than on what you like best. This tendency to accentuate the negative and to neglect the positive is extremely common among people who experience body-image distress. It's like playing, "Mirror, mirror on the wall, what's my worst part of all?"

3. THE WISHING WELL TEST

This test concerns your perceptions of your body "as it is" and your body "as you wish it could be." Each item on the test deals with a different physical characteristic. For each characteristic, think about how you would describe yourself as you *actually look*. Then think about how you *wish* you looked. The difference between the two reveals how close you come to your personal ideal. In some instances, your looks may closely match your ideal. In other instances, they may differ considerably. Some of your ideals may be very important to you; in other areas, your ideals may be less significant. For each item, rate not only how closely you resemble your personal ideal (Part A), but also how important your ideal is to you (Part B).

THE WISHING WELL TEST

For each item, first rate how much you look like your preferred ideal. Then rate how important your ideal is to you. Enter your ratings on the line to the left of each scale.

1. A. My ideal height is:

0	1	2	3
Exactly As I Am	Almost As I Am	Fairly Unlike Me	Very Unlike Me

B. How important to you is your ideal height?

0	1	2	3
Not Important	Somewhat Important	Moderately Important	Very Important

2. A. My ideal skin complexion is:

0	1	2	3
Exactly As I Am	Almost As I Am	Fairly Unlike Me	Very Unlike Me

B. How important to you is your ideal skin complexion?

0	1	2	3
Not Important	Somewhat Important	Moderately Important	Very Important

3. A. My ideal hair color is:

0	1	2	3
Exactly As I Am	Almost As I Am	Fairly Unlike Me	Very Unlike Me

B. How important to you is your ideal hair color?

0	1	2	3
Not Important	Somewhat Important	Moderately Important	Very Important

4. A. My ideal hair texture and length are:

0	1	2	3
Exactly As I Am	Almost As I Am	Fairly Unlike Me	Very Unlike Me

B. How important to you is your ideal hair texture and length?

0	1	2	3
Not Important	Somewhat Important	Moderately Important	Very Important

5. A. My ideal facial features (eyes, nose, ears, facial shape) are:

0	1	2	3
Exactly As I Am	Almost As I Am	Fairly Unlike Me	Very Unlike Me

B. How important to you are your ideal facial features?

0	1	2	3
Not Important	Somewhat Important	Moderately Important	Very Important

6. A. My ideal muscle tone or definition is:

0	1	2	3
Exactly As I Am	Almost As I Am	Fairly Unlike Me	Very Unlike Me

B. How important to you is your ideal muscle tone or definition?

0	1	2	3
Not Important	Somewhat Important	Moderately Important	Very Important

7. A. My ideal body proportions are:

0	1	2	3
Exactly As I Am	Almost As I Am	Fairly Unlike Me	Very Unlike Me

B. How important to you are your ideal body proportions?

0	1	2	3
Not Important	Somewhat Important	Moderately Important	Very Important

8. A. My ideal weight is:

0	1	2	3
Exactly As I Am	Almost As I Am	Fairly Unlike Me	Very Unlike Me

B. How important to you is your ideal weight?

0	1	2	3
Not Important	Somewhat Important	Moderately Important	Very Important

9. A. My ideal physical strength is:

0	1	2	3
Exactly As I Am	Almost As I Am	Fairly Unlike Me	Very Unlike Me

___

B. How important to you is your ideal physical strength?

0	1	2	3
Not Important	Somewhat Important	Moderately Important	Very Important

___

10. A. My ideal physical coordination is:

0	1	2	3
Exactly As I Am	Almost As I Am	Fairly Unlike Me	Very Unlike Me

___

B. How important to you is your ideal physical coordination?

0	1	2	3
Not Important	Somewhat Important	Moderately Important	Very Important

___

Scoring Your Wishing Well Test

There are ten physical characteristics for which you rated how much you differ from your personal ideal and how important your ideal is to you.

1. For *each* characteristic, multiply your rating from Part A (how much you differ from your ideal) by your rating from Part B (the importance of your ideal). Their product can range anywhere from 0 to 9. For example, if your ideal height is

exactly as you are (0) and your height is moderately important to you (2), your score on Item 1 is 0 × 2 = 0.

2. Now add your scores for all ten items. This total is your Wishing Well score and can range from 0 to 90.

3. Enter your score on your Profile and mark the appropriate box.

Self-Discovery: "How Do I Measure Up?"

The Wishing Well Test offers insights into *why* you dislike certain physical aspects of yourself. Dissatisfaction means that you don't have what you want. If you aspire to physical ideals that you believe you lack, you are going to have a negative body image. Of course, we all fall short of one ideal or another. Nobody's perfect. But the more we value some ideal, the more it hurts if we don't live up to it. Your Wishing Well score takes into account both (A) whether you think you measure up and (B) how much it matters to you.

If your score places you in either the High or Very High category, then what you see when you look in the mirror greatly disappoints you. Your body image may be ruled, as psychoanalyst Karen Horney would say, by "a tyranny of shoulds." Your perfectionistic standards for your appearance are a driving force behind your negative body image.

If your Wishing Well score is in the Average range or lower, you aren't necessarily free from "shoulds." There are probably a few ideals that you value and expect yourself to embody, and occasions when you give yourself grief for not measuring up to these standards. However, soon you will discover that your problem lies less in how you actually look than in how you think you *ought* to look.

This program will help you recognize how your personal ideals are interfering with your self-acceptance. Wishing for physical perfection is not wishing well! Once you recognize the "tyranny" of your ideals, you can take steps to lessen their power over you.

4. THE DISTRESSING SITUATIONS TEST

Many of us endure *negative emotions* about our appearance. These feelings might include anxiety, despair, disgust, anger, shame, envy, or embarrassment. Different situations trigger negative body-image feelings for each of us. For example, Laurie always feels self-conscious at the pool, whereas Everett never thinks about how he looks in a bathing suit. He feels awful after getting a haircut, while a visit to the beauty salon actually makes Laurie feel better.

The next test asks you to think about your reactions to fifty different situations. Use the scale of 0 to 4 to indicate how often you have had negative feelings about your appearance in each setting. Of course, there may be situations on the list that you have not encountered or those that you avoid. If so, simply indicate how often you believe that you *would* have negative body-image feelings *if* you were in those situations.

THE DISTRESSING SITUATIONS TEST

How often do (would) you have negative feelings about your appearance in each of the following situations?

0 = Never; 1 = Sometimes; 2 = Moderately Often; 3 = Often; 4 = Almost Always

HOW
OFTEN?

_____   1. At social gatherings where I know few people

_____   2. When I am the focus of social attention

_____   3. When people see me before I've "fixed myself up"

_____   4. When I am with attractive people of my sex

_____   5. When I am with attractive people of the other sex

_____   6. When someone looks at parts of my appearance that I dislike

_____   7. When people can see me from certain angles

_____   8. When someone compliments me on my appearance

_____   9. When I think someone has ignored or rejected me

_____ 10. When the topic of conversation pertains to appearance

_____ 11. When someone comments unfavorably on my appearance

_____ 12. When somebody else's appearance gets complimented and nothing is said about my appearance

_____ 13. When I hear someone criticize another person's looks

_____ 14. When I recall any kidding or unkind things people have said about my appearance

_____ 15. When I am with people who are talking about weight or dieting

_____ 16. When I see attractive people on television or in magazines

_____ 17. When I am trying on new clothes at a store

_____ 18. When I am wearing certain "revealing" clothes

_____ 19. If I'm dressed differently than others at a social event

_____ 20. When my clothes don't fit just right

How often do (would) you have negative feelings about your appearance?

0 = Never; 1 = Sometimes; 2 = Moderately Often; 3 = Often; 4 = Almost Always

HOW
OFTEN?

_____	21. After I get a new haircut or hairstyle
_____	22. For women: When I am not wearing any makeup
_____	23. If my hair isn't fixed just right
_____	24. If my friend or partner doesn't notice when I'm "fixed up"
_____	25. When I look at myself in the mirror
_____	26. When I look at myself nude in the mirror
_____	27. When I see myself in a photograph or videotape
_____	28. When I have my photograph taken
_____	29. When I haven't exercised as much as usual
_____	30. When I am exercising
_____	31. After I have eaten a full meal
_____	32. When I get on the scale to weigh myself
_____	33. When I think I have gained some weight
_____	34. When I think I have lost some weight
_____	35. When I am already in a bad mood about something else
_____	36. When I think about how I looked earlier in my life
_____	37. When I think about what I wish I looked like
_____	38. When I think about how I may look in the future
_____	39. When anticipating or having sexual relations
_____	40. When my partner sees me undressed
_____	41. If my partner touches me in body areas that I dislike
_____	42. If my partner doesn't show sexual interest

How often do (would) you have negative feelings about your appearance?

0 = Never; 1 = Sometimes; 2 = Moderately Often; 3 = Often; 4 = Almost Always

HOW
OFTEN?

——————— 43. When I am with a certain person
(Specify whom: ——————————————)
——————— 44. At particular times of the day or evening
(Specify when: ——————————————)
——————— 45. During particular times of the month
(Specify when: ——————————————)
——————— 46. During particular seasons of the year
(Specify when: ——————————————)
——————— 47. During certain recreational activities
(Specify which: ——————————————)
——————— 48. When I eat certain foods
(Specify which: ——————————————)
——————— 49. Any other difficult situation? ——————————
——————— 50. Any other difficult situation? ——————————

Scoring Your Distressing Situations Test

This test produces a Distressing Situations score:

1. Add your ratings on the first 48 items. Ignore items 49 and 50.

2. Check to be sure your score falls between 0 and 192.

3. Enter your score on your Profile, and mark the appropriate box.

Self-Discovery: "What Situations Make Me Miserable?"

Thus far, you've evaluated what you dislike about your body, and you've discovered some of the idealized images that cause your dissatisfaction. Now let's consider what situations and events trigger your negative body-image feelings. Your Distressing Situations score represents the total provocation of your misery.

Did your score reach High or Very High levels? If so, you spend considerable time feeling bothered or upset about your appearance. You feel self-conscious about your looks much of the time and expend a lot of effort trying to fix what you think is wrong or trying to avoid situations that spark distress. Some days may be so filled with body-image frustration that your life seems like a minefield—every event harbors the potential for an explosion of negative emotions and experiences. You tire of your struggle to manage your distress and probably criticize yourself for not handling it better.

In this program, we will target your most troublesome situations, those in which you are conditioned to react—almost reflexively—with negative feelings. When you develop the skill and confidence to master these situations and events, you will be empowered to respond differently.

Those of you with Average or Low scores on this test may still have body-image difficulties. You too have your Achilles' heels—times and places that bring intense discontent with your appearance. Should you try to turn these situations around? Absolutely. Even if your distress is limited to a few sets of circumstances, who needs the grief?

5. THE BODY-IMAGE THOUGHTS TEST

In the course of our daily lives, we all have thoughts about our own appearance, some of which are listed in the Body-Image Thoughts Test. Please read each thought and rate how frequently, if at all, it has occurred to you *during the last week.* Don't take any thought too literally. Your thoughts might be similar in content, only with different words. For instance, you may not have the exact thought "I am unattractive," but you may have equivalent thoughts like "I'm ugly" or "I look terrible."

The first list contains negative thoughts; the second positive ones. Use the rating scale to note how often you've had each thought in the past week.

THE BODY-IMAGE THOUGHTS TEST

In the *last week,* how often have you had each of these thoughts?

0 = Never;   1 = Sometimes;   2 = Moderately   Often;   3 = Often; 4 = Very Often

A.   *NEGATIVE THOUGHTS:*

_____   1. My life is lousy because of how I look.
_____   2. My looks make me a nobody.
_____   3. I don't look good enough to be here (i.e., in some specific situation).
_____   4. Why can't I ever look good?
_____   5. It's just not fair that I look the way I do.
_____   6. With my looks, nobody is ever going to love me.
_____   7. I wish I were better looking.
_____   8. I *must* lose weight.

In the *last week,* how often have you had each of these thoughts?

0 = Never; 1 = Sometimes; 2 = Moderately Often; 3 = Often;
4 = Very Often

A. *NEGATIVE THOUGHTS:*

_____   9. They think I look fat.
_____   10. They're laughing about my looks.
_____   11. I'm not attractive.
_____   12. I wish I looked like someone else.
_____   13. Others won't like me because of how I look.
_____   14. I'll never be attractive.
_____   15. I hate my body.
_____   16. Something about my looks has to change.
_____   17. How I look ruins everything for me.
_____   18. I never look the way I want to.
_____   19. I'm so disappointed in my appearance.
_____   20. I feel unattractive so there must be something wrong with my looks.
_____   21. I wish I didn't care about how I look.
_____   22. Other people notice "right off the bat" what's wrong with my body.
_____   23. People are thinking I'm unattractive.
_____   24. They look better than I do.
_____   25. I especially think that I'm unattractive when I'm with attractive people.
_____   26. I can't wear stylish clothes.
_____   27. My body needs more definition.
_____   28. My clothes just don't fit right.
_____   29. I wish others wouldn't look at me.
_____   30. I can't stand my appearance anymore.
_____   31. Any other frequent negative thought? Specify: _____

_____   32. Any other frequent negative thought? Specify: _____

B. *POSITIVE THOUGHTS:*

_____   1. Other people think I'm good-looking.

_____   2. My appearance helps me to be more confident.

_____   3. I am proud of my body.

_____   4. My body has good proportions.

_____   5. My looks seem to help me socially.

_____   6. I like the way I look.

_____   7. I still think I'm attractive even when I'm with people more attractive than me.

_____   8. I'm at least as attractive as most people.

_____   9. I don't mind people looking at me.

_____   10. I'm comfortable with my appearance.

_____   11. I look healthy.

_____   12. I like the way I look in my bathing suit.

_____   13. These clothes look good on me.

_____   14. My body isn't perfect, but I think it's attractive.

_____   15. I don't need to change the way I look.

_____   16. Any other frequent positive thought? Specify: _____

_____

_____   17. Any other frequent positive thought? Specify: _____

_____

Scoring Your Body-Image Thoughts Test

Here you compute both a Negative Thoughts score and Positive Thoughts score:

1. Add your ratings for items 1–30 in Part A, the Negative Thoughts section. Ignore items 31 and 32. Enter this score, which can range from 0 to 120, on your Profile.

2. Now, add your answers for the first 15 items of Part B, the Positive Thoughts section (omit items 16 and 17). The score you enter on your Profile can range from 0 to 60.

3. For each score, mark the correct box on the Profile grid.

Self-Discovery: "What Do I Think When I Think About My Looks?"

The Body-Image Thoughts Test helped you "read your own mind." It's crucial to discover how often certain thoughts, both positive and negative, run through your head. If your Negative Thoughts score was High or Very High, you tend to think the worst and you think it often. When contemplating your appearance, your mind floods with disapproval. You've convinced yourself that your self-criticisms are really true. You fret over your "flaws." You stew over what other people think of your appearance and probably believe they judge your looks as harshly as you do. Once immersed in your negative body-image thoughts, you find it difficult to "change the channel."

Average scores here don't necessarily mean you are free from negative thinking. You may either be gentler in your self-criticisms or point your negativity at a more limited target. In the latter case, when you take shots at yourself, your thoughts are more like a few well-aimed bullets than scattershot. Though it doesn't hurt everywhere, you are still wounded.

Now let's examine the extent to which you allow yourself to have pleasant, approving thoughts about your body. How high is your Positive Thoughts score? The higher the better. If your score puts you in the Low or Very Low category, you have few good things to say to yourself. Why are you so empty-minded when it comes to thoughts about your physical assets? The basic reason may be that you don't believe there's anything good to be said. Or maybe you push any positive thoughts aside with a "Yes but . . . ," followed by self-criticism. For example, "I look pretty good in my new clothes, *but* I'm still too fat."

If you can appreciate the physical assets that other people have, why not your own? Another reason for a shortage of positive body-image thoughts could be that you have been raised to believe that only vain, self-centered people think such things. As a result, if you have a complimentary thought about your looks, you give yourself a brief guilt trip and quickly dismiss the positive thought. This program will teach you how to give yourself permission to acknowledge and enjoy your best features.

The combination of chronic negative thoughts plus infrequent positive thoughts reflects an unhappy imbalance. If, in the privacy of your own mind, you berate your appearance, some self-approving thoughts would at least help you recover from the onslaught of self-criticism. That's food for thought!

6. THE BODY/SELF RELATIONSHIP TEST

We are accustomed to talking about our relationships with people—with family, friends, colleagues, and acquaintances. Although we seldom think about it this way, we also have a relationship with our bodies. The final body-image test contains a series of statements about how you might think, feel, or behave in relation to your body. Some of the statements deal with your physical appearance; others refer to your physical activities and health. On the Body/Self Relationship Test, you are asked simply to rate, from 1 to 5, how well each statement describes you.

THE BODY/SELF
RELATIONSHIP TEST

How well does each statement describe you?

1 = Definitely Disagree; 2 = Mostly Disagree; 3 = Neither Agree Nor Disagree; 4 = Mostly Agree; 5 = Definitely Agree

_____ 1. My body is sexually appealing.

_____ 2. I like my looks just the way they are.

_____ 3. Most people would consider me good-looking.

_____ 4. I like the way I look without my clothes.

_____ 5. I like the way my clothes fit me.

_____ 6. I dislike my physique.

_____ 7. I am physically unattractive.

_____ 8. Before going out in public, I always notice how I look.

_____ 9. I am careful to buy clothes that will make me look my best.

_____ 10. I check my appearance in a mirror whenever I can.

_____ 11. Before going out, I usually spend a lot of time getting ready.

_____ 12. It is important that I always look good.

_____ 13. I am self-conscious if my grooming isn't right.

_____ 14. I take special care with my hair grooming.

_____ 15. I am always trying to improve my physical appearance.

_____ 16. I usually wear whatever is handy without caring how it looks.

_____ 17. I don't care what people think about my appearance.

_____ 18. I never think about my appearance.

_____ 19. I use very few grooming products.

_____ 20. I easily learn physical skills.

_____ 21. I am very well-coordinated.

_____ 22. I am in control of my health.

_____ 23. I am seldom physically ill.

How well does each statement describe you?

1 = Definitely Disagree; 2 = Mostly Disagree; 3 = Neither Agree Nor Disagree; 4 = Mostly Agree; 5 = Definitely Agree

_____ 24. From day to day, I never know how my body will feel.
_____ 25. I am a physically healthy person.
_____ 26. I would pass most physical-fitness tests.
_____ 27. My physical endurance is good.
_____ 28. My health is a matter of unexpected ups and downs.
_____ 29. I do poorly in physical sports or games.
_____ 30. I often feel vulnerable to sickness.
_____ 31. I know a lot about things that affect my physical health.
_____ 32. I have deliberately developed a healthy lifestyle.
_____ 33. Good health is one of the most important things in my life.
_____ 34. I don't do anything that I know might threaten my health.
_____ 35. I do things to increase my physical strength.
_____ 36. I often read books and magazines that pertain to health.
_____ 37. I work to improve my physical stamina.
_____ 38. I try to be physically active.
_____ 39. I know a lot about physical fitness.
_____ 40. Being physically fit is not a strong priority in my life.
_____ 41. I am not involved in a regular exercise program.
_____ 42. I take my health for granted.
_____ 43. I make no special effort to eat a balanced and nutritious diet.
_____ 44. I don't care to improve my abilities in physical activities.

Scoring Your Body/Self Relationship Test

This test is a little trickier to score than the others were. Because it is really four tests in one, you will calculate four separate scores. Also, due to the fact that some test items are worded positively and others are worded negatively, you must use the specific formulas I give you. Each formula requires that you sum ratings on particular items, subtract the sum of ratings on other items, then add a certain number of points. (Points are added to adjust for the wording of certain items.) Just follow the formulas and you will have your scores for the four subtests.

A. To determine your *Appearance Evaluation* score:

Step 1. Add your ratings on items 1–5 _____

Step 2. Add your ratings on items 6–7 _____

Step 3. Subtract the amount in Step 2 from the amount in Step 1 _____

Step 4. Add 12 points to the Step 3 amount   +12

Score = _____

On your Profile enter the amount in Step 4. Make sure it falls somewhere from 7 to 35. Mark the box for your score on the Profile grid.

B. To determine your *Appearance Orientation* score:

Step 1. Add your ratings on items 8–15 _____

Step 2. Add your ratings on items 16–19 _____

Step 3. Subtract the amount in Step 2 from the amount in Step 1 _____

Step 4. Add 24 points to the Step 3 amount   +24

Score = _____

Enter the final amount on your Profile. It should fall somewhere between 12 and 60. Mark the correct box on your Profile.

C. To determine your *Fitness/Health Evaluation* score:
   Step 1. Add your ratings on items
           20–27   _____
   Step 2. Add your ratings on items
           28–30   _____
   Step 3. Subtract the amount in Step 2
           from the amount in Step 1   _____
   Step 4. Add 18 points to the Step 3
           amount   +18
                              Score =   _____

Enter the final amount on your Profile. Your score should be a number between 11 and 55. Mark the proper box on your Profile.

D. To determine your *Fitness/Health Orientation* score:
   Step 1. Add your ratings on items
           31–39   _____
   Step 2. Add your ratings on items
           40–44   _____
   Step 3. Subtract the amount in Step 2
           from the amount in Step 1   _____
   Step 4. Add 30 points to the Step 3
           amount   +30
                              Score =   _____

Enter the amount in Step 4 on your Profile. Your score should fall between 14 and 70. Mark the correct box on your Profile.

Self-Discovery: "If I Dislike Parts of Me, How Do I Feel About All of Me?"

An important principle of gestalt psychology is that "the whole is not equal to the sum of its parts." For example, just because you dislike several parts of your appearance doesn't mean that you cannot accept your looks overall. On the other hand, you may hate only one physical attribute, such as your weight or some facial feature, yet believe this "flaw" ruins everything. Your Appearance Evaluation score (Part A) reveals your overall perception, "the big picture."

Is your Appearance Evaluation score Low or Very Low? If so, your vision of your body is clouded. Your dissatisfactions obstruct your perception of your looks as a whole. You may think of yourself as ugly, or find the idea that anyone might see you as attractive to be pretty foreign. You need to develop a more accurate view of your appearance, its parts *and* its totality.

What if, despite a Low or Very Low Body Areas Satisfaction score, you scored in the Average or High categories on Appearance Evaluation? That's good news. It implies that, to some extent, you are able to keep your specific dissatisfactions in check and feel okay about your looks overall.

Self-Discovery: "How Much Do I Bank on My Looks?"

Your Appearance Orientation score (Part B) reveals how invested you are in your looks, how much you emphasize your appearance over other qualities or traits you possess.

Was your score in the High or Very High range? If so, then you are highly appearance-oriented. You place excessive importance on your looks and probably devote lots of time, mental energy, and behavioral activity to your appearance (not to mention the money you spend on your looks). For you, attractiveness is a continual pursuit. In your mind, your appearance defines a large part of who you are as a person.

But think about this for a moment: If you experience considerable body-image dissatisfaction and distress, then you've made a heavy investment in something that's not paying off. We invest big to reap big dividends. Unfortunately, large investments risk sizable losses as well. The wise investor diversifies to minimize such losses. You need to invest your sense of self-worth in other areas besides your appearance.

An intense appearance orientation magnifies whatever feelings you have about your appearance. To paraphrase a familiar nursery rhyme: When you feel good, you feel very, very good; when you feel bad, you feel horrid. For fashion models, whose income depends on their looks, a pimple, wrinkle, or rash can cost them hundreds or thousands of dollars. For you, the price is psychological. How much do you depend on your looks? Too much?

Although being appearance-oriented motivated many of you to read this book in the first place, I'm sure some of you actually scored Average or lower on Appearance Orientation. This doesn't mean you consider your looks to be irrelevant in your life. It probably reveals either or both of two facts:

First, because our society works overtime teaching us to invest in our appearance, few of us escape the lesson. The vast majority of us, male and female, are quite appearance-oriented, so that even an average level of investment in your appearance relative to your peers may be an overemphasis when judged objectively. Second, some people who score Low on Appearance Orientation may care about their appearance

THE PERSONAL BODY-IMAGE PROFILE FOR WOMEN

Score the tests as explained in the text. Enter each test score in the blank provided below. Then, to classify your score from "Very Low" to "Very High," mark an X in the appropriate box on the Profile.

BODY-IMAGE TEST	Score	Very Low	Low	Average	High	Very High
1. Body Areas Satisfaction Test	___	8–22	23–25	26–27	28–32	33–40
2. Mirror Image Test						
A. Mirror Discomfort	___	1–10	11–25	26–35	36–69	70–100
B. Mirror Image Satisfaction	___	8–22	23–25	26–27	28–32	33–40
3. Wishing Well Test	___	0–8	9–17	18–26	27–50	51–90
4. Distressing Situations Test	___	0–50	51–72	73–80	81–110	111–192
5. Body-Image Thoughts Test						
A. Negative Thoughts	___	0–8	9–17	18–21	22–39	40–120
B. Positive Thoughts	___	0–16	17–26	27–32	33–39	40–60
6. Body/Self Relationship Test						
A. Appearance Evaluation	___	7–17	18–23	24–25	26–29	30–35
B. Appearance Orientation	___	12–40	41–46	47–48	49–53	54–60
C. Fitness/Health Evaluation	___	11–33	34–40	41–42	43–47	48–55
D. Fitness/Health Orientation	___	14–41	42–49	50–52	53–59	60–70

THE PERSONAL BODY-IMAGE PROFILE FOR MEN

Score the tests as explained in the text. Enter each test score in the blank provided below. Then, to classify your score from "Very Low" to "Very High," mark an X in the appropriate box on the Profile.

BODY-IMAGE TEST	*Score*	Very Low	Low	Average	High	Very High
1. Body Areas Satisfaction Test	____	8–25	26–28	29–30	31–33	34–40
2. Mirror Image Test						
A. Mirror Discomfort	____	1–10	11–20	21–30	31–65	66–100
B. Mirror Image Satisfaction	____	8–25	26–28	29–30	31–33	34–40
3. Wishing Well Test	____	0–8	9–17	18–26	27–50	51–90
4. Distressing Situations Test	____	0–24	25–43	44–49	50–65	66–192
5. Body-Image Thoughts Test						
A. Negative Thoughts	____	0–7	8–15	15–17	18–32	33–120
B. Positive Thoughts	____	0–13	14–21	22–25	26–34	35–60
6. Body/Self Relationship Test						
A. Appearance Evaluation	____	7–19	20–24	25–26	27–29	30–35
B. Appearance Orientation	____	12–36	37–42	43–44	45–50	51–60
C. Fitness/Health Evaluation	____	11–36	37–42	43–44	45–50	51–55
D. Fitness/Health Orientation	____	14–41	42–49	50–52	53–59	60–70

but see no point in trying to improve it. These people feel their best is still not good enough. Ask yourself: Have I abandoned my looks because I think trying to improve my appearance is hopeless?

Self-Discovery: "Is There More to Me than Meets the Eye?"

Your Fitness/Health Orientation score (Part C) indicates your degree of investment in something about your body besides its attractiveness. People who are strongly oriented toward their physical health and fitness care about their appearance but also about what their body can *do*. They are active. They exercise regularly. They make conscious, healthy choices about what they eat. They strive to maintain a lifestyle that will prevent illness and promote health. For them, the beauty of the body is also beneath its surface.

How does your Fitness/Health Orientation level compare with your Appearance Orientation level (from Part B)? Don't compare your numerical scores, compare the categories in which they fall (i.e., Very Low to Very High). Are you equally invested in appearance and fitness/health? If you stress your appearance more than your fitness and health, you will need to put more effort into your physical well-being. Contrary to the line from one of comedian Billy Crystal's well-known characters, it is *not* "better to look good than to feel good!"

If you are strongly invested in your health and fitness, you should ask yourself *why* you are pursuing good fitness. In other words, if you avidly exercise and carefully select your diet, is health your goal? Or is your goal to *look* thin, *look* muscular, or *look* healthy? Sometimes Fitness/Health Orientation is truly Appearance Orientation in disguise. This is a judgment call only you can make. Be honest with yourself.

Self-Discovery: "Is My Body Image Fit and Healthy?"

I hope your Fitness/Health Orientation score places you in the High or Very High category. I hope you *act* healthy in order to *be* healthy. More importantly, I hope you feel that your investment in healthy living is paying off. To find out, check your Fitness/ Health *Evaluation* score (from Part D). Higher scores reflect a favorable payoff: You feel fit and healthy. Lower scores indicate dissatisfaction with how well your body functions: You feel out of shape or unhealthy. Later in this program we'll find ways to strengthen and enjoy your physical well-being.

TRANSLATING SELF-DISCOVERIES INTO POSITIVE CHANGES

After answering all the questions in the body-image tests, my clients and research participants often report a clearer understanding of their body-image experiences. Like them, perhaps your body image has come into sharper focus. You may notice patterns that were not apparent to you before. Having charted your Personal Body-Image Profile, you can literally picture both your vulnerabilities *and* your assets.

You can look at the revelations of your Profile in two different ways. From one view, you can chastise yourself: "I can't believe my body image is so lousy. I'm really screwed up." From another, certainly more helpful point of view, you can see exactly what you need to change.

Stating What You Need

Now it's time to translate your self-discoveries into specific needs for body-image improvement. On "My Body-Image

Needs Helpsheet," which follows on pages 95–96, write down at least three important needs you can identify from your results of each body-image test. I have organized the Helpsheet into specific areas to make this easier for you. With this exercise, you will begin to translate the insights you gained from your tests into a personal plan for change.

Here are some examples from Laurie's list:

"I need to stop hating my hips."

"I need fewer self-critical thoughts about my weight."

"I need to get more comfortable with my looks at social events (especially at the pool)."

"I need to be able to look in the mirror and not get upset."

"I need to spend less time trying to decide what to wear before going out."

"I need to emphasize my looks less and start paying more attention to my physical fitness."

"I need to quit comparing myself to every good-looking person I see (especially in the magazines)."

Here are some excerpts from the list that Everett compiled:

"I need to quit hassling myself for having some hair loss."

"I need to accept the fact that I'm no muscle man."

"I need to spend less time criticizing myself (my nose) when I'm looking in my mirror."

"I need to give myself more credit for the fact that I exercise regularly and am in pretty good shape."

"I need to stop thinking that women consider me to be boring because of my looks."

"I need to appreciate the fact that I have nice skin."

"I need to be friendlier to tall guys. It's not their fault they are taller than I am."

"I need to help myself and stick with my body-image therapy program."

HELPSHEET FOR CHANGE

My Body-Image Needs

Physical characteristics I need to feel better about:

I need to _____ .

I need to _____ .

I need to _____ .

Feelings I need to control or eliminate:

I need to _____ .

I need to _____ .

I need to _____ .

Physical ideals I need to emphasize less:

I need to _____ .

I need to _____ .

I need to _____ .

Negative thoughts I need to get rid of:

I need to _____.

I need to _____.

I need to _____.

Positive thoughts I need to have more of:

I need to _____.

I need to _____.

I need to _____.

Situations I need to learn to handle better:

I need to _____.

I need to _____.

I need to _____.

Appearance-oriented behaviors I need to change:

I need to _____.

I need to _____.

I need to _____.

Fitness/health-oriented behaviors I need to change:

I need to _____.

I need to _____.

I need to _____.

Other things I need to change to improve my body image:

I need to _____.

I need to _____.

I need to _____.

ACHIEVING SELF-DISCOVERIES IN EVERYDAY LIFE

Your Personal Body-Image Profile highlights your characteristic experiences—how you generally think, feel, act, and so forth. However, not all of your upsetting body-image experiences are alike. Each occurrence or "episode" of body-image distress has its own unique elements. It consists of specific thoughts, emotions, and behaviors that unfold in a particular situation and in response to certain events. Body-image change requires that you analyze and understand the elements of each distressing episode precisely when it happens. To accomplish this, you will keep a special diary of your body-image experiences. Your diary will work like a videotape that captures and records the moment-to-moment expression of your body image.

The Power of Self-Monitoring

Most therapists believe that before people can overcome their problems, they must learn to perceive their own inner world and their own actions with detachment and accuracy. If you no longer want to be depressed, anxious, or angry, you must be able to put the experience in context, to step back from it, and ask: What am I feeling? What am I doing? What just happened to cause me to feel and do these things? What am I saying to myself about this situation?

These questions are the key to a powerful technique called *self-monitoring*. Self-monitoring is like eavesdropping on yourself. It entails becoming consciously aware of your own immediate experience, observing exactly what is going on inside and out. When you self-monitor, you become immediately alert to body-image feelings when they occur. You recognize exactly what emotions you're having. You determine what it is about a particular situation that initially triggers your negative feelings. You realize exactly what thoughts you are having and how you are viewing the situation. You also examine how you behave in response to these thoughts and feelings.

Self-monitoring may sound simple, but it takes some practice to master. Most people with a negative body image focus only on feeling bad, on being upset, and on blaming their appearance for their unhappiness. They feel what they feel and do what they do, without stepping out of the experience to dissect it. Self-monitoring is a skill, and skills develop through rehearsal. However, the benefits that it brings make learning to self-monitor well worth the effort.

At first, your negative body-image feelings may hinder your self-monitoring. For this reason, I always start my clients off by having them monitor experiences from the recent past rather than those that are currently unfolding. Once you are familiar and comfortable with the process, you will be able to use your new skill when you need it most, which is in the heat of the moment.

You may believe that you already self-monitor. Many of my clients respond to the idea of self-monitoring with, "But I'm *always* analyzing my looks. I'm *always* focused on how lousy I feel about my body." Being aware of your appearance or being immersed in distress is *not* self-monitoring. Such intensely subjective awareness is not enough for change to occur. You must also develop a more *objective* view of your experiences.

Some of my clients argue further, "Hey, I know exactly what's happening during these episodes. I'm ugly and that upsets me." I understand how they feel. If you have hated your body for a long time, it's difficult to separate the hatred from whatever it is that you hate. If you've convinced yourself that your faulty body is the problem, then your negative body-image feelings will seem justified. However, I ask that you bear with me on this. You *can* become open, observant, and objective enough to monitor your emotions, your thoughts, your actions, and the events going on around you. As impossible as it may seem right now, you can change your body-image experiences. You are not condemned to feel ugly and upset forever!

Some of my clients also tell me that they don't have "episodes." They claim they're perennially upset about their looks. "Life is one big, awful episode," they say. Yes, I realize you may continue to dislike the same aspect of your appearance, but you are not thinking about it at every waking moment, nor are you constantly upset about it. Like a sleeping dragon, sometimes your dissatisfaction is dormant. At other times it is full of fire. Something happens to awaken your discontent. As you dwell on it, your emotions become *especially* negative and intense. This is what I mean by an "episode."

The ABCs of Your Body-Image Experiences

Take a few minutes now to recall several episodes of body-image distress from the recent past, especially those that you expect to occur again. Recurrent episodes indicate an especially troublesome situation for you. For each episode, you will identify three fundamental elements of the experience and record them in your Body-Image Diary. These three elements unfold as the *A-B-C Sequence,* as depicted in the figure on the next page.

"A" stands for the *Activators.* What events were occurring that activated or triggered your negative feelings about your appearance? In your Body-Image Diary, write down a brief description of the particular situation that immediately preceded your distress. Be as specific as possible.

"B" stands for your *Beliefs*. What thoughts were going through your mind at the time? Try to re-create the mental conversation you were having with yourself. How were you perceiving or interpreting the situation? What were you telling yourself? Recalling thoughts out of their immediate context can be difficult. Remind yourself by filling in the blank: "I was thinking _____," or, "I was probably thinking _____."

"C" stands for the *Consequences*. What were your emotional and behavioral reactions? In your diary, you will describe these consequences in terms of what I call the *Emotional TIDE*. This acronym will help you analyze the four essential aspects of the situation's consequences. Let me explain:

THE A-B-C SEQUENCE OF
YOUR BODY-IMAGE EXPERIENCES

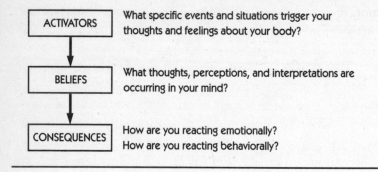

ACTIVATORS — What specific events and situations trigger your thoughts and feelings about your body?

BELIEFS — What thoughts, perceptions, and interpretations are occurring in your mind?

CONSEQUENCES — How are you reacting emotionally? How are you reacting behaviorally?

Your Emotional TIDE

The letter "T" of TIDE stands for the *Types* of emotions you experienced in the situation. What did you feel? Depression? Anxiety? Anger? Shame? Disgust? Embarrassment? Envy? In your Body-Image Diary, name the exact feeling or feelings that you had during the episode.

The letter "I" of TIDE refers to the *Intensity* of emotions.

Rate how strong your emotional experience was at its peak, from 0 for Not at All Intense to 10 for Extremely Intense.

The "D" in TIDE stands for *Duration* of the episode. How long did the episode of body-image distress last? About how many minutes, hours, or days passed until you felt noticeably better and were not so bothered by your body image?

And, finally, the "E" of TIDE refers to the *Effects* of the episode on your behavior. This is extremely important. What did you do as a consequence of your distress? For example, did you try to remove yourself from the situation? Did you become inhibited and withdrawn? Did you try to fix or conceal the bodily focus of your distress? Did you take your feelings out on others? Did you take them out on yourself? Your behavioral reactions at this point in the sequence often represent reflexive efforts to cope with or defend yourself against your unwanted emotions. Over the years, you have developed habitual ways to try to put out the fire. Unfortunately, many times you only fan the flames of your discontent.

I chose the term "Emotional TIDE" because the *more* emotions you experience at a *greater* intensity for a *longer* duration with more *numerous* behavioral effects, then the more powerful the episode—like being swept up in a turbulent tide.

Keeping Your Body-Image Diary

Using a personal Body-Image Diary to self-monitor is *essential* to your success in overcoming a negative body image. I recommend that you write out the format of the diary in a personal notebook that you keep handy. My clients do this and find it much more convenient than photocopying the Help-sheet form on page 103 and then having to keep up with umpteen unbound sheets of paper.

Before you start keeping your diary, I'd like you to do two things:

First, review the five sample diary entries at the end of this chapter. Two of these examples are from Laurie and Everett, whom you met at the beginning of this chapter. After reviewing all five examples, reread your answers on the Distressing Situations Test and the Body-Image Thoughts Test. This will give you plenty of personal reminders of the Activators and the Beliefs that lead to your own upsetting Consequences.

Second, complete your Body-Image Diary for as many different *recent* episodes of distress as possible. During the next two or three days, recall and enter at least ten to fifteen recent episodes to become skilled at monitoring your ABCs. With this practice, the self-monitoring sequence will become very familiar and natural. For each episode, vividly re-create the experience as if it were happening in the present. Close your eyes and picture the situation. Replay your "memory videotape" of the experience—the events, your thoughts, your emotions, and your actions.

After spending a few days analyzing the A-B-C Sequence and Emotional TIDE of ten to fifteen past episodes, you'll be ready for current self-monitoring. For the rest of the week, monitor any episode that occurs. Make a diary entry as soon as possible afterward. Don't try to change the episode; just mentally monitor your experiences as they unfold. Then, record them in your diary. As you monitor these experiences, you will probably generate more items to add to your Body-Image Needs Sheet.

It is crucial that you continue to self-monitor and maintain your diary *throughout the program*. We'll use your detailed accounts of your body-image experiences in many helpful ways as you progress through the remaining six steps of the program.

MY BODY-IMAGE DIARY

Date: _____

A-B-C Sequence

Activators (Triggering events and situations):

_____

_____

_____

Beliefs (Thoughts and perceptions of the situation):

_____

_____

_____

_____

_____

Consequences (Emotional **TIDE**):

Types of emotions: _____

_____

Intensity of emotions (0 to 10): _____

Duration of the episode: _____

Effects of the episode on your behavior:

_____

_____

_____

_____

THE BODY-IMAGE DIARY
FOR *Laurie*

Date: *6-19*

A-B-C Sequence

Activators (Triggering events and situations):

I'm in the checkout line at the grocery. There are 2 guys behind me who are laughing a lot.

Beliefs (Thoughts and perceptions of the situation):

They must be laughing at me!! They're making fun of me—joking about my big fat butt. I hate myself! I've got to get out of here.

Consequences (Emotional **TIDE**):

Types of emotions: *Embarrassed—then angry (at them)—then depressed.*

Intensity of emotions (0 to 10):   *9*

Duration of the episode: *3 or 4 hours*

Effects of the episode on your behavior:

I cried in the car driving home. I skipped dinner and stayed in my room reading diet books. I refused to tell my husband what was wrong.

THE BODY-IMAGE DIARY
FOR *Everett*

Date: *12/4*

A-B-C Sequence

Activators (Triggering events and situations):

Getting my hair cut.

_____

Beliefs (Thoughts and perceptions of the situation):

My stylist cut too much off! She's ruined me. I hate her! She did it on purpose—just like before. God, I look stupid!! (So what else is new?)

Consequences (Emotional **TIDE**):

Types of emotions: *Anger*

Disgust

Intensity of emotions (0 to 10):   *8*

Duration of the episode: *off and on for 2 days*

Effects of the episode on your behavior:

Spent hours messing with my hair. I phoned the stylist to complain—I got nasty with her. I wore my "Atlanta Braves" cap to work 2 days straight.

THE BODY-IMAGE DIARY
FOR *Carolyn*

Date: _May 25_

A-B-C Sequence

Activators (Triggering events and situations):

Trying on new outfits at the department store in the mall.

Beliefs (Thoughts and perceptions of the situation):

Nothing ever fits me. My chest and shoulders are too skinny. I look like a 10-year-old boy! The sales clerk is lying when she says I look nice.

Consequences (Emotional **TIDE**):

Types of emotions: _Ashamed_

Intensity of emotions (0 to 10): _4_

Duration of the episode: _45 minutes_

Effects of the episode on your behavior:

I left the store without buying anything. Went home and soothed myself by eating a quart of butter pecan ice cream.

THE BODY-IMAGE DIARY
FOR *Steve*

Date: *3-30*

A-B-C Sequence

Activators (Triggering events and situations):

I was making out with Jill and she was rubbing my chest and arms.

Beliefs (Thoughts and perceptions of the situation):

She can feel how unmuscular I am. She'll be turned off. When she stopped rubbing my arms I was glad—but figured she quit because she didn't like how they felt.

Consequences (Emotional **TIDE**):

Types of emotions: *Anxiety (self-conscious)*

Intensity of emotions (0 to 10):   *6*

Duration of the episode: *20 min.*

Effects of the episode on your behavior:

I stopped making out with her. To get out of the situation, I told Jill I needed to go study.

THE BODY-IMAGE DIARY
FOR *Melissa*

Date: *Sept. 9*

A-B-C Sequence

Activators (Triggering events and situations):

Thumbing through "Cosmo" (looking at the models).

Beliefs (Thoughts and perceptions of the situation):

Thought about how much I've aged. Thought about how wrinkled my Mom is now. Thought about the ugly scar on my chin. Wish I could afford plastic surgery.

Consequences (Emotional **TIDE**):

Types of emotions: *Depressed*

Intensity of emotions (0 to 10):   *5*

Duration of the episode: *30 minutes*

Effects of the episode on your behavior:

Went to bed early—just to try to get it out of my mind.

Maybe you're thinking you will skip the diary keeping or do it later after reading another chapter or two. Bad idea! This is very important. If you were my client, you would bring your diary to every session. We would review it and learn from it each time. Later, you will rely on the self-discoveries from your diary to promote positive changes in your body image. Because I sincerely want to help you change, I urge you to get started on your Body-Image Diary today.

I'll see you in Step 3 next week.

STEP 2

Progress Check: How Am I Helping Myself?

• You have completed, scored, and interpreted six body-image tests. With your Personal Body-Image Profile, you are gaining valuable insight into the strengths and vulnerabilities of your body image.

• You are using your Body-Image Diary to monitor and analyze the A-B-C Sequence—Activators, Beliefs, and Consequences (including the Emotional TIDE)—of your body-image experiences as they unfold. Having spent a few days to record your most common, distressing episodes from the past, you are now monitoring your current episodes. You are faithfully entering them in your Body-Image Diary.

• Having translated your test results into what you need to change, as further revelations turn up in your Body-Image Diary, you are adding to your Body-Image Needs Helpsheet.

Weight, Warts, and All!

Getting Comfortable with Your Body

IT WAS MY FIRST session with Deborah. As the tears rolled slowly down her cheeks, she told me how unhappy she was about her body.

"Little things set me off. One minute I'm fine, and the next thing I know, I'm feeling really ugly. I despise my hair. I despise my face. I despise my flat chest. Whenever I'm around guys or with my friends, I become unbelievably self-conscious. Lots of times I refuse to go places or do things because I can't stand the way I look."

When I asked Deborah to describe how she felt about having all these bad experiences, she repeated how much she detested various aspects of her body. She recounted episodes of self-loathing. Perhaps my question had been too subtle. So I tried again.

"Deborah, I know that there are things you really dislike about your body. I understand how upset you can become in certain situations. But tell me, how do you *feel* about being this way? What's it *like* having a negative body image?"

This time she got it. "I *hate* hating my body. I'm really tired of feeling ugly. I'm really sick of getting upset. I don't like myself for being this way. Maybe the best way to describe it is that I don't feel in control. I don't feel in control of what I look like, and I don't feel in control of my emotions. I feel totally frustrated and helpless."

In our first session, I asked Kevin the same question. He thought about it for a moment and then offered this analogy:

"It's like there's this part of me, lurking inside my head, that sometimes just takes over. I want it to stop, but it's really powerful. I want to run away from it, but I can't—not for very long anyway. I struggle with it and get pretty uptight. I feel trapped by it, like I'm not really in charge of myself."

THE HUMAN NEED FOR CONTROL

Although they used different words to describe what having a negative body image feels like, Deborah and Kevin voiced a common problem. Both talked about not feeling in control— about feeling frustrated, helpless, powerless, or trapped. Do any of their words describe your personal body-image struggle?

Psychologists have conducted numerous scientific studies revealing that a sense of control is crucial to people's well-being. Even if we are not truly in control of every aspect of our lives, we need to feel that, for the most part, we are. We need to believe that we can anticipate and manage the obstacles and opportunities that come our way. When we think we lack control over important events—for example, how successful we are at work or whether people will like us—we become upset. We feel anxious if we are unsure of our ability to control what happens to us. We feel depressed if we are convinced that we have no control. We feel angry if our attempts to take control are unfairly hindered.

Step 3 of your program will help you regain the emotional control that your negative body image has taken from you. Your current dissatisfaction with your own body is victimizing you—and victims are never happy. By learning to take control of your feelings, you will discover that body-image misery doesn't need to be an integral part of your life.

Appearance Control Versus Emotional Control

To achieve a positive body image, you will need to regain control at two different levels. The first level pertains to your appearance itself. Exactly how much you invest in controlling your looks was revealed in Step 2 by your Appearance Orientation score. If your score was fairly high, you spend lots of time, energy, or money to manage what you look like, enlisting clothing, hairstyles, makeup, diets, or perhaps even cosmetic surgery in efforts to make the most of your looks. If your Appearance Orientation score was low, you may have quit trying to manage your appearance because you are convinced that you have no control. Only if you believe that your efforts are successful will you feel better about your body.

The second, more important level of control pertains to your emotional experiences. You struggle to control your negative feelings about your body by seeking experiences that will make you feel attractive and avoiding situations that will make you feel unattractive. Successful control over your feelings is *real* control—control that matters.

Fixing your body doesn't necessarily fix how you feel about it. Many of us have mastered techniques for improving our appearance; otherwise we'd all be walking around looking like we just got out of bed. However, fewer of us are skilled at managing our body-image emotions. In this chapter, you will begin to take emotional control or, in the language of your Body-Image Diary, you will begin to turn the TIDE of your body-image distress toward becoming more comfortable with your body.

Before beginning any journey, it's helpful to know where you are going and the route you will take. Therefore, before you start to carry out Step 3, please read all the way to the end of this chapter. Then you will be well prepared for the actual journey.

Learning to Take Control

Some people incorrectly assume that emotional control is inborn—either you have it or you don't. Emotional control is really a set of skills that you learn. Thus far, your life has been your only teacher. As I explained in Step 1, what you experienced growing up has most likely conditioned you to react negatively to your appearance—to feel bothered by the image of your body, whether in your mind or your mirror. Body-image therapy is your new teacher, showing you how to reverse your previous conditioning.

Learning any new skill—whether it's learning to do a new dance, make great lasagna, or develop body-image control—is easiest if the process is broken down into simple steps. With practice, you will build competence and confidence in controlling your emotional reactions to your looks.

BODY-AND-MIND RELAXATION

The first step toward developing control over your body-image emotions is *Body-and-Mind Relaxation*. The plain truth is that you cannot feel tense or upset *and* simultaneously be relaxed. Think about it—when was the last time you were cool, calm, and collected and at the same time felt distressed and out of control? Because relaxation is the physical and mental opposite of distress, mastering Body-and-Mind Relaxation is the essential foundation for becoming more comfortable with your appearance. You can also use it to put the brakes on any "runaway train" of negative thoughts and feelings about your looks, enabling you to apply other specific techniques for controlling your body image.

Learning Body-and-Mind Relaxation is quite simple and straightforward. It consists of four ingredients that work together to create very pleasant physical and mental experiences of well-being.

Muscle relaxation: When we are bothered or upset, our bodies react by contracting our muscles. The muscles store this distress, so we may continue to feel tense or agitated even after the worst of our emotional storm has passed. In fact, this lingering muscular tension makes it more likely that we will become emotionally upset again—about our body image or about something else. So controlling muscle tension is important for emotional control.

Diaphragmatic breathing: When we are uptight, our breathing becomes more erratic. This irregular breathing, in turn, creates bodily sensations that lead us to feel even less in control. Deep, rhythmic diaphragmatic breathing, on the other hand, enhances our sense of control and deepens our relaxation.

Mental imagery: What we picture in our mind's eye has a profound effect on our emotions. Picturing our appearance as flawed or frightful triggers unsettling emotions. The ability to control these upsetting images and to paint pleasant images greatly improves our inner sense of well-being.

Self-instructions: Like mental images, words are powerful in their capacity to evoke emotions. Think of the words "ugly" and "gross." How do they make you feel? How about the words "peaceful" and "confident?" People who meditate use certain words, called "mantras," to foster serenity. In Body-and-Mind Relaxation, you will find words that will help you express and experience greater contentment and control.

Your Special Time and Place

To learn Body-and-Mind Relaxation, you are going to need to create a thirty-minute quiet period in your day. During your relaxation time, you should have no other obligations or distractions.

Sitting in rush-hour traffic may be a good place to benefit from the skill of Body-and-Mind Relaxation, but it's a terrible place to try to learn it. As real estate salespeople say, "location is everything." You will need to create a special place, one that is very serene and where you'll not be interrupted. A private den or bedroom is usually a good spot. Ideally, your place should have a comfortable chair, recliner, or futon. If you decide to use your bed, prop several pillows behind you so that you can sit up comfortably with your legs outstretched.

Tell family or friends that you do not wish to be disturbed for a full half hour. Pick a time when you are neither especially tense nor especially tired. Unplug your telephone. Turn off any television or radio that would be a distraction. Dress comfortably. Loosen any tight clothing or jewelry.

Many of my clients are busy people who cannot imagine taking time out of their day to "do nothing." Actually, taking the time to develop emotional control is one of the best investments you can make in long-term productivity. Some of my clients also worry that taking time for themselves is "selfish." Making yourself a priority for some time each day is actually healthy, ultimately helping you be the best that you can be with others, as well. The benefits of Body-and-Mind Relaxation reach beyond body image into all aspects of your life.

Your Script to Relax

When I teach Body-and-Mind Relaxation to my clients, I always give them an audiotape of the following script. It isn't possible to read it and relax simultaneously, so eventually you will need a recorded version. Later, I'll tell you how to make or buy a tape. For now, just read through the script to see how it flows. Notice the four main ingredients: muscle relaxation, deep breathing, mental imagery, and calming self-instructions.

Settle into the chair. . . . Get really comfortable. . . . Gently close your eyes. . . .

Take five slow deep breaths. Breathe evenly from your diaphragm [the lowest part of your chest at your abdomen]. *Breathe so that your stomach slowly rises and falls. . . . Notice the soothing flow of air in and out of your lungs. . . .* [Continue this deep, regular breathing throughout the exercise.]

To begin, make a tight fist with both of your hands. [If your nails are long, just turn your fingers under, put them on the outside of your palm, and press.] *Pay close attention to the tightness in those muscles of your hands. Notice the tension. Study it. . . . Now, let go of the tension and just relax those muscles. Notice the tension flowing out. . . . Notice the difference between the relaxation that you feel now in those muscles and the tension that you felt only a moment ago. . . .*

Okay, do this again. Make sure when you tense your muscles that you tense only those muscles and not other muscles in your body. You're making a tight fist now with both hands. Study the tension in those muscles. . . . Now let go and relax. Notice the sensations of relaxation. . . . Let your hands be completely loose and limp. . . .

Next, tense your biceps and only your biceps. As if you're showing off your muscles, bring your arms up and flex your biceps. Study the tension that you feel in each of your upper arms. Your left arm . . . Your right arm . . . Notice these sensations. Notice the difference as you relax. Just let go of the tension; let your arms drop. . . . Notice the pleasant difference. . . .

Now, tense your triceps [the muscles just under your biceps]. *Turn your arms so that your palms are facing up and extend your arms in front of you and tense them. Notice the tension there in your triceps—a tight, uncomfortable feeling. Study this tension; concentrate on it. . . . Now, let go and relax these muscles, noticing the difference as the tension leaves and the relaxation and comfort take its place. . . . Focus on this pleasant difference between the earlier tension and the current relaxation. . . .*

The next muscles are in your shoulders and upper part of your back. Simply extend your arms in front of you and pull your shoulders forward, stretching forward. Notice the tension in your shoulders and the upper part of your back. Study the sensations. . . . Now be very aware of the difference as you let go completely and relax these muscles. . . . Just settle back, noticing the heavier, warmer feeling in these muscles. . . .

Now push your shoulders back. Do this by leaning forward slightly and moving your arms back so as to push your chest out. Notice the tension in your shoulders. . . . Now feel the difference as you relax those muscles. . . . Let go completely and relax. . . .

The next series of muscles are in the neck. [These muscles are a bit easier to strain than most, so I want you to tense them only enough to feel the muscles tighten but not hard enough to hurt yourself.] *First, simply push your head down so that your chin almost touches your chest. Notice the unpleasant tightness in your neck. Study this sensation. . . . Now, slowly lift your head and completely let go of the tension. Notice the relaxation flowing into those muscles. . . . Be aware of the contrast between the tension that you felt a moment ago and the pleasant relaxation you feel right now. . . .*

Sit forward slightly and lean your head back. Push your head back with your face upward, noticing the tension underneath your chin and in your neck. Focus on the sensations there. . . . Now face forward again and relax those muscles. Notice any sensations that you associate with relaxation. . . . Just let the relaxation soothe you. . . .

Tilt your head to the left, until you feel a tightness in the muscles on the right side of your neck. . . . Notice how it feels as you bring your head back up, as you let go of that tension and just relax. . . . Now tilt your head to the right. Focus on the tightness in the muscles on the left side of your neck. . . . Now bring your head back up, release the tension, and relax. . . . Just enjoy the sensations. . . .

Next, we'll move to the muscles of your face. Let's begin with the muscles around your mouth. Open your mouth as wide as you can as if you were yawning. Feel the tension around your mouth and in your jaw. . . . Now, let go and enjoy. . . . Simply enjoy your sensations of relaxation. . . .

And now push your lips together as hard as you can. Again, notice the uncomfortable tightness in the muscles around your mouth. . . . Okay, let go totally and relax these muscles. . . . Just feel the relaxation there. . . .

Press your tongue against the roof of your mouth, noticing the tight sensations in your mouth, your tongue, your jaw. . . . And now, completely relax. . . . Just let that tension flow out and be gone. . . .

Now, scrunch up your nose so that all the muscles around your nose become tense. Notice the tight, tense sensations in those muscles. . . . Feel the pleasant difference as you relax those muscles. . . . Notice the sensations of relaxation there. . . .

Close your eyes tightly to tense the muscles there. Concentrate on the tension. . . . Feel the difference as you relax the muscles around your eyes. . . . Just release all of the tension. . . .

Next, tense the muscles of your forehead by frowning. Notice the tightness there. . . . And now relax. . . . Just enjoy the sensations of warmth beginning to flow through your face. . . .

You are continuing to breathe from your diaphragm. Your slow, even breathing makes your stomach go up . . . and down . . . up . . . and down. . . . Simply think the word "peaceful" as you inhale. Think the word "calm" as you exhale. Ready now, "peaceful" . . . and "calm" . . . "peaceful" . . . and "calm" . . . "peaceful" . . . "calm" . . . "peaceful" . . . "calm.". . . . As you breathe so smoothly and deeply, you become more and more relaxed. . . .

The next muscles to tense are the muscles in your stomach. Without changing your slow, even pattern of breathing, just pull your stomach in and notice the uncomfortable tightness of these muscles. . . . Now, as you exhale, let go of that tension and relax. . . .

As you continue breathing so smoothly and deeply, tense your stomach muscles again—this time by pushing your stomach out. Really notice the tension there. . . . Now, while exhaling, totally relax those muscles. . . . Notice the sensations of warmth, heaviness, and relaxation throughout your midsection. . . .

Next, as you inhale, tighten the muscles in your buttocks. Study the tension. . . . And while exhaling, let go and relax those muscles. . . . Simply enjoy any sensations of warmth, heaviness, and relaxation in these muscles. . . .

Now, focus your attention on your legs. Extend your legs in front of you and raise them just slightly in the air, tensing the muscles of your thighs. Feel the uncomfortable strain in your thighs. . . . But notice the difference as you exhale and let go of that tension. Lower your legs and completely relax. . . . Feel the warm flow of relaxation moving through your thighs. . . .

Now, point your toes back toward your head so that the muscles around your ankles and your calves become tense. Just tip your feet back slightly. Notice the hard tightness in your calves. . . . And while exhaling, release that tension and simply relax. . . . Now point your toes away from you, and again sense the tension in your feet and your lower legs. . . . And while exhaling, simply let go and relax. . . . Just let all the tension flow out of your legs. . . .

Now, deepen the relaxation that you feel throughout your entire body by taking three or four smooth breaths from the diaphragm. . . . Just breathe evenly . . . comfortably. . . . Feel the relaxation flow through your body from your hands . . . up through your arms . . . to your shoulders . . . up through your head and neck . . . and down your chest . . . through your midsection . . . all the way down your legs . . . into your feet. Each complete inhalation and exhalation of air increases the depth of relaxation. . . .

As you breathe smoothly, allow yourself to become aware of any slight tension that you feel in any muscle in your body. . . . Simply tense that muscle and release the tension as you've done before.

[Pause for 30 seconds]

Let yourself enjoy the wonderful inner sensations of relaxation as they flow through your body. In your enjoyment, you are becoming more and more relaxed . . . sinking into the chair . . . feeling peaceful and calm, contented, very pleasant feelings. . . . Use your breathing to enhance your relaxation even more, sinking more comfortably and deeply into relaxation. Each time you exhale, feel more tension flowing out of your body and more calm, peaceful feelings flowing into your body.

[Pause for 30 seconds]

And now, let's invite your imagination to paint a pleasurable picture in your mind to help you feel even more calm and content and relaxed. Simply place yourself, in your mind, in a springtime scene, on the beach or in the mountains or in the countryside—whichever pleases you most.

Begin to paint your mental picture very vividly and experience your pleasant scene as if you were really there. . . . You hear the melody of birds, singing so sweetly. . . . You see the colors of nature around you. . . . You feel the soothing, gentle warmth of the sun. . . . Against your skin you feel a soft breeze that caresses your body. . . .

[Pause for 30 seconds]

Simply enjoy your pleasant scene. . . . You have not a worry in the world, absolutely nothing to do but simply relax . . . feeling so relaxed and peaceful. . . . You are giving way totally to the experience.

[Pause for 30 seconds]

Now, in your mind's eye, picture a small circle of your favorite color located in the center of your body. . . . This circle contains feelings of well-being, of contentment, of confidence, of being in control. . . . Using your deep, slow breathing, make the circle grow, ever so gradually. . . . The expanding circle fills you more and more. . . . It fills you more and more with your very real experience of contentment and confidence and control. . . . As you inhale, let the circle expand. . . . And as you exhale, let the experience of contentment and confidence and control spread and radiate throughout your body. . . . Allow the feeling to grow, to spread, to fill you up completely . . . more and more as you breathe in . . . and out. . . . So peaceful and calm . . . very content, very confident, very much in control.

[Pause for 60 seconds]

Gradually, counting backward from 10 to 1, feel yourself— refreshed and alert—slowly reactivating your body. . . . 10, 9, 8 . . . moving your hands a little bit whenever you're ready . . . 7, 6, 5 . . . moving your feet . . . 4, 3 . . . and moving your legs . . . and 2, 1 . . . slowly moving your head. . . . And now, whenever you're ready, open your eyes.

Making Your Own Tape for Body-and-Mind Relaxation

Sounds pretty relaxing, doesn't it? You can see why it's important to put the script on audiotape. Having a tape with your
own voice telling you how to relax can be especially helpful.
Ultimately, once you have mastered Body-and-Mind Relaxation, *you* will be the one talking to yourself *in your own mind*. If
dissatisfaction with your voice is one of your body-image
problems, however, using your own voice on the tape may not
be a good idea at this stage in the program. Ask a friend or
loved one, someone whose voice is comforting to you, to
make the tape for you.

First, you'll need a simple cassette recorder—preferably
one with a built-in microphone—and a ninety-minute cassette tape, with forty-five minutes of recording time on each
side. You will use about thirty-five minutes of one side.

Next, locate a very quiet place. You want no interruptions
or background noises while you are recording. When you are
listening to your completed tape, coughs, sneezes, and sniffles
won't be particularly relaxing to hear. Nor will you want to
listen to your phone ringing, your neighbor's dog yapping, or
your toilet flushing!

Before recording, read through the script at least once to
get the feel of it. The italicized script should be read softly, in an
even (almost monotonous) tone without lots of vocal inflec-
tions. Pay attention to the special punctuation in the script.
Words enclosed in brackets [like this] are instructional information and should not be read aloud on your tape. Ellipses (*that
look like this . . .*) mean that you should insert a five-second
pause. When you encounter an ellipsis, simply let the tape
continue while you silently count out five seconds. There

are also specific instructions in the script designating some longer pauses.

Stopping or pausing and then restarting the recorder sometimes will leave distracting clicks on the recording. Experiment with your machine to see how to make the cleanest possible recording. You may need to record the script in one uninterrupted reading.

If you're feeling especially creative, softly play some background music while recording the script. Try a comforting classical piece, such as Pachelbel's Canon in D or Hadyn's Cello Concerto in C: Adagio. Other mellow possibilities include New Age music by instrumentalists such as George Winston, David Lanz, Michael Jones, or Will Ackerman. Some people enjoy using tapes of natural sounds, like the ocean or rainfall. Whatever you select, keep it soothing and simple. Save John Philip Sousa and the Rolling Stones for other occasions.

Making your own tape is easy and can be fun to do. However, if you prefer, a copy of the Body-and-Mind Relaxation tape that I have recorded professionally is available from Guilford Publications for $12.95. To order, call 1 (800) 365-7006 and request catalog item #9652.

Practicing Body-and-Mind Relaxation

Each day, once a day, for the next week, give yourself the full Body-and-Mind Relaxation experience. Here's exactly what I want you to do:

1. On Days 1 to 4, let your tape guide you through the experience.

2. Then, on Days 5 and 6, take *yourself* through the experi-

ence without using the tape. On page 125, I have summarized the steps of Body-and-Mind Relaxation for your easy reference.

3. Finally, Day 7, I want you to skip the part involving the tensing of your muscles. To achieve Body-and-Mind Relaxation, use only slow breathing, pleasant imagery, and mental phrases like "peaceful and calm," "pleasant and content," and "I'm so relaxed."

Charting Your Progress: The Body-and-Mind Relaxation Helpsheet

Even the very first time you experience Body-and-Mind Relaxation, you should have deeply pleasant feelings of enhanced well-being. But remember, relaxation is a skill to be mastered through repeated practice. You will get better and better at it each time. To monitor your progress and maximize your benefits, you need to keep a record of your relaxation sessions. Before you begin a session, and then again afterward, I want you to ask yourself two questions: How physically relaxed do I feel? How contented, confident, and in control do I feel?

First, rate your current level of *physical relaxation* anywhere from 0, for extremely tense and uptight, to 100, for completely relaxed. Then, rate your current level of *mental relaxation* from 0 to 100. A rating of 0 means you feel extreme mental discontent, you are totally lacking in confidence, and you feel not at all in control. A 100 means you feel completely contented, confident, and in control.

On page 126 is your Body-and-Mind Relaxation Helpsheet for keeping track of your physical and mental experiences. There are enough spaces provided for one week of daily practice. But because you will continue to practice relaxation as an ongoing part of this program, you may want to photo-

SUMMARY OF STEPS IN
BODY-AND-MIND RELAXATION

1. Breathe slowly and deeply (from the diaphragm).
2. Tense and relax hands.
3. Tense and relax biceps.
4. Tense and relax triceps.
5. Tense and relax shoulders (forward then backward).
6. Tense and relax neck (forward then backward).
7. Tense and relax neck (left then right).
8. Tense and relax mouth/jaw (open wide, then press lips, then press tongue).
9. Tense and relax nose.
10. Tense and relax eyes.
11. Tense and relax forehead.
12. Focus on breathing slowly and deeply.
13. Repeat the mental phrases "peaceful" and "calm."
14. Tense and relax stomach (pull in, then push out).
15. Tense and relax buttocks.
16. Tense and relax upper legs.
17. Tense and relax lower legs (feet forward, then backward).
18. Use breathing and mental phrases to relax entire body.
19. Vividly imagine your pleasant scene.
20. Use breathing, plus mental imagery of your inner expanding circle of color, plus mental phrases to radiate relaxation throughout your body.
21. "Wake up" count from 10 to 1.

BODY-AND-MIND RELAXATION HELPSHEET

Use this form to record your experiences as you learn and practice your Body-and-Mind Relaxation. Before and after each relaxation session, rate your physical and mental experiences:

1. *Physical Relaxation:* How physically relaxed do I feel?
2. *Mental Relaxation:* How contented, confident, and in control do I feel?

The scale for rating each experience is as follows:

0	25	50	75	100
Not At All				Completely

Date	Time	Relaxation Ratings				Noteworthy
		Physical		Mental		Experiences
		Before	*After*	*Before*	*After*	
___	___	___	___	___	___	_____
						_____
___	___	___	___	___	___	_____
						_____
___	___	___	___	___	___	_____
						_____
___	___	___	___	___	___	_____
						_____
___	___	___	___	___	___	_____
						_____
___	___	___	___	___	___	_____
						_____
___	___	___	___	___	___	_____

copy the Helpsheet for future use or copy the format of the Helpsheet into the notebook that you use as your Body-Image Diary.

By entering your "Before" and "After" ratings each time, you will be able to see how much progress you are making. Use the Helpsheet to note any special experiences that you become aware of. For example, you may realize that your facial muscles are quite tense and usually require a repetition of the exercise to relax them more fully. You may discover that your mental imagery is especially helpful in enhancing your sense of well-being.

Several years ago, a client told me he played his relaxation tape while driving to and from work. That's practice all right—a dangerous practice. On occasion, you may find that you become so relaxed, you fall asleep. If you use your car as a quiet place to relax, just make sure it's not moving!

Over time, your relaxation will come more easily and quickly and will be experienced even more deeply. After only one week of practice, you will be ready to learn how to use Body-and-Mind Relaxation specifically to control and melt away body-image distress. So, best wishes for a relaxing week!

MELTING AWAY YOUR MISERY

Some of you may be tempted to jump to this section without having practiced Body-and-Mind Relaxation. You may be thinking that relaxing sounds too easy to spend much time on or too pleasant to be therapeutic. Yes, Body-and-Mind Relaxation is both simple and pleasant, but only through practice can you achieve effective and long-lasting control over your body-image emotions.

Having spent a week cultivating your Body-and-Mind Relaxation, now we'll look at how you can use your new skill to feel more positive and secure about your appearance, and to have more control over your episodes of body-image distress. The method that you will use to achieve these two goals is called *systematic desensitization*.

Although pronouncing it may not be so easy, systematic desensitization is a straightforward therapy that dozens of scientific studies have proven can help people feel less distressed and more in control of their lives. As a therapist for over twenty years, I have seen my clients reap enormous benefits from systematic desensitization. Some have used desensitization to overcome problems other than that of an unhappy body image. I recall one woman who used it to overcome her longstanding fear of airplane flights and enjoy her family vacation in Hawaii. Countless clients of mine have used desensitization to transcend their anxiety over taking tests. Many have reduced chronic social anxieties that prevented them from giving a speech or interfered with their asking for dates. Desensitization not only helped these people to *feel* different, it enabled them to *be* different.

Making New Connections with Desensitization

How does systematic desensitization work? Basically, it "reprograms" your responses to stressful situations. As a result of past experiences, you've learned to associate certain emotional reactions with particular events, situations, or objects. This is called *classical conditioning*. Many people have been conditioned to feel anxiety, shame, or other negative emotions when they think about particular aspects of their appearance or look at themselves in a mirror. Recall the Distressing Situations Test that you took in Step 2 and the Activators you've listed in the A-B-C Sequences in your Body-Image Diary. Many of the situations and events that you identified trigger your conditioned emotional reactions. This may have gone on for so long that your reactions have become habitual and automatic, like reflexes.

With systematic desensitization, you can take conscious control over your conditioning and weaken the subliminal connection that has been forged between your appearance and your negative feelings. Through *counterconditioning,* you will replace the troublesome connection with a more positive one. Training yourself to control your emotions—and stopping your emotions from controlling you—clears the way for an increasingly positive body image.

To desensitize your body image, I will ask you to "turn on" your Body-and-Mind Relaxation while, at the same time, you picture specific aspects of your appearance or imagine being in certain situations. Desensitization is a very gradual process, and you will begin by imagining things that you already feel relatively comfortable with, and gradually move on to images with which you are less comfortable. (By the way, if you ordered my Body-and-Mind Relaxation tape, you'll see that Body-Image Desensitization is taught on Side 2.)

Constructing Your Body-Image Hierarchies

To design your own personalized Body-Image Desensitization program, you need to develop two important lists, called "hierarchies." The first will be your Hierarchy of Body Areas. The second will be your Hierarchy of Distressing Situations. You will arrange the items on each list in a particular order, from those that you associate with no body-image distress to those that you associate with the most discontent or distress. You should also have available your completed Body Areas Satisfaction Test (from page 63) and Distressing Situations Test (from pages 75–77), as well as your Body-Image Diary.

Your Hierarchy of Body Areas

First let's develop your Hierarchy of Body Areas. On the Helpsheet that follows, there are six spaces for listing specific body areas. Review your Body Areas Satisfaction Test and locate one part of your body about which you feel relatively *satisfied*. Write this area on the bottom line numbered 0. Now you will select at least five areas or aspects of your appearance with which you are *dissatisfied*. Use a scale from 0 to 10 to specify how much discontent or distress you associate with each area. Thus, at the top of the hierarchy, Number 5, will be the body area or feature that bothers you the most. Number 4 will be somewhat less distressing, Number 3 even less disturbing, and so forth. It's a good idea to have each step up the hierarchy involve about the same increase in "distress points."

HELPSHEET: MY HIERARCHY OF BODY AREAS

Body Area	Rating of Discontent or Distress (0–10)
5. _____ (most distressing body area)	_____
4. _____	_____
3. _____	_____
2. _____	_____
1. _____	_____
0. _____ (a satisfying body area)	_____

Expect to do some juggling of items as you construct your Hierarchy of Body Areas. You may modify the form to insert more than six areas if needed.

To see what a completed hierarchy looks like, the following is the Hierarchy of Body Areas that Laurie developed as she was preparing for desensitization.

LAURIE'S HIERARCHY OF BODY AREAS

Body Area	Rating of Discontent or Distress (0–10)
5. Shape of my hips and rear (most distressing body area)	10
4. Size of my thighs	8
3. Muscle tone of my stomach	6
2. My teeth	4
1. Freckles on my arms	2
0. My hair (a satisfying body area)	0

YOUR HIERARCHY OF DISTRESSING SITUATIONS

Now I want you to develop the second hierarchy—your Hierarchy of Distressing Situations. Here you will list the events and situations you typically associate with negative body-image feelings. Create your hierarchy by carefully reviewing your Body-Image Diary and your answers to the Distressing Situations Test in Step 2.

Again, using the Helpsheet, you will build your hierarchy

from bottom to top. The bottom line, Number 0, is reserved for a situation in which you have no body-image distress or perhaps even have positive body-image feelings. List at least five more situations that trigger varying degrees of body-image distress and assign them from 1 to 10 distress points. The top line, Number 5, should be your most distressing situation. As before, try to have relatively equal increases in distress points at each step of your hierarchy. Insert more situations if you need to.

HELPSHEET: MY HIERARCHY OF DISTRESSING SITUATIONS

Situation   Distress Rating
                                                  (0–10)

---

5. _____   _____
   (most distressing situation)

4. _____   _____

3. _____   _____

2. _____   _____

1. _____   _____

0. _____   _____
   (nondistressing situation)

As illustrations, on the next page are Laurie's and Everett's completed Hierarchies of Distressing Situations.

LAURIE'S HIERARCHY OF DISTRESSING SITUATIONS

Situation	Distress Rating (0–10)
5. Weighing myself	10
4. Wearing my leotard at the gym	9
3. When I'm bloated, right before my menstrual period	7
2. With Pat, my good-looking friend	4
1. Whenever I am smiling so broadly that my teeth are obvious to others	2
0. I'm really dressed up and Dave tells me how nice I look	0

EVERETT'S HIERARCHY OF DISTRESSING SITUATIONS

Situation	Distress Rating (0–10)
5. When anybody comments on my hair loss	10
4. Being seen when my hair is wet, which accentuates how bald I look	8
3. Talking to a woman who is taller than I am	6
2. Having people see my profile (i.e., look at my nose from the side)	5
1. The first few days after getting a haircut	3
0. Going on a three-mile run in the park	0

BODY-IMAGE DESENSITIZATION: IN YOUR MIND'S EYE

You've mastered Body-and-Mind Relaxation skills and developed your hierarchies. Now let's put them to use in Body-Image Desensitization. You will carry out *three* kinds of desensitization, each according to specific instructions. It is essential that you conduct your sessions exactly as described.

Your first desensitization sessions will be based on your Hierarchy of Body Areas. You'll be systematically using *mental imagery* to picture each body area in your hierarchy. Here's how:

• First, seat yourself in a quiet, private place where you won't be interrupted by anyone (including the phone) for at least thirty minutes. Eyes closed, spend about five minutes turning on your Body-and-Mind Relaxation. At this point, you should be sufficiently skilled to relax without playing your tape.

• Begin at the bottom of the hierarchy—at Number 0, a body area you find satisfactory. In your mind's eye, picture very clearly that area of your body for about fifteen seconds. Be aware of how you feel.

• Return to your relaxing. Use slow breathing, mental imagery (pleasant scenes and your expanding circle of contentment), and self-instructional phrases ("calm," "peaceful," and "relaxed"). Enjoy this experience for about thirty seconds.

• Now clearly imagine Body Area 0 again, this time for about thirty seconds. Notice how you feel.

• Then return to relaxation for another half minute.

• Imagine Body Area 0 for a full minute. Notice your feelings.

• Return to your Body-and-Mind Relaxation, including your pleasant imagery, for another half minute.

• Next create a mental image of Body Area 1 on the hierarchy. Picture it clearly for fifteen seconds. Notice how you feel.

• Return to relaxation, deepening it further. When you are very relaxed, continue.

• Imagine Body Area 1 for thirty seconds. Notice your feelings.

• Return to deepening your relaxation.

• Then, after relaxing for a while, repeat your image of Body Area 1, this time for a full minute. Again notice your feelings.

• Shift to your relaxation again.

Continue these steps all the way up your hierarchy. The procedure is simple and predictable. First, you will relax, then imagine a body area for fifteen seconds. Relax again, then imagine the area for thirty seconds. Relax again, then imagine the area for one minute. Relax again, then move up to the next area in your hierarchy.

Each time you imagine an area, just be aware of how you feel. If you begin to notice tension or negative emotions, simply use your relaxation skills (slow breathing, pleasant imagery, muscle tension release, calm and peaceful mental phrases) to melt away any discomfort that occurs as you imagine the body area. You should move up to the next body area in the hierarchy *only* after you have been able to remain reasonably relaxed when imagining the lower items in the hierarchy.

Most people will not reach the top of their hierarchy during the first session. In fact, that would *not* be advisable. After about thirty minutes of desensitization, you should end the session. Always finish with two or three minutes of pleasurable relaxation, including imagery of your expanding inner circle of contentment. Later in the day, or the next day, begin again, starting with the last area you were able to imagine without distress.

Each day over the next few days, I want you to schedule and experience desensitization, proceeding step-by-step all the way to the top of your Hierarchy of Body Areas. Use the Helpsheet on page 137 to log your experiences and your progress. Keeping track of your progress reinforces the changes you are making. When you've mastered the hierarchy, have one more session in which you go from bottom to top, imagining each area for a full minute while actively maintaining your relaxation. Once you are able to do this, you will have begun to weaken the connection between your negative emotions and your mental images of your body.

BODY-IMAGE DESENSITIZATION: IN YOUR MIRROR'S REFLECTION

Once you've mastered Body-Image Desensitization "in your mind's eye," you're ready to graduate to *Mirror Desensitization*. The steps are the same as before, except that instead of looking at your body in your mind's eye (in your imagination), you will look at yourself in a mirror. You actively use your relaxation skills to maintain feelings of calm and contentment and to melt away any feelings of tension, distress, or discontent you experience when viewing your appearance.

For Mirror Desensitization you will, of course, need a mirror. Use a full-length mirror, not a hand-held mirror or the one on your medicine cabinet—they're too small. If you don't own a full-length mirror (perhaps because mirrors trigger your negative body-image feelings), then borrow one

BODY-IMAGE
DESENSITIZATION HELPSHEET

Body Areas "In My Mind's Eye"

Using your Hierarchy of Body Areas, indicate each area successfully completed during desensitization. Note any important experiences (feelings, thoughts, or difficulties). Remember, you start at the bottom and work up.

Body Area	Imagery Duration	Date Completed
5. _____	For 1 min.	_____
	For 30 secs.	_____
	For 15 secs.	_____
4. _____	For 1 min.	_____
	For 30 sccs.	_____
	For 15 secs.	_____
3. _____	For 1 min.	_____
	For 30 secs.	_____
	For 15 secs.	_____
2. _____	For 1 min.	_____
	For 30 sccs.	_____
	For 15 secs.	_____
1. _____	For 1 min.	_____
	For 30 secs.	_____
	For 15 secs.	_____
0. _____	For 1 min.	_____
	For 30 secs.	_____
	For 15 secs.	_____

Observations and experiences:

from a friend or invest in one of your own. (Don't worry—
you will soon feel just fine seeing your reflection in a mirror.)
Make sure the mirror is of good quality—not one that produces a distorted reflection. The goal here is to enable you to
feel in control, *not* to make you feel like you're in a carnival
fun house.

Situate your mirror in a private place, like your bedroom or
bathroom, where you will not be interrupted during your
sessions. For Mirror Desensitization, you will not be seated in
your usual relaxation spot. If you wish, start out there until
you are completely relaxed, but then move to stand in front of
the mirror, at a distance of three or four feet.

From my professional experience, I know that most people
are reluctant to carry out Mirror Desensitization. Given the
choice, I suspect many people would prefer oral surgery over
having to look at themselves in a full-length mirror! They say
that they feel silly or self-conscious looking at themselves in the
mirror. Recall that in Step 2 of the program, you rated your
discomfort with looking at yourself in the mirror. Most of my
clients in body-image therapy report high levels of anxiety
while looking at their reflection—a 50 or more on a 100-point
discomfort scale. This unsettling reaction is certainly understandable—after all, if you dislike your appearance, looking at
your reflection will trigger a negative body-image experience,
just as someone who dislikes spiders is going to feel anxiety
looking at a spider. Being uncomfortable looking at your own
body, even in the complete privacy of your bedroom or bathroom, is a symptom of your body-image problem.

Body-Image Desensitization teaches you to confront rather
than avoid body-image distress. By confronting it, you can
control it and overcome it. In fact, the more you might want
to *avoid* Mirror Desensitization, the more you truly *need* it to
neutralize your negative body image. It's okay if you think

Mirror Desensitization sounds intimidating—even crazy. Your mirror will survive. And so will you!

You will be carrying out Mirror Desensitization twice. The first time, wear comfortable indoor clothing. After you have completed your entire hierarchy while fully clothed, repeat the process while undressed and without any makeup—viewing your natural, unadorned appearance. I suggest that you practice desensitization in the buff immediately after a soothing bath or shower.

Begin with Body Area 0 at the bottom of your hierarchy. Briefly look at this area in the mirror, for about fifteen seconds, then close your eyes and relax for a while. Open your eyes and look at the area a bit longer, for about thirty seconds. Again, close your eyes and continue to relax. Then, view your body area in the mirror for a full minute, and relax afterward.

Continue the desensitization process as before, gradually and successfully moving up your Hierarchy of Body Areas until you've completed it. Use the Helpsheet on page 140 to record your experiences after each session. Remember, always end each session with calming imagery and deep breathing. And don't try to move too quickly through the hierarchy. Complete it over three or four separate sessions. As before, after you've mastered the hierarchy, have a final victory session to repeat the entire hierarchy, viewing each area for a minute while actively maintaining a comfortable, relaxed state of body and mind.

BODY-IMAGE DESENSITIZATION: FOR DISTRESSING SITUATIONS

Now you should be ready for the finale—your last series of desensitization sessions. Earlier, you built a Hierarchy of Distressing Situations that lists events that you associate with

BODY-IMAGE
DESENSITIZATION HELPSHEET

My Mirror's Reflections

Using your Hierarchy of Body Areas, indicate each area successfully completed during desensitization. Note any important experiences (feelings, thoughts, or difficulties). Remember, you start at the bottom and work up.

Body Areas	Mirror-Viewing Duration	Dates Completed	
		Clothed	Undressed
5. _____	For 1 min.	_____	_____
	For 30 secs.	_____	_____
	For 15 secs.	_____	_____
4. _____	For 1 min.	_____	_____
	For 30 secs.	_____	_____
	For 15 secs.	_____	_____
3. _____	For 1 min.	_____	_____
	For 30 secs.	_____	_____
	For 15 secs.	_____	_____
2. _____	For 1 min.	_____	_____
	For 30 secs.	_____	_____
	For 15 secs.	_____	_____
1. _____	For 1 min.	_____	_____
	For 30 secs.	_____	_____
	For 15 secs.	_____	_____
0. _____	For 1 min.	_____	_____
	For 30 secs.	_____	_____
	For 15 secs.	_____	_____

Observations and experiences:

increasing levels of body-image distress. Over the next few days, carry out desensitization with this hierarchy. By now, you know what to do. Beginning with Situation 0, alternate relaxation with clear mental pictures of each situation listed in your hierarchy. Picture each event or situation in as detailed and realistic a manner as possible, as if it were really happening. Then actively use your Body-and-Mind Relaxation skills to melt away any tension or distress. As before, break the hierarchy up into several successful sessions, and use a copy of the Helpsheet on page 143 to record your progress. After you've mastered the final step, give yourself one more experience of accomplishment by repeating the entire hierarchy. Celebrate your great progress!

SUCCESS STORIES

Harnessing the power of desensitization to control body-image experiences is a promising application of the technique. If you are reading this chapter for the first time and have not yet learned Body-and-Mind Relaxation or carried out Body-Image Desensitization, you may be a bit skeptical. Skepticism is fine, as long as you don't let it get in the way of your progress.

How did Laurie and Everett do in Step 3 of the program? Both practiced Body-and-Mind Relaxation each day for about a week before proceeding to Body-Image Desensitization. Everett was initially resistant, thinking he already knew how to relax. After some practice, he learned he could attain even deeper relaxation. He also found that he was able to stay cool in situations that really used to rattle him.

Laurie recognized the benefits of applying relaxation from the start. Whenever she began to worry about her appearance, she just stopped and did a little Body-and-Mind

Relaxation: "My head used to flood with feelings about being fat. I never tried to control them. I just dwelled on them and let them upset me. Now I have more emotional control." Mirror Desensitization was very difficult for Laurie. She had to confront how uptight she got while looking at her body, especially her naked body, in the mirror. Nevertheless, she persevered, and desensitization helped her better accept her body.

Everett seems to have benefited the most from body-image desensitization for distressing situations. He used it to feel more comfortable in contexts where he worried about people noticing his hair loss or his nose: "I'm becoming less self-conscious now. I use my mental image of the color circle. Lots of times when something happens that used to make me feel ugly, I fill my mind with purple-colored confidence. It works!"

Body-and-Mind Relaxation is also an effective tool to control tension and distress arising from the other hassles of your daily life. When your negative feelings start to get the better of you, you can use this skill to back off and reestablish control. You can even go one step further. Develop hierarchies and desensitize yourself to situations that repeatedly trigger personal anxieties other than those related to your body image. Whether you fear driving on the expressway, speaking in public, going to the doctor for a physical exam, or asking someone for a date, desensitization can really help.

Throughout the rest of this program, keep on practicing what you've learned in Step 3. Apply it to your body image. Apply it to your life.

BODY-IMAGE
DESENSITIZATION HELPSHEET

My Distressing Situations

Using your Hierarchy of Distressing Situations, indicate each situation successfully completed during desensitization. Note important experiences (feelings, thoughts, or difficulties). Remember, you start at the bottom and work up.

Distressing Situations	Imagery Duration	Date Completed
5. _____	For 1 min.	_____
	For 30 secs.	_____
	For 15 secs.	_____
4. _____	For 1 min.	_____
	For 30 secs.	_____
	For 15 secs.	_____
3. _____	For 1 min.	_____
	For 30 secs.	_____
	For 15 secs.	_____
2. _____	For 1 min.	_____
	For 30 secs.	_____
	For 15 secs.	_____
1. _____	For 1 min.	_____
	For 30 secs.	_____
	For 15 secs.	_____
0. _____	For 1 min.	_____
	For 30 secs.	_____
	For 15 secs.	_____

Observations and experiences:

STEP 3

Progress Check: How Am I Helping Myself?

• At this point in the program, you are continuing to track your episodes of body-image distress as they occur. You are recording the Activators, your Beliefs, and the Consequences of these events in your Body-Image Diary. Among the Consequences that you are monitoring is your Emotional TIDE—the Types, Intensity, Duration, and Effects of your emotions.

• You have learned Body-and-Mind Relaxation, and you are practicing it as often as possible—each day if you can. You are using your Body-and-Mind Relaxation Helpsheet to follow your progress.

• Having developed your body-image hierarchies, you have applied your relaxation skills to systematic Body-Image Desensitization. You have carried out desensitization for body areas that you dislike—both in your "mind's eye" and in front of your mirror. You have completed desensitization for situations that trigger body-image distress. You have recorded your progress on your Body-Image Desensitization Helpsheets.

• You are applying your skills in everyday life. You are learning to take control of your body-image emotions as they emerge in specific situations.

Reasonable Doubt

Questioning Your Appearance
Assumptions

"Nothing's beautiful from every point of view."
Horace, first century B.C.

IMAGINE THE FOLLOWING SCENARIO. How would you feel?
What would you do?

*You are married. Sometimes your spouse is quite considerate of you.
But more typically your spouse is critical and finds fault with your
looks. Daily you are subjected to insults: "You look totally pathetic.
I'm ashamed to be with you." Just when you think you look fine, your
spouse points out your imperfections. Before going out together for the
evening, your partner demands that you spend hours on your appearance, only to "reward" your efforts with, "So that's the best you can
do?" All evening, your spouse tells you that everyone is noticing how
unattractive you are. Finally, upon returning home, your partner
angrily blames your looks for ruining the entire evening.*

You probably wouldn't accept such demeaning treatment
passively. Rather, you have several alternatives for action. You
might try to avoid your partner whenever possible. You might

confront your partner and insist that the criticisms cease—or else! For your ultimate recourse, you'd find a good divorce attorney.

I trust that you can see my metaphor in this scenario. Your supercritical companion is none other than YOU. The constant stream of nasty remarks is your own inner voice talking. However, you can't avoid yourself. You can't divorce yourself. That leaves only one alternative. You must confront your insulting inner voice. You must challenge and change the faulty "mental tapes" that you replay every day. There is no "or else."

WHAT DO YOU SAY WHEN YOU TALK TO YOURSELF?

Curiously enough, when people try to explain their personal problems, they often neglect the significant role that their own thinking, or what psychologists call *cognition,* plays as a source of their unhappiness. In the first century A.D., the philosopher Epictetus wisely observed, "What disturbs people's minds is not events but their judgments on events." This is the basic tenet of cognitive therapy. How you feel when you look in the mirror depends on what you see. And what you see depends on what you focus on and what you say to yourself about it.

Cognitive therapy involves changing problematic thought patterns—patterns that cause us to feel inappropriately anxious, sad, angry, disgusted, embarrassed, guilty, or ashamed. All of these feelings can be warranted in response to certain situations, but many people burden themselves with excessive amounts of distress. Psychologist Albert Ellis asserts that people needlessly hold on to various "irrational beliefs," such as "I must never make a mistake," "It is essential that everyone like me and approve of me," or "I should never get angry, or feel envy or jealousy." These extreme beliefs are self-defeating philosophies that we've learned over the course of our lives. We adhere to these beliefs without ever stopping to question them or even realize how they intensify and perpetuate our unpleasant emotions. Dr. Ellis argues that since most of our negative emotions are the result of our own faulty thinking, we can learn to challenge and change our thinking, and develop more rational and productive attitudes. This applies to body image, as well. We need not be the passive victims of our illogical assumptions about our appearance.

Psychiatrist Aaron T. Beck is another pioneer of cognitive therapy. Dr. Beck maintains that our emotions are a natural outgrowth of our cognitive *interpretations* of an experience. How you feel about events depends on the specific, personal meanings you attach to them. Basic emotions—joy, sadness, anxiety, anger, and shame or embarrassment—are closely tied to certain types of interpretations we make of events in our lives. Our body-image emotions work in precisely the same way. Our cognitions determine our feelings in general and our body-image emotions in particular.

You feel joy when you perceive that something of value has been gained, and you feel sad when you realize that something of value has been or might be lost. For some people, divorce brings the joyful expectation of freedom; for others, it brings the sorrow of failure and loss. With respect to your body image, you feel content or happy if you believe your looks match your physical ideals, and you feel dejected if you think your appearance will *never* be acceptable.

You feel anxious when you believe that some unpleasant event might occur, like getting laid off from work—unless, of course, you've got a better job lined up. If you anticipate that you can exert control over a potential adversity, then you will feel less anxiety. Body-image anxiety stems from expectations that bad things like social criticism or rejection might happen because of how you look.

You feel angry when you interpret events as obstacles that unjustly interfere with your getting what you deserve or have strived for. For example, if your partner doesn't compliment you as much as you think he or she "should," you'll feel annoyed and resentful. Similarly, you become angry about your appearance if you tell yourself that your looks cheat you out of what's fair. You are resentful of your appearance if it doesn't "cooperate" in your looking the way you "should."

You feel ashamed or embarrassed when you think that there is something unacceptable about you that's noticeable to others. Less relevant than what others really think about this "something" is what *you* think about it or what you *think* others think. You might experience some degree of humiliation upon learning, after the party, that your pants' zipper was at "half-mast" the entire evening. You may convince yourself that you can never face those people again because they regard you as a complete fool, thereby intensifying your humiliation. The same body-image emotion occurs when you decide that your physical "flaws" have become obvious to others. The emotion is intensified by your belief that the revelation of your flaws ruins everything.

Cognitive Therapy and the Voices Within

Cognitive therapists recognize that our emotions stem from how we talk *to* ourselves *about* ourselves. If someone catches us thinking out loud as we try to solve a problem or rehearse some anticipated social situation, we might get embarrassed and try to explain away our seemingly silly behavior. Yet we all talk to ourselves in the privacy of our own thoughts. Each of us has ongoing *internal dialogues,* or conversations in our mind. These inaudible dialogues comprise thoughts or statements about ourselves and interpretations of actual or potential events in our lives.

Our internal dialogues usually occur without our even realizing that we are talking to ourselves. We carry on these conversations as automatically as walking, driving, or brushing our teeth. This is because the mental processes that drive these habits are so well-learned that they require no deliberate or conscious thought. Social psychologist Dr. Ellen Langer at Harvard refers to this automatic-pilot process as "mindlessness."

Mindlessness has its advantages and disadvantages. It certainly makes us more efficient; we can effortlessly and simultaneously do several routine things without really thinking about them. Although driving a car obviously requires a certain amount of attentiveness, an experienced driver shifts gears, gives turn signals, or hits the brakes when the light changes to red—all without consciously deciding what to do. Such unconscious, reflexive thought and behavior work in our favor. Among the greatest liabilities of mindlessness, however, is that we fail to see the connections between our silent assumptions, thoughts, and beliefs, and our emotional experiences. Put simply, we don't know our own minds.

Decades of scientific research have confirmed that how we talk to ourselves in our internal dialogues can have a very powerful impact on how we feel. Although our inner conversations are inaudible to others, at some level we do "hear" them ourselves. But most of us only notice the feelings that result from these dialogues, which—especially if they are negative and intense—can command most of our attention.

Private Body Talk

To overcome your body-image distress, you must first become aware of your inner conversations, especially those that deal with your physical appearance, which I term *Private Body Talk*. Let me give you an example of Private Body Talk:

Arlene and Darlene are identical twins. One day, the twins are together in a public restroom. Before leaving, each looks at herself in the mirror. Darlene leaves feeling despondent and bad about herself. Arlene, in contrast, leaves feeling especially confident and positive about herself. Remember, these two women look *exactly* alike. What happened here?

While looking in the mirror, Darlene had the following Private Body Talk: "Oh, I look so ugly. Nobody will ever like me if I don't lose ten pounds. My pointed chin is really stupid looking. Everybody who sees me today will think I'm repulsive." Understandably, Darlene walked away feeling as if she wanted to hide.

Contrast her Private Body Talk with the inner conversation of her identical twin. Arlene thought: "Hmm, I look kind of nice today. I really like this new lipstick. It makes me want to smile, which shows my nice teeth. I might look even better if I lost a few pounds, but the world won't come to an end if I don't. I look pretty good anyway. My blue eyes really stand out when I wear this blue blouse."

Obviously, the twins' different emotional experiences were provoked by profoundly different Private Body Talk.

FEELING IS BELIEVING

In this chapter and the one that follows, you will apply cognitive therapy to your own unhappy body image. In Step 2 of your program, I explained how your body-image experiences typically unfold in an A-B-C Sequence. You remember that "A" stands for *Activating* events—those events or situations that ultimately trigger your emotional reactions. The "C" refers to the emotional *Consequences*—whether feelings of sadness, distress, or dissatisfaction, or feelings of happiness, pleasure, and confidence resulted. The "B" that falls in the middle refers to your *Beliefs*—the thoughts you express in your internal dialogues about an event as it unfolds. What happens during the "B" stage will largely determine your emotional responses to the activating events. What happens at "B" will also influence how you try to defend yourself against your negative emotions. "B" is where people often have problematic Private Body Talk—irrational, self-defeating conversations with themselves. In your Body-Image Diary, you have no doubt recorded examples of your own derogatory dialogues.

One answer to the question "Why does my appearance upset me so much?" is to be found in your Private Body Talk. You are torturing yourself with a continuing flow of nasty remarks. But to change your self-defeating inner conversations, you must ask another crucial question: "Why do I engage in such disparaging dialogues in the first place?" You need to understand the factors that influence what you say in your Private Body Talk.

Returning to the case of the twins, why did Arlene have an inner conversation that boosted her confidence, while Darlene's Private Body Talk made her want to hide her body from the world? Because twins are not treated identically, even in the same social environment, we could guess that Arlene's parents or peers may have interacted with her more favorably than they did with her sister. Maybe Arlene's relatives preferred her and complimented her looks more. Perhaps Darlene was cruelly teased about her appearance by a classmate or a boyfriend, or maybe she had a more relentless bout with adolescent acne than Arlene did.

Maybe, maybe, maybe. . . . We could speculate forever about discrepancies in the twins' personal histories that may have led to their body-image differences. What is certain is that different physical and social histories exert a lasting effect on our current thoughts, feelings, and actions. Though our early life experiences may never occur again, they have left their mark embedded in our memories and in how we think about ourselves. Being taunted at age six by someone who, for whatever reason, considered your looks deserving of ridicule cannot really "hurt" you today. Those taunts are long over. However, such a traumatic event may have taught you something—something that fed upon itself and remains with you still. This "something" is responsible for your negative Private Body Talk, which, in turn, causes you to feel day-to-day body-image distress.

SILENT ASSUMPTIONS ABOUT YOUR APPEARANCE

Whether through personal trauma ("Hey, Porky Pig!") or "normal" socialization by our culture ("Blondes have more fun"), all of us have acquired certain basic beliefs or *assumptions* about the importance of our physical appearance in our lives. Cognitive psychologists call such basic assumptions *schemas*. Schemas help determine what we consider to be "reality." Over time, our schemas become so ingrained in us that we cease to be aware of them; they become "truths" that we take for granted. Schemas serve as templates or guides in the inner workings of our mind. Schemas influence what we pay attention to, how we think about events in our lives, and how we think about ourselves. We have schemas about all sorts of things—about success and failure, about love and relationships. And we have schemas that dictate how we think about physical appearance—our own appearance and that of others.

In Step 1, you learned that all of us possess appearance-based assumptions that shape our perceptions of others. Social stereotypes are essentially the appearance schemas for "social cognition," or how we think about others. For example, suppose you believe that fat people lack self-discipline with food. As a result, you are more likely to notice their eating behavior and infer that they are probably overindulging again. A thinner person consuming the same amount wouldn't attract your attention or provoke such conclusions. If, on the other hand, you assume that obesity is strongly controlled by genetics, then you will be less prone to make disparaging inferences about fat people.

Our body-image emotions emerge from schemas we hold about our own physical characteristics. I call these schemas *Appearance Assumptions*. Your Appearance Assumptions are your unstated, often unrecognized beliefs about the relevance and the influences of your looks in your life. Your Appearance Assumptions serve as "self-evident truths" that guide your Private Body Talk. They are usually quiet, behind-the-scene forces, but they are very powerful. Most likely, you never seriously question their accuracy. You probably ignore, resist, or readily dismiss any evidence that your Appearance Assumptions might be off base or incorrect. Your assumptions are your body-image "rulers"—in both senses of the word. They are the dictators of your Private Body Talk as well as the yardsticks you use to determine how your appearance measures up.

The Ten Appearance Assumptions

Based on my research on the psychology of physical appearance and my clinical work with clients who have negative body
images, I have identified ten common Appearance Assumptions. Because people live rather unhappily by these guiding
principles, I consider these assumptions to be the Ten Commandments of a negative body image. I have listed them on a
Helpsheet on page 155 for your first self-discovery assignment
in this chapter. Please take a moment now to fill out this
Helpsheet. Then we'll discover what your answers mean.

Now let's review your answers. A rating of 4 or 5 indicates
that you agree with a particular statement. How many of these
statements reflected your personal beliefs?

In my professional experience, I encounter individuals
who, despite their profoundly negative body image, adamantly
deny that they subscribe to any of the ten Appearance Assumptions. However, if I present the statements in a different
light, these people discover that some of the assumptions do
fit. So, carefully review any of the statements you rated with a
1, 2, or 3. Ask yourself: Do I ever *act* as if I believe this
statement? Or, alternatively: Based on how I act, *would someone
who knows me think* that I believe the statement?

Now how many Appearance Assumptions did you endorse?
Although they may seem to you like obvious "givens," or "just
the way things are," *all* of them are faulty. Singly or collec-
tively, these silent assumptions serve as a premise for the kind
of Private Body Talk that produces body-image distress.

SELF-DISCOVERY HELPSHEET

The Ten Appearance Assumptions

Read each statement below and decide how much you agree with it. Then, use the 1 to 5 rating scale to express how closely the statement matches your own personal belief. Be completely honest with yourself.

1 = Strongly Disagree; 2 = Mostly Disagree; 3 = Neither Disagree Nor Agree; 4 = Mostly Agree; 5 = Strongly Agree

_____   1. What I look like is an important part of who I am.

_____   2. The first thing that people will notice about me is what's wrong with my appearance.

_____   3. One's outward physical appearance is a sign of the inner person.

_____   4. If I could look just as I wish, my life would be much happier.

_____   5. If people knew how I *really* look, they would like me less.

_____   6. By controlling my appearance, I can control my social and emotional life.

_____   7. My appearance is responsible for much of what has happened to me in my life.

_____   8. I should always do whatever I can to look my best.

_____   9. The media's messages in our society make it impossible for me to be satisfied with my appearance.

_____   10. The only way I could ever like my looks would be to change how I look.

The Oppressive Power of Appearance Assumptions

I won't ask that you simply accept on faith what a disastrous effect these Appearance Assumptions have on your body image. I will give you scientific proof. In my computer are data from a random sample of 300 people who answered the Appearance Assumptions questionnaire and took the same body-image tests that you completed in Step 2. I divided these people into two groups: those who clearly agreed with most of the Appearance Assumptions and those who disagreed with these assumptions. Let's call these two groups "Assumers" and "Doubters." Then, on three of the body-image tests, I compared Assumers and Doubters to see what percentage of each had a negative body image. The results, summarized in the figure on page 157, are compelling.

On each of the three body-image tests, the vast majority (about three-fourths) of Assumers had a negative body image. On the Body/Self Relationship Test, their overall Appearance Evaluation was unfavorable. On the Body Areas Satisfaction Test, they disliked most areas or aspects of their appearance. On the Distressing Situations Test, they indicated that they often experienced intensely negative body-image emotions in many situations. Contrast these obviously unhappy Assumers with people who are Doubters of the Appearance Assumptions. On each of the three tests, Doubters seldom had a negative body image. In fact, about 85 percent to 90 percent had a *positive* view of their overall appearance, were *satisfied* with most areas of their body, and had *fewer* episodes of body-image distress.

This evidence should help convince you just how potent Appearance Assumptions are. Appearance Assumptions fuel self-critical Private Body Talk, which, in turn, gives rise to

HOW DO APPEARANCE ASSUMPTIONS AFFECT YOUR BODY IMAGE?

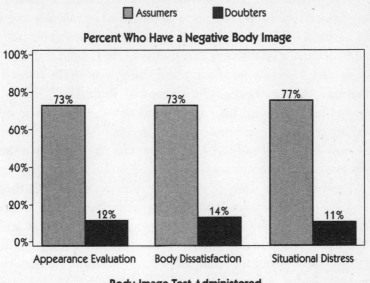

emotional distress. Assumers like Everett and Laurie, described below, have Private Body Talk that always seems to disrupt their peace of mind. Doubters, on the other hand, keep a "clear head" about their looks. Your becoming less of an Assumer and more of a Doubter will spare you considerable misery.

Everett

As you will recall, Everett hates his height, his nose, and his receding hairline. Among his Appearance Assumptions, Everett firmly believes Assumption 2, that the first thing people notice about him is one or all of these characteristics. In his mind, his nose stands out as his most conspicuous feature.

Understandably then, he begins each social encounter by noticing whether or not the *other* person is noticing his nose. If the person looks at his face, he concludes that he or she is awed by his nasal monstrosity. If the person is not looking at his face, he concludes that his nose is too hideous to behold.

In turn, Everett becomes self-conscious and tells himself that the other person finds him repulsive. Reflexively, Everett covers his nose with his hand—until he realizes he may be calling even more attention to his "defect." Self-defensively, he now turns his head and looks away. Then he thinks that the person must see how awkward he is.

Everett is not able to focus on the *social* conversation because of interference from his *inner* conversation. He often ends this kind of interaction abruptly, feeling anxious and disgusted with himself. Everett is so ill at ease during initial face-to-face encounters that, as much as possible, he tries to transact his sales business over the phone so that prospective clients cannot see his "terrible" nose. Even then, Everett worries what they will think when they eventually do meet him. Then they'll see it all—the nose, the thinning hair, and his short stature. Appearance Assumption 2 drives Everett's dread of first meetings.

Laurie

Laurie strongly believes Assumptions 5 and 8. She believes that she has a duty to look her best and to conceal her pear-shaped hips and her "tubby tummy" from view, so she disguises her shape with loose-fitting clothes. She is certain that anyone who sees her stomach and "thunder thighs" will find them very unappealing and, as a result, will find her unappealing as well.

Once a neighbor dropped by her apartment unexpectedly, when Laurie was wearing snug shorts and a tank top, and she refused to answer the door until she had changed into her oversized shirt. "I can't let her see me looking like this," Laurie thought. "She'll know how fat I really am."

Laurie is sure that if she doesn't always look her best, even her husband's interest in her will wane. To Laurie, the fact that Dave seems sexually attracted to her means she's succeeding at her "beauty duty." After enjoying a few passionate kisses, though, her thoughts inevitably shift to the frightening experience of his seeing her naked. "He'll really be grossed out," she worries. Laurie recalls her shame when her high-school boyfriend patted her tummy and also when he caressed her hips and thighs. He never said anything, but in her mind, he didn't have to. She "knew" what he was thinking and why he stopped seeing her: "My massive gut and butt just ruined everything!"

Appearance Assumptions in Action

Can you see how Everett and Laurie's Appearance Assumptions directed the flow of their attention, thoughts, feelings, and actions? Now it's your turn to examine how your assumptions spawn problematic Private Body Talk. On the Helpsheet on pages 161–162, list the assumptions you endorsed with a rating of 4 or 5. Then, write down what each assumption leads you to focus your attention on and to think (in your Private Body Talk). Consult your Body-Image Diary for illustrations of how your assumptions come into play. Finally, write down how they make you feel about your appearance. You will discover that there is a direct connection between each Appearance Assumption you endorse and the body-image distress you sometimes feel. Laurie's Helpsheet samples some of her assumptions and serves as an illustration.

SELF-DISCOVERY HELPSHEET

Laurie's Appearance Assumptions in Action

When I assume: #5 *(My real looks make me unlikable)*

Then I focus on: *Hiding all flaws*

And I think: *"What if people see them anyway?"*

And I feel: *Paranoid, defensive*

When I assume: #8 *(I should always look my best.)*

Then I focus on: *If anything looks less than ideal.*

And I think: *"I need to fix it."*

And I feel: *Worried, anxious, preoccupied*

When I assume: #2 *(My flaws are 1st thing people see.)*

Then I focus on: *My flaws and others looking at me.*

And I think: *"They think I look awful."*

And I feel: *Awful! Self-conscious—ugly.*

When I assume: #1 *(My looks are me)*

Then I focus on: *My appearance—constantly!*

And I think: *About what's wrong and how to fix it.*

And I feel: *Too obsessed; too "vain" pressure.*

SELF-DISCOVERY HELPSHEET

My Appearance Assumptions in Action

When I assume: _____

Then I focus on: _____

And I think: _____

And I feel: _____

_____

When I assume: _____

Then I focus on: _____

And I think: _____

And I feel: _____

_____

When I assume: _____

Then I focus on: _____

And I think: _____

And I feel: _____

_____

When I assume: _____

Then I focus on: _____

And I think: _____

And I feel: _____

_____

When I assume: _____

Then I focus on: _____

And I think: _____

And I feel: _____

When I assume: _____

Then I focus on: _____

And I think: _____

And I feel: _____

When I assume: _____

Then I focus on: _____

And I think: _____

And I feel: _____

When I assume: _____

Then I focus on: _____

And I think: _____

And I feel: _____

When I assume: _____

Then I focus on: _____

And I think: _____

And I feel: _____

INTERCEPTING YOUR ASSUMPTIONS:
YOUR NEW INNER VOICE

From the early insights of Sigmund Freud to contemporary research conclusions, a century of collective wisdom makes it clear that happiness comes from striving to experience ourselves honestly and fairly. Playing distorted mind games with ourselves, even unconsciously, contributes to our discontent. Cognitive therapy is the newest generation of therapies to help people accomplish honest self-awareness and self-acceptance.

Cognitive therapy helps you search for, listen to, and nurture what I call your *New Inner Voice*. This voice is one of fairness, tolerance, logic, patience, and determination. It doesn't give a damn whether you are fat or thin, tall or short, disfigured or flawless, able-bodied or physically disabled, or where you are on anybody's scale of physical attractiveness. This New Inner Voice cares about you as a whole person. It speaks a different Private Body Talk—one that is as reasonable and supportive as your old inner voice has been unjust and disparaging.

Your Appearance Assumptions are fundamental to your way of thinking. As you've seen from my research findings, these "commandments" govern how you think and feel about your looks and ultimately about yourself. Their rule decrees that you should have certain negative body-image thoughts and forbids you to have other, healthier Private Body Talk.

Weakening the power of your Appearance Assumptions is not easy. Their reign is longstanding and, on the surface, Appearance Assumptions seem deserving of their sovereign position. The first words spoken by your New Inner Voice will merely question your assumptions, consciously challenging their authority over your thoughts and feelings. Each assumption paints a picture, and your New Inner Voice must ask "What's wrong with this picture?" Let's examine the ten Appearance Assumptions, one by one.

Assumption 1: What I Look Like Is an Important Part of Who I Am.

This sounds perfectly reasonable, doesn't it? But you must ask, "*How* important are my looks? Is appearance one of the most important parts of my identity? More important than my ability to have satisfying relationships? More important than my intelligence? More important than my personality? Which is more important—my outward appearance or my *liking* my appearance?"

Remember what you learned in Step 1: How physically attractive someone is has little bearing on his or her personality or self-esteem. Our looks are only as important as we let them be.

Dora's New Inner Voice talks to her about this assumption:

My looks aren't everything. I need to focus more on liking my looks and less on what I look like. It's my body image that's an important part of who I am. My success at work, at tennis, and at being a loving mother have nothing to do with my looks. What I *do* is the most important part of who I am.

Assumption 2: The First Thing that People Will Notice About Me Is What's Wrong with My Appearance.

You may be right. For a small percentage of individuals, this assumption is valid. People will indeed stop and take notice if you have green hair or an alligator tattooed on your forehead. But then, you probably welcome the attention. What about distinctive features that are less a matter of personal choice? If you are extremely obese, have a pronounced facial disfigurement, or are missing a limb, only blind people will fail to notice. But so what? Just because people notice this characteristic doesn't mean that all is ruined, or that they will hate you, or that you have no right to exist. What happens *after* they notice is up to you. Your behavior—your friendliness, kindness, and conversation—is much more powerful than whatever is "wrong" with your looks.

Assumption 2 is incorrect for most people most of the time. In reality, *you* are the one focusing on what you don't like about your looks. You're doing the noticing; other people usually couldn't care less. They've got better things to think about.

Oliver's New Inner Voice helps him keep perspective:

So what if people notice that I am short? What difference does that really make? Life goes on! I'm a pretty likable, outgoing guy. People tell me that I'm funny, not that I'm funny looking.

Assumption 3: One's Outward Physical Appearance Is a Sign of the Inner Person.

This assumption is all about stereotypes. Although we might like to believe we can accurately judge books by their covers, we cannot. Both the scientific evidence and the experiences of daily life contradict this assumption. We manage to maintain this false assumption by selectively remembering only occasions when our first impressions based on looks turn out to be right, while forgetting all the times these impressions were off base.

Consider your own experiences. How often has somebody good-looking turned out to be generous rather than self-centered? How often have big, muscular guys turned out to be cooperative rather than bullies? How many blondes do you know who are not the least bit ditsy? How many short men do you know who don't have a chip on their shoulder? Do you know any fat folks who are hard-working rather than lazy? I suspect you've even known a few people with deep-set, dark, and penetrating eyes who turned out not to be serial killers!

Assuming that outward appearance reveals inner worth will lead you to think that people constantly judge you by your appearance. This in turn may cause you to place so much stock in your looks that you become anxious and obsessive. You must persuade yourself that the assumption is a gross exaggeration.

Nellie's New Inner Voice is the voice of reason:

I know I pay too much attention to outer appearances, especially my own. I don't have to look perfect for people to see my inner qualities. Whenever possible, I need to remind myself that my *actions* tell people who I truly am.

Assumption 4: If I Could Look Just as I Wish, My Life Would Be Much Happier

The biggest problem with this assumption is its converse implication: Unless I look the way I want to (i.e., thinner or taller or with my nose fixed), I cannot be happy. Your *wish,* not your appearance, creates your unhappiness. Your wish sells you short. Good-looking people are not necessarily happier than less attractive people. Physically attractive folks have their wish lists too.

Can you recall experiences in your life in which the more you wished for something, the less you appreciated what you had? The more you wish for a new Mercedes, the more your current car seems like a total rattletrap. So you spend big bucks and get a new Mercedes. Before long, it's your old Mercedes, which seems like a junk heap compared to the new Rolls Royce you wish you had. I call this the "Wish-Wash Syndrome." Wishing causes you discontent, which you believe can be washed away by getting what you wish. Instead, one fulfilled wish leads to your wishing for something else. Discontent returns, and the cycle continues.

Todd's New Inner Voice keeps him in touch with reality. It reminds him that his goal is to achieve a better body image, not to have a different body:

> I finally realized that my appearance doesn't prevent my happiness. I do. I make myself unhappy trying to lose weight. When I lose it, I make myself unhappy worrying about gaining it back. Once I accept myself and learn to like my looks, my life will be happier.

Assumption 5: If People Knew How I *Really* Look, They Would Like Me Less.

Buying into this assumption can send you into hiding— concealing parts of your body you think others will view negatively. You worry about what you assume to be the "naked truth." The problem is that this assumption becomes an "untested truth."

Consider Ann, who had a slightly crooked toe. She always went to bed with her socks on, telling her husband that her feet got cold. She feared that if her husband saw her toe, he would be repulsed by it (and by her). At the beach, she always kept her shoes on, certain that exposing her toe would invite stares that she couldn't handle. Finally, Ann was able to convince herself to bring her toe out of hiding and show it to her husband. He reassured her he loved her—crooked toe and all. Then, together they went for a barefoot walk on the beach.

Disproving Assumption 5 requires that you test it. Hiding only makes you feel worse. First try an indirect test. Ask yourself how often your liking someone was undermined by your discovering some imperfection in his or her appearance. How often have you said, "Now that I've seen Sally without her makeup, I have no use for her?" Or, "I hadn't realized Jimmy had hair on his back. I'll be sure to avoid him from now on."

Later in the program, I'll help you come out of hiding and test this assumption directly. Right now, your New Inner Voice needs to remind you that *you* are the one who likes you less because of some physical feature you are ashamed of; if people knew how you really look, their opinions about you would not, in fact, change.

Hear the New Inner Voice that coaxed Abbie out of hiding:

I worried that I'd be hurt if people knew how I really look. I worried that if they see how hairy my arms are, their opinion of me will go down. But worrying itself makes me feel bad. I'm really tired of always having to wear long sleeves. Could I really feel that much worse if I stopped hiding what I look like? Is it possible that I've built this up to be a bigger deal than it really is?

Assumption 6: By Controlling My Appearance, I Can Control My Social and Emotional Life.

You do have some control over your appearance. The use of clothing, cosmetics, hairstyling, a healthy diet, and regular exercise can be helpful tools for managing your appearance, which in turn can help you feel good about yourself. The risk, however, is relying too heavily on these tools. Like a carpenter who cannot build a house using only a hammer, you cannot construct a happy life using only your looks.

Another problem with this assumption is the fact that appearance management works only if it improves your body image. A closet packed with expensive, stylish clothes is useless if you don't like how you look in them. They may help you hide what you dislike about your body, but as you saw for Assumption 5, hiding doesn't change your body image. It only reinforces your belief that your unadorned appearance is unacceptable.

Your own experiences are probably the best evidence against the assumption that you can control your social and emotional life by controlling your appearance. If all those appearance-managing efforts are so effective, then why do you still have a negative body image? Let's rephrase Assumption 6 to make it more accurate: By controlling my *body image,* I can better control my social and emotional life.

Sue's New Inner Voice helps her adjust her thinking:

I can see that spending too much time and money to "fix" my appearance is misdirected effort. Constantly trying to change my looks is only a Band-Aid. It never ends—a different hairstyle, a new brand of cosmetics, another outfit, the latest diet. In the long haul, what has all this actually accomplished? I'm still unhappy with my looks. If I really want to feel better, I need to focus on changing my feelings instead of my looks. Then I'll have more control over my life.

Assumption 7: My Appearance Is Responsible for Much of What Has Happened to Me in My Life.

People tend to overestimate the power of physical appearance—both its detrimental and its beneficial effects. Perhaps, during childhood, you were teased about your weight or some other physical feature. In adolescence, acne may have placed you at a disadvantage in the dating game. Perhaps you looked just fine—but not as striking as your brother, or sister, or best friend. It's true that your appearance has influenced some things in your life, but most events in your life have had absolutely nothing to do with your looks. Most events were the result of your personality, decisions, actions, and intellect. You are not a passive victim of your appearance.

History is packed with evidence that beauty is not a prerequisite for success. Neither Abraham Lincoln nor Winston Churchill would qualify as a handsome hunk. With a port-wine birthmark on his bald head, Gorbachev emerged as a world leader. Golda Meir, Eleanor Roosevelt, and Margaret Thatcher were hardly beauty queens. Review the evidence from your own interpersonal experiences. Can you think of people you loved, liked, or admired for reasons that were totally unrelated to their looks?

Sam has always had a slight build, about which he was teased as a youth. He embraced Assumption 7 until he came to realize that the most important influences in his life were his shy personality and his love of nature. Sam's New Inner Voice says:

My appearance has affected events in my life, but I am ultimately responsible for how I've chosen to deal with those events. Besides, my history is already written. My present and future need not be altered by my appearance.

Assumption 8: I Should Always Do Whatever I Can to Look My Best.

Why? What do you believe will happen if you always look your best? What will happen if you don't? The words "should" and "always" in this assumption imply that looking your best is your *duty*. Conversely, the assumption implies that by not looking your best you have failed. Another problem here is that looking your best is highly subjective. You will always be able to imagine ways you could look even better! Nobody can possibly look their best all the time. Why would you want to set yourself up for failure by expecting the impossible?

Do you expect *other people* have the best imaginable appearance on all occasions? Would you consider a friend a failure if he or she wore less than perfect clothing or had a hair out of place? For the sake of your friendships, I hope you don't hold your friends to such extreme and impractical standards. Similarly, I doubt you would tolerate that expectation from a friend. So if you would not expect this of others, or tolerate their expecting it of you, why should you require yourself to look your best at all times?

Ursula devotes an excessive amount of time to her appearance and is still unhappy. So she started using her New Inner Voice to speak out against this perfectionism:

> I like looking nice, but I could stand to loosen up some. I don't have to look perfect all the time. When I look less than my best, nobody ever tells me I should look better. I'm the one pressuring myself. I'm the one giving myself grief. Instead of doing whatever I can to always look my best, I need to do whatever I can to accept my looks. It's okay to look acceptable, instead of exceptional.

Assumption 9: The Media's Messages in Our Society Make It Impossible for Me to Be Satisfied with My Appearance.

If you hold this assumption, you will feel powerless and will see little point in trying to overcome your negative body image. The forces opposing you will seem too great. It's true that the media convey strong and unhelpful images about physical appearance. They tell you that if you want to be happy and successful, you either must be naturally very attractive or must purchase all the products and services available to come as close to physical perfection as you can. The bottom-line message is that good looks are everything and should be pursued at all costs.

You don't have to be a rocket scientist to see that these messages are extreme and distorted. If media messages were omnipotent, nobody would have a positive body image. There are many roads to success and happiness that do *not* require your being a 10 on a 10-point scale of physical perfection. Much worse than not being a 10 is *worrying* about not being a 10.

Although they fuel your body-image worries, the media don't point a gun at your head and say, "Believe everything we say, or else!" What you believe is entirely up to you. A character in the movie *Network* protested the media's injustices by screaming from a rooftop to the passive public below, "I'm mad as hell, and I won't take it anymore!" You don't have to take it anymore. Your Private Body Talk does not have to echo the voices of the media.

Should you sell your radio and television, give up movies, and stop reading magazines? Should you join a nudist colony and boycott all products that alter appearance? Should you find a rooftop and scream, trying to change our appearance-preoccupied world? Probably not. The world could certainly use some changes, but your power and your happiness depend on *you*. You can see and hear the media's messages *without* accepting them as the rules you must live by. Begin to let go of Assumption 9 by realizing that the messages are only as powerful as you allow them to be. You do not have to regard yourself as a victim.

Back in Step 2, Melissa recorded an episode of distress in her Body-Image Diary that was triggered by comparing herself with the models in *Cosmopolitan*. Melissa's assertive New Inner Voice helps her "not take it anymore":

> I'm tired of trying to look like all these perfect bodies in the media. Just because they are there doesn't mean I have to look like them. They are professional models, and I have no interest in being a model. I'm going to work like hell to accept myself. The media don't make it impossible for me to accept my looks. I do.

Assumption 10: The Only Way I Could Ever Like My Looks Would Be to Change How I Look.

This assumption drives people to cosmetic surgeons, to weight-loss programs, and to the stores offering the "latest look." Many of my new clients cannot fathom ever feeling good about themselves unless they change their weight. They want me to help them lose ten or fifteen pounds so that they can have a positive body image. When I suggest that we *first* work toward a positive body image and *then* decide about weight loss, they stare at me in disbelief. How could I be so stupid?

I understand perfectly the basis of Assumption 10. If something is broken, it should be fixed. If you believe that your appearance is "broken" and the products and the technology exist to "fix" it, then you should fix it. Maybe you modified your weight. Maybe you bought new clothes or altered your hairstyle. You may even have had electrolysis or cosmetic surgery. These changes felt pretty good—for a while anyway. However, you haven't permanently fixed how you feel about your appearance. So I ask you, what's really broken?

Challenge this assumption head on! What's broken is your body image, and that's what needs repair. As you learned from the research I described earlier, in the introductory chapter, you *can* change your body image without changing your body. An accurate version of Assumption 10 is: "The only way I could ever like my looks would be to change my body image."

Erica has invested a great deal of time and money in trying to be beautiful, but although she's always "fixing" her appearance, she still feels unattractive. Her New Inner Voice urges her to focus more on her body image than on her body:

> I've spent much of my life trying to change what I look like. I've got nice clothes and flattering cosmetics. I know how to manage my weight. What I need to do is focus on the real problem and the real solutions. Fixing my appearance feels good at the moment, but it doesn't last. The only way I can like my body is to work directly on my body image. That's what really needs fixing.

CULTIVATING YOUR NEW INNER VOICE

You've now heard several New Inner Voices questioning the assumptions that many people have about their appearance, its importance, and its consequences. These voices speak a language that puts appearance in a realistic perspective, a language that helps people take responsibility for how they think and feel, no matter what they look like. These voices affirm that body image is much more influential than the body's actual appearance, which is why changing appearance alone is often a fruitless, impermanent solution to being unhappy with your looks.

Finding your own New Inner Voice is essential to developing a positive body image. This voice of reason and tolerance is already within you, although right now it may be only a whisper in your mind. Consciously give this voice the words it needs to speak more clearly and forcefully. And then listen to it!

Laurie and Everett discovered several Appearance Assumptions that set them up for body-image distress. They knew that developing "reasonable doubt" of these beliefs would require more than a casual commitment to stop assuming. Merely realizing "I shouldn't think those things" would be of little consequence in changing the status quo. Change would only come—and did come—from their actively *doing* something about their assumptions. You, too, can change.

Following is a Helpsheet for cultivating the New Inner Voice that will chip away at your Appearance Assumptions. Use your own words to create a reasonable doubt of each assumption listed. Don't expect to believe fully everything you write. Write down what you would like to be able to believe—what makes sense. After you've written down the words on the Helpsheet, read them aloud. At an emotional level, your New Inner Voice may sound rather strange. That's okay for now. Take a few minutes each day to read them aloud again. Soon this voice will begin to sound familiar, and its wisdom will become increasingly apparent. In Step 5, you'll have more opportunities to develop your New Inner Voice, and by the end of the program you will be fluent in this new language.

HELPSHEET FOR CHANGE

Questioning My Appearance Assumptions

Assumption 1:   What I Look Like Is an Important Part of Who I
                 Am.
    My New Inner Voice says:

_____

_____

_____

_____

Assumption 2:   The First Thing that People Will Notice about Me
                 Is What's Wrong with My Appearance.
    My New Inner Voice says:

_____

_____

_____

_____

Assumption 3:   One's Outward Physical Appearance Is a Sign of the
                 Inner Person.
    My New Inner Voice says:

_____

_____

_____

_____

Assumption 4:   *If I Could Look Just as I Wish, My Life Would Be Much Happier.*
My New Inner Voice says:

_____

_____

_____

_____

Assumption 5:   *If People Knew How I Really Look, They Would Like Me Less.*
My New Inner Voice says:

_____

_____

_____

_____

Assumption 6:   *By Controlling My Appearance, I Can Control My Social and Emotional Life.*
My New Inner Voice says:

_____

_____

_____

_____

Assumption 7:   *My Appearance Is Responsible for Much of What Has Happened to Me in My Life.*
My New Inner Voice says:

_____

_____

_____

_____

Assumption 8:   *I Should Always Do Whatever I Can to Look My Best.*

My New Inner Voice says:

_____

_____

_____

_____

Assumption 9:   *The Media's Messages in Our Society Make It Impossible for Me to Be Satisfied with My Appearance.*

My New Inner Voice says:

_____

_____

_____

_____

Assumption 10:   *The Only Way I Could Ever Like My Looks Would Be to Change How I Look.*

My New Inner Voice says:

_____

_____

_____

_____

STEP 4

Progress Check: How Am I Helping Myself?

• You are dutifully practicing your Body-and-Mind Relaxation skills and using them to control distress in your daily life.

• If you have not completed your Body-Image Desensitization, you are continuing to progress up your hierarchies from Step 3.

• You are regularly recording the A-B-C Sequence of your negative body-image experiences in your Body-Image Diary.

• Having identified your basic Appearance Assumptions, you are learning to recognize and challenge the ways in which these Appearance Assumptions command your Private Body Talk and, ultimately, your day-to-day body-image emotions. Increasingly, you can see that your assumptions are debatable and unhealthy.

• You are working on your New Inner Voice—a voice that does not passively accept your Appearance Assumptions. You are finding the right words for your New Inner Voice—words that challenge each assumption and words that support you in your efforts to change.

Critical Thinking

Correcting Your
Body-Image Errors

SPRING HAS SPRUNG IN Virginia Beach. As each day brings a sunny warmth to the oceanfront, it also calls forth beach-going bodies of all sizes, shapes, and shades, colorfully clad in very little and armed with towels, chairs, coolers, and lotions. For Laurie, the arrival of spring each year brings distress. Shopping for meager, fashionable strips of cloth that she could wear for some fun in the sun is no fun at all. Laurie's thoughts are not of exposing her body to the sun's soothing rays, gentle sea breezes, or cool ocean currents. Instead, weight-worried Laurie thinks only of exposing her body to the critical eyes of others. She dwells on how her looks will compare with the all-too-perfect, bikinied bodies that will surround her. And that feels awful!

Night after night in his neighborhood tavern, Everett sits at his customary barstool, sips his beer, and watches the women laugh and talk. Everett is too shy to talk to them, except in the imaginary conversations he scripts in his mind. If Everett were to muster the courage for a simple hello or to request a dance, he knows exactly what would happen: These lovely ladies would take one quick look at his five-foot-five-inch body, crowned by his balding head, and they'd be gone in a flash. "Who needs the grief?" he sighs in defeat. As it is, he figures that they gather in the ladies' room and laugh about his looks.

DISCOVERING YOUR BODY-IMAGE ERRORS

In Step 4, you learned how your appearance-related assumptions establish the basic roadmaps of your Private Body Talk. On their own, your thoughts will always travel the well-worn paths directed by your underlying assumptions. However, your Appearance Assumptions never function alone. There is a second set of factors that influence the course of thoughts about your body. Called *cognitive errors,* they are the specific mental mistakes that occur during your inner dialogues. These mistakes drive your body-image thoughts the wrong way up one-way streets, into wrong turns, down dead ends where it is impossible to turn around, and along winding paths that take you nowhere. It's no wonder that you run out of gas on such a frustrating journey.

Cognitive errors are not the same as Appearance Assumptions. Appearance Assumptions set the stage for the *general* focus of your attention and thought. Cognitive errors are the *specific* manifestations of how you think about your looks. Appearance Assumptions set you up for faulty Private Body Talk, and your cognitive errors carry it out.

Cognitive therapists help clients recognize their cognitive errors and purge them from their internal dialogues. In Step 5, you will learn effective strategies to eliminate your cognitive errors and develop fair, accurate, logical, and rational thinking. The result of such cognitive change is emotional liberation. Disturbing body-image emotions, such as recurrent anxiety, anger, depression, and shame, will be provoked less often. And when they do arise, they will be less intense, shorter lived, and less disruptive of your daily life.

In my therapy practice as well as in my research, it has become apparent to me that people with a negative body image tend to make the same mental mistakes. I have identified twelve separate *Body-Image Errors*, which I call the "Dirty Dozen." Because they are the enemies of a healthy body image, you must come to know them well. Then, you'll be prepared to do battle with them later in this chapter.

After teaching you to recognize these twelve errors, defining them for you, and illustrating how they might appear in your Private Body Talk, I will provide you with examples in which a person commits each error. Then you will determine, on a scale from 0 to 4, how much the error described applies to your own Private Body Talk. Even though you will not match the case examples in every detail, such as gender or focal concern, a specific Body-Image Error may still reflect your own particular pattern of thinking. You may wish to review the thoughts recorded in your Body-Image Diary and compare them with the descriptions of the Dirty Dozen.

Body-Image Error 1: Beauty-or-Beast

"Beauty-or-Beast" thinking occurs when you regard your appearance in terms of extremes—as either very attractive or very ugly. This is called *dichotomous thinking:* You're either rich or poor, smart or stupid, happy or miserable, good-looking or hideous. Many people think of their weight this way: "Either I'm the perfect weight or I'm fat." The truth is that reality is not a matter of either/or. Reality is on a continuum, and in between black and white there are many shades of gray. As you can see, Beauty-or-Beast thinking leads you to arrive at exaggerated conclusions about your appearance.

BEAUTY-OR-BEAST IN PRIVATE BODY TALK

Automatic negative thoughts here take the form of extreme statements about one's appearance. A person fearful of becoming fat gains a few pounds and concludes, "I am a blimp." Or, someone concerned with being too thin loses a few pounds and thinks, "I am a beanpole." After a less-than-perfect haircut, you may think you look like the lead character in a horror flick.

In another common version of Beauty-or-Beast thinking, you may consider a physical feature as either "okay, I guess" or "ugly." Although less extreme than full-blown dichotomous thinking, this variation still leads to Private Body Talk that prevents positive body-image feelings. In this dichotomy, you either feel neutral or apathetic about your looks, or you feel very discontented. When you are feeling neutral, your Private Body Talk is usually more silent, because "my looks are nothing to notice, not worth thinking about."

BEAUTY-OR-BEAST IN ACTION: CHARLES'S CASE

Charles has recurring facial acne. With any minor outbreak, he becomes intensely self-conscious. He stands in front of the mirror and picks at his face—physically and mentally. In his Private Body Talk, he ruminates about how unattractive he is and how his face is totally ruined. In his mind's eye, Charles looks "reasonably okay" without acne but grotesque with it. As a result, the only time he gives any serious thought to his appearance is during an outbreak. Seldom does Charles have any positive feelings about his looks.

SELF-DISCOVERY

How often do you think about your looks in exaggerated, either/or terms? Rate how often you commit the Beauty-or-Beast error.

0	1	2	3	4
Never	Occasion-ally	Moderately Often	Often	Very Often

Body-Image Error 2: The Unreal Ideal

In Step 1, we examined the various "standards" of appearance championed by our culture—for weight, height, shape, muscularity, complexion, and for hair color, texture, and style. Magazines, movies, and television bombard us so heavily with these all-too-perfect images that we cannot escape being affected by them. When we absorb these messages to the extent that we internalize society's standards as our own body-image ideals, we become vulnerable to the "Unreal Ideal." Your score on the Wishing Well Test in Step 2 is an index of how much you disparage your looks for not living up to these ideals. My research has revealed that this Body-Image Error is among the most common and most distressful mental mistakes that people make.

In 1983, I conducted an experiment in which I had subjects view pictures of people in photo albums and answer a variety of questions. Some subjects got a photo album filled with physically attractive people; the rest got an album picturing average or less-attractive individuals. Afterward, I asked my subjects to rate their own looks. Those who had been exposed to the photos of good-looking people reported feeling less attractive than did the subjects who had viewed plainer-looking people. This result is what psychologists call the "social-comparison contrast effect." By comparing ourselves against lofty standards, we end up devaluing ourselves. Comparing causes despairing!

UNREAL IDEALS IN PRIVATE BODY TALK

Gauging your physical worth by Unreal Ideals causes you to become preoccupied with your inadequacies. You dwell on what you *don't* look like and on what you don't like about your looks. Your Private Body Talk will be filled with what I call "too" thinking. "I'm *too* short or *too* fat or *too* this or *too* that." The Unreal Ideal error often produces internal dialogues full of words such as "should," "must," and "ought." For example, "I *should* have more definition in my chest." "I *ought* to have a smaller waist."

A common variation of the Unreal Ideal error is "wishful thinking": "I wish I had longer fingers and smaller feet." "I really wish I were thin." "I wish my chest were bigger." Although the words differ somewhat, you are still focusing on not measuring up to your ideals.

UNREAL IDEALS IN ACTION: OLIVIA'S CASE

Olivia feels terrible about her appearance whenever she looks in the mirror. Sometimes she feels outright disgust; other times, she feels hopeless and dispirited. Examining her Private Body Talk, Olivia realizes that she evaluates her appearance against very particular standards—those of "perfect" feminine beauty, like the models seen in most media ads. This ideal is the tall, very slender female, with large and sparkling eyes, luscious lips, a thick and flowing mane, and finely sculpted facial structure. Because Olivia's appearance does not match this ideal, she cannot feel attractive. She focuses on her so-called shortcomings and mentally criticizes her height, weight, overall body proportions, and her "tree-trunk legs"—strong, sturdy legs that you'll seldom see in a magazine ad. Olivia feels dissatisfied because she judges herself against an unattainable standard of beauty and, of course, always falls short of it.

SELF-DISCOVERY

How much have you absorbed society's standards in judging your appearance? You might want to flip back to your answers on the Wishing Well Test in Step 2. Rate below how often you use an Unreal Ideal to evaluate your appearance.

0	1	2	3	4
Never	Occasionally	Moderately Often	Often	Very Often

Body-Image Error 3: Unfair-to-Compare

In the "Unfair-to-Compare" error, you go beyond evaluating your body against the standards represented by professional models or mental images of perfection. Here, you pit your appearance against that of real people you encounter in everyday life. However, your comparison is by no means made with a random selection of people. It's lopsided—made only with people you see as having the physical qualities that you find attractive and wish you had—and thus biased against you from the very start.

For example, suppose you wish you had thick blond hair. If you pick someone for comparison whom you perceive to have an absolutely wonderful head of blond hair, you've essentially predetermined your conclusion about your own hair. Someone has to lose at this comparison game, and you set it up always to be you. You fall prey to the social-comparison contrast effect that I described earlier. If you compare yourself to a taller person, you will always come up short.

The Unfair-to-Compare pattern is usually unfair in another respect. People who commit this error seldom pick just any physical quality for comparison; typically, they choose the characteristic they like least in themselves, the one they worry about the most. So the Unfair-to-Compare error essentially adds insult to injury.

UNFAIR-TO-COMPARE IN PRIVATE BODY TALK

The routine ruminations that result from this error include the "too" thinking and the wishful thinking that also accompany the Unreal Ideal error. However, the Unfair-to-Compare error involves comparisons with real people, not glossy or celluloid images. When you make this mental mistake, not only do you have negative feelings toward your body, but you may also experience negative feelings like envy and jealousy toward the person with whom you compare yourself. You may think, "They make me look bad." You may feel intimidated around them, try to avoid them, spread rumors about them, or perhaps even retaliate with some unkind remark. After all, if you could denigrate them in some way, you might be able to restore your own sense of adequacy. Obviously, Unfair-to-Compare thinking is unfair to everyone.

UNFAIR-TO-COMPARE IN ACTION: GLORIA'S CASE

Gloria's negative feelings about her appearance are strongest when she's with others whom she considers to be attractive. She always notices how people look, especially if they are attractive.

Here's an example of her Private Body Talk: "I hate trying on clothes in the store. There's always some really pretty salesperson or customer around that makes me look so plain." (In reality, some are prettier than Gloria and some are not.) In another version, Gloria muses, "I just felt awful about myself at the party. With all those well-dressed, good-looking women there, I looked terrible." (In reality, some were more dressed up than Gloria and some were not.) Or she thinks, "I'm really uncomfortable around handsome men. I'm not pretty enough for them." Says who?

As a result of Gloria's faulty thought patterns, she often feels self-conscious and anxious in social situations. If you were to watch her interact with people, you might sense Gloria's tension and underlying hostility toward anyone who happens to be physically attractive.

SELF-DISCOVERY

How often do you measure your physical adequacy in relation to how good others look? Rate how often you compare your appearance to good-looking people around you.

0	1	2	3	4
Never	Occasion-ally	Moderately Often	Often	Very Often

Body-Image Error 4: The Magnifying Glass

With the "Magnifying Glass" thought pattern, you focus on some aspect of your appearance that you dislike and then exaggerate its importance—as if you had placed your body under a magnifying glass. It's hard to think about your appearance without focusing on this one unsatisfactory feature, which comes to represent almost all of your appearance. So what do you see when you look in the mirror? A giant flaw.

Imagine that you have purchased a beautiful new car. It's your favorite color, and it has all the options you've ever dreamed of. You wash it often, check the fluids religiously, and keep its interior spotless. One day, you are driving behind a dump truck, which spills some gravel onto your beloved automobile. The result is a dime-sized dent right in the middle of the hood. Understandably, you are upset. Now whenever you look at your car, the little dent takes on the dimensions of the Grand Canyon. As you drive along, your eyes focus more on the dent in your hood than on the road. When friends admire your new car, your reply is "Yeah, but look at this awful dent." They probably would never have noticed the blemish, but now you can't seem to see anything else. As a Body-Image Error, the Magnifying Glass means that you are always looking at your body's "dents."

THE MAGNIFYING GLASS IN PRIVATE BODY TALK

The Magnifying Glass exemplifies what psychologists call *selective attention*. Whenever you think about your body, you zoom in on whatever you dislike most about your looks. You equate your entire appearance with your "chipmunk cheeks," "flabby thighs," or "knobby knees." Because you dwell disproportionately on the defects you see, your Private Body Talk sounds like a broken record. At some level, you're really tired of listening to this record, but you keep on playing it anyway.

THE MAGNIFYING GLASS IN ACTION: NANCY'S CASE

Nancy knows she's not genuinely unattractive, but she believes that her eyes are too small and close set and that they ruin her looks. When she looks in the mirror or even just ponders her appearance, her thoughts focus almost exclusively on her eyes, and within seconds, she has a sinking feeling. When a friend compliments Nancy on how she looks in her new hairstyle, Nancy is pleased but immediately thinks, "I'd sure look better if I didn't have these beady eyes."

SELF-DISCOVERY

Consider how much this Magnifying Glass error happens in your own Private Body Talk. How often do you focus on and exaggerate the importance of your "flaws?"

0	1	2	3	4
Never	Occasion-ally	Moderately Often	Often	Very Often

Body-Image Error 5: The Blind Mind

The Magnifying Glass Error involves overemphasis. The "Blind Mind" error is the other side of the coin—what you ignore or minimize. The Magnifying Glass and the Blind Mind errors operate together to produce a "tunnel vision" perspective on your appearance. In my automobile analogy, the car's wonderful features were either forgotten or seemed irrelevant in light of the dent. When your mind is "blind," you overlook those physical features you don't feel bad about, as if only perceived defects are worth your attention.

THE BLIND MIND IN PRIVATE BODY TALK

You would think that someone with a negative body image would want to try to feel better by playing up his or her assets.

The Blind Mind error prevents this. A large portion of the body is often neglected or dismissed as "not worth thinking about." Ironically, these unappreciated assets may be the very features that others find most attractive about a person. In her Private Body Talk, a woman with a very pretty face says to herself, "Oh, yes, I guess my face is okay, but who cares since I have such awful hair?"

Many people commit the Blind Mind error as the result of a fear of vanity. They fear that liking something about their own looks would make them vain or conceited. So, if they ever find themselves appreciating one of their physical qualities, a chastising voice in their Private Body Talk commands that they change the channel of their thoughts.

THE BLIND MIND IN ACTION: IRA'S CASE

Ira has a nice physique, a radiant smile, and wonderful, warm eyes. But in his preoccupation with a scar on his chin, Ira is oblivious to his physical assets. Thus, Ira has blind spots in his thinking; he ignores any features that are *not* annoying to him. Ira's wife thinks he is absolutely adorable. She often tells him that he has the sexiest eyes she's ever seen. Ira laughs and tosses aside her sincere compliments, suggesting that she get glasses.

SELF-DISCOVERY

To detect your body-image blind spots, review your physical characteristics from head to toe. You may want to reexamine your answers on the Body Areas Satisfaction Test from Step 2. Ask yourself how many of these areas you seldom notice or think about. Then rate how often you commit the Blind Mind error.

0	1	2	3	4
Never	Occasion- ally	Moderately Often	Often	Very Often

Body-Image Error 6: Ugly-by-Association

This error occurs when feelings of unattractiveness about one attribute spill over to other physical features. This error of overgeneralizing operates on the principle of "guilt by association." In the "Ugly-by-Association" error, otherwise "innocent" aspects of your appearance are ordained unattractive simply because they exist on the same body as parts you dislike.

UGLY-BY-ASSOCIATION IN PRIVATE BODY TALK

In the Ugly-by-Association thought pattern, your inner dialogues are "looking for trouble." First, your Private Body Talk zeros in on some unacceptable characteristic. You begin to feel unattractive and dissatisfied. Then you ask yourself "Just *how* ugly am I?" or "What *else* is wrong with my looks?" Of course, these questions are emotionally loaded. In answering, you begin to overgeneralize, feeling uglier each time you locate another unacceptable feature. And the uglier you feel, the more likely you are to notice physical features that aren't "perfect."

UGLY-BY-ASSOCIATION IN ACTION: TED'S CASE

When Ted focuses on his fifty-year-old face, he spots some wrinkles and thinks, "God, I look old." Then he begins his quest to locate all the aging aspects of his body. He searches for anything sagging, graying, or thinning as evidence of his unattractiveness. No doubt Ted will find whatever he is looking for, and his search will culminate with the sweeping conclusion that he's undeniably over the hill.

SELF-DISCOVERY

Rate how often you commit the Ugly-by-Association error. How often does your discontent with one aspect of your body lead you to find fault with other aspects?

0	1	2	3	4
Never	Occasion- ally	Moderately Often	Often	Very Often

Body-Image Error 7: The Blame Game

Another compelling cognitive error that fuels negative body-image thoughts and feelings is the "Blame Game." Often, people who have negative feelings about some perceived flaw in their appearance incorrectly assume that this attribute is directly responsible for certain disappointments that they experience. This is the psychological phenomenon of *scapegoating*.

Of course, as I discussed in the first chapter, one's looks *can* influence life events. The fact that Michael is six-foot-five is likely to help him be chosen for a basketball team over a person who is five-foot-three. Without a doubt, obese individuals are sometimes discriminated against in our society. In the Blame Game, however, a person scapegoats his or her physical appearance for setbacks that occur, even in the absence of evidence. This mental mistake is often very subtle and may lead you to think more negatively about some aspect of your appearance when you are in an uncomfortable situation or after some social disappointment. At such times, it is natural to try to understand why things happen as they do. But it is clearly wrong to assume automatically that your appearance is responsible.

THE BLAME GAME IN PRIVATE BODY TALK

In the Blame Game, you think, "If I didn't look so _____, then (something bad) wouldn't have happened." If you don't get the job or date or promotion you wanted, you blame your looks. Your automatic Blame Game thoughts allege that your looks have ruined, screwed up, or interfered with something you hoped for in your life.

THE BLAME GAME IN ACTION: IRENE'S CASE

Irene went to a party and met a man to whom she was quite attracted. Later on, he left the party with another woman. In her disappointment, Irene's Private Body Talk blamed her appearance for the so-called rejection: "It was my skinny body and stupid curly hair. Who'd be interested in somebody who looks like a celery stalk?" She concluded, "It's my body's fault that he left with someone else. There is something really wrong with me. My looks aren't good enough." (Unbeknownst to Irene, the fellow had left the party with his sister.)

SELF-DISCOVERY

In Step 4, did you endorse Appearance Assumption 7—the general belief that your appearance is responsible for much of what has happened in your life? If so, then you probably play the Blame Game often. That Appearance Assumption predisposes you to scapegoat your looks in your Private Body Talk. Rate how frequently you play the Blame Game in your day-to-day life.

0	1	2	3	4
Never	Occasion- ally	Moderately Often	Often	Very Often

Body-Image Error 8: Mind Misreading

People who have a negative body image often use the following reasoning: "If *I* think I look bad, then *others* must think I look bad too. Others see me exactly as I see myself." Psychologists call this mental process *projection,* because it involves projecting our own thoughts and beliefs into the minds of others. In fact, others may have entirely different ideas. That's why I label this error "Mind Misreading." Irene committed this error when she assumed that the man at the party had rejected her because he found her homely, when in reality she was projecting her own feelings of unattractiveness onto him. You can see that Mind Misreading and the Blame Game may often operate together.

Mind Misreading doesn't require the occurrence of a dramatic event or disappointment. You may believe that other people are thinking what you are thinking about your body even though nothing bad has actually happened. Again, you have no solid proof of others' thoughts, but you assume the worst.

MIND MISREADING IN PRIVATE BODY TALK

With Mind Misreading, you think you can get into someone else's head and understand exactly what's going on in there. You think you know what the person is looking at—your big hips, crooked teeth, baggy eyes, protruding ears—whatever *you* loathe about your looks. You believe that you're eavesdropping on the person's private thoughts. "They see how overweight I am and can't stand to look at me. They think I'm a lazy slob and wish they didn't have to talk to me." Obviously, what's going on here is projection. Because *you're* worried about your weight, you assume others must be thinking about it too.

MIND MISREADING IN ACTION: VICKIE'S CASE

As a result of breast cancer, Vickie had a double mastectomy. Now, whenever she and her husband are out on the dance floor, she "just knows" everyone is thinking about how flat-chested she is. Whenever her coworkers don't comment on a new outfit she's wearing, she tells herself, "They think it looks stupid on me." And whenever Vickie's husband isn't in the mood to make love, she gets upset. She's sure he's repulsed by the scars on her chest. Vickie spends a lot of time feeling self-conscious about her body, because she has convinced herself that others are silently as critical of her appearance as she is.

SELF-DISCOVERY

Review what you dislike most about your appearance. Ask yourself how often you Mind Misread and infer that others are noticing and thinking about your physical "flaws." Record your rating below.

0	1	2	3	4
Never	Occasion-ally	Moderately Often	Often	Very Often

Body-Image Error 9: Misfortune Telling

The Blame Game and Mind Misreading errors reflect your inferences about past and current events. "Misfortune Telling" deals with the private predictions that you make—how you think your appearance will affect your future. People with intense body dissatisfaction expect that their physical shortcomings will have dire effects on their lives. When you engage in Misfortune Telling, you expect your looks will foster frequent disappointments. You may apply this kind of faulty reasoning to short-term situations ("No one at the party will want to talk to me") or long-lasting issues ("I'll never be taken seriously in my career").

MISFORTUNE TELLING IN PRIVATE BODY TALK

With Misfortune Telling, you may use extreme words like "always" or "never" when you anticipate the adverse effects of your looks. For example, you think, "With my homely mug, I'll *never* be loved." Or, "I look too old *ever* to get a promotion." Or, "As long as I'm overweight, my mother will *never* respect me." Or, "If I get any balder, *all* my friends will start to tease me."

MISFORTUNE TELLING IN ACTION: EDWARD'S CASE

Edward had an automobile accident that severed his left arm at the elbow. In addition, he is about fifty pounds heavier than weight charts recommend. Edward thinks of himself as a "one-armed blob." His Private Body Talk often includes statements of doom like "I'm so hideous no woman will ever fall in love with me." Edward's Misfortune Telling involves predicting that others will think negatively of him—a sort of future Mind Misreading. However, his assumptions are not about a *specific* person's thoughts or feelings. Rather, his sweeping assumptions encompass what *all or most* people will think and do.

SELF-DISCOVERY

How often do you engage in Misfortune Telling—expecting looks to cause future negative consequences? Remember, Misfortune Telling concerns short-term, situational expectations, as well as those about the rest of your life.

0	1	2	3	4
Never	Occasion-ally	Moderately Often	Often	Very Often

Body-Image Error 10: Beauty Bound

When you restrict your goals or activities because of what you dislike about your body, you are a prisoner of your negative body image. "Beauty Bound" thinking is reflected in self-statements that you *cannot* do certain things because of what you look like. Quite powerful, this error engenders actions that are especially self-defeating and diminish your quality of life.

BEAUTY BOUND IN PRIVATE BODY TALK

Beauty Bound thinking usually begins with "I can't . . ." You tell yourself you can't go certain places or be with certain people because you don't look good enough. You tell yourself that, because of your looks, you can't wear certain clothes or certain colors. You prohibit your own participation in certain activities—from parties, from an exercise class, from the beach or pool, from clothing stores, or from wearing jeans. Usually your "I can't" thinking takes the form of "I look too _____ to do that." Often, Beauty Bound thinking involves temporary restrictions, such as "Until I get a tan, I can't go to the pool." Other instances of this error reflect more permanent prohibitions: "With my scrawny arms, I'll never be able to wear short-sleeved shirts."

By now, you are realizing that the various Body-Image Errors often conspire together to create your distress. Beauty Bound thinking may compound other cognitive errors. For example, a woman who thinks "I can't go to the party because my hair looks weird" is restricting her activities (Beauty Bound thinking) because she assumes that others at the party would react negatively to her looks (Misfortune Telling). Similarly, a man whose Beauty Bound thinking says, "I'm too fat, so I can't eat in front of other people," is also Misfortune Telling by assuming that others will judge him as fat and reject him for eating.

BEAUTY BOUND IN ACTION: EVELYN'S CASE

Evelyn detests her weight and is also preoccupied with the dark hair on her arms. As the result of her Private Body Talk, Evelyn does not allow herself to do various things in her daily life. Her automatic thoughts include: "Unless I lose twenty pounds, I can't possibly wear shorts to the picnic." Or, "I'm too fat to go to the job interview." Or, "I can't attend the weight-loss exercise class until I lose weight." Regarding the hair on her arms, Evelyn thinks, "Unless the house is on fire, I'd never go outside without long sleeves to hide my arms." She often bleaches the hair to make it less visible. Even so, she once refused to be in a friend's wedding because she would have had to wear a sleeveless gown.

SELF-DISCOVERY

How often do your Beauty Bound beliefs prevent you from doing things? Rate how frequently you restrict your activities because of your feelings about how you look.

0	1	2	3	4
Never	Occasion-ally	Moderately Often	Often	Very Often

Body-Image Error 11: Feeling Ugly

The "Feeling Ugly" error entails what psychologists call *emotional reasoning:* We "reason" purely on the basis of how we feel. The starting point is an emotion, and the end point is a faulty conclusion that justifies (and strengthens) the emotion. For example, you are anxious and think, "I *feel* like something bad is going to happen." So you conclude, "Something bad *is* going to happen." Specifically, the Feeling Ugly error usually follows the "logic" that "because I *feel* ugly, I must *be* ugly." The Feeling Ugly error is especially significant because it perpetuates and worsens the body-image distress already ignited by some other cognitive error.

Let's consider an analogy. Suppose you and a friend are on a leisurely stroll through the woods. Everything is pleasant until your friend wonders aloud if there could be any snakes around. Not being especially fond of such creatures, you notice your accelerating heartbeat and your hastened pace. You look around and see plenty of places where snakes could hide: There are rocks and logs where they could lie in wait for you, and overhanging branches from which they could conduct an aerial assault. "These woods are a snake haven," you conclude. "I'm sure there are hundreds slithering about. Let's get out of here!" Because you are feeling afraid, you decide that snakes must be there somewhere—despite having no evidence of them. You "reasoned" from your fear that something *must* be wrong. What's really wrong is that you inferred "facts" from feelings.

FEELING UGLY IN PRIVATE BODY TALK

The Private Body Talk that emanates from Feeling Ugly is an emotional dialogue that confuses feelings with facts. The Feeling Ugly pattern of thinking goes something like "No wonder I feel so ugly, just look at me! Look how homely (or fat, or skinny, or short, or huge-breasted, or disfigured . . .) I am! I look wretched!"

For most people with a negative body image, this Private Body Talk makes perfect sense; it doesn't seem illogical at all. What you must realize here is that your feelings of distress come *first,* and you "conveniently" use your perceived flaws to justify your distress. Other people with the same physical features do not necessarily feel as bad as you do. An inferiority complex does not come on the same gene that gives you a short stature or a receding hairline or a little extra padding for your rear end.

FEELING UGLY IN ACTION: ROBERTO'S CASE

Roberto has a brownish birthmark that's about an inch in diameter on the right side of his neck. Once in a while, someone will ask him how it got there—people are understandably curious—or unknowingly will tell him that he has dirt on his neck. On these occasions, he Mind Misreads and is sure the person thinks he looks ridiculous. As a result, Roberto starts to feel unattractive and self-conscious. And, based on this feeling, he "knows" that he must certainly look defective. He "knows" that his birthmark is truly repugnant. When Roberto is feeling ugly, that's the only truth he will consider. His girlfriend tells him again and again that she finds him very attractive, but he privately dismisses her reassurances, saying to himself, "I know how I feel; I know I'm odd-looking. Besides, she probably feels sorry for me and is just trying to be nice."

SELF-DISCOVERY

Do you commit the Feeling Ugly error of emotion-based reasoning? Rate how often you conclude that you (or something about you) must be unattractive merely because you feel that way.

0	1	2	3	4
Never	Occasion-ally	Moderately Often	Often	Very Often

Body-Image Error 12: The Moody Mirror

Like the Feeling Ugly error, the "Moody Mirror" pattern involves emotional reasoning, but the two errors differ in a fundamental way. With Feeling Ugly thinking, we acknowledge our feelings of unattractiveness and decide they must be true reflections of how we look. The Moody Mirror mistake begins with negative feelings about *something else*—being upset or in a bad mood for reasons unrelated to our appearance. Then, our bad mood spills over to affect our body-image experiences.

Your brain has stored in memory different Private Body Talk "tapes" that it runs again and again, producing predictable emotional experiences. These tapes remain silent until something happens to turn them on. Negative emotional states—such as anxiety, sadness, frustration, or shame—can activate these dormant dialogues, especially those cast in a similar emotional hue. So what happens with the Moody Mirror is that your mood seeks an easy target, and you begin to denigrate your looks.

THE MOODY MIRROR IN PRIVATE BODY TALK

The Moody Mirror doesn't produce inner conversations that are particularly distinguishable from other Private Body Talk we've heard. The key question to ask in detecting the presence of the Moody Mirror error is: "When I am bothered or upset about something apart from my looks, am I prone to pick on what I dislike about my appearance?"

THE MOODY MIRROR IN ACTION: RACHEL'S CASE

Rachel has a very stressful job in a department store. By midafternoon, she typically feels tense and disgruntled. Although she begins each day feeling comfortable with her appearance, when she returns from work, she's preoccupied with her hair and her weight and spends thirty minutes in front of the mirror engaging in self-critical Body Talk. Before going out for the evening, she tries on outfit after outfit without any satisfaction. Clearly, Rachel's body image has become the victim of her lousy mood.

SELF-DISCOVERY

How often do your bad moods spill over to affect your thoughts and feelings about your appearance? Rate your experience of this last error—the Moody Mirror pattern.

0	1	2	3	4
Never	Occasion- ally	Moderately Often	Often	Very Often

SUMMING UP YOUR BODY OF THOUGHT

On page 205, you'll find a Self-Discovery Helpsheet that lists the Dirty Dozen errors we've discussed. Transfer to this Helpsheet the twelve ratings you made, indicating the extent to which you commit each error. Then carefully add these ratings to obtain your Total Error Score.

How to Interpret Your Body-Image Error Score

Total Body-Image Error scores can range from 0 to 48. Make sure your score falls within this range. Total scores are divided into five smaller ranges, or levels. Level 1 is least problematic; Level 5 reflects the most severe body-image difficulties. Based on your score, determine which level defines your current cognitive condition and the likely body-image difficulties you have as a result:

LEVEL 1: TOTAL SCORE = 0 TO 5

Congratulations! You are an especially clear body-image thinker, more error-free than 90 percent of the population. You have a generally positive body image and experience only occasional or mild body-image distress.

SELF-DISCOVERY HELPSHEET

Summing Up Your Body of Thought

From the "Self-Discovery" section for each of the twelve Body-Image Errors, locate your 0 to 4 rating. Write each rating below to the left of the error. Then sum your ratings to get a total score.

Rating	*Body-Image Error*
_____	1. Beauty or Beast
_____	2. The Unreal Ideal
_____	3. Unfair-to-Compare
_____	4. The Magnifying Glass
_____	5. The Blind Mind
_____	6. Ugly-by-Association
_____	7. The Blame Game
_____	8. Mind Misreading
_____	9. Misfortune Telling
_____	10. Beauty Bound
_____	11. Feeling Ugly
_____	12. Moody Mirror
_____	= TOTAL ERROR SCORE

LEVEL 2: TOTAL SCORE = 6 TO 12

If you score in this range, the good news is that you commit fewer errors than at least 60 percent of the population. The bad news is that you make enough mental mistakes to provoke mild to moderate body-image distress in a few important situations.

LEVEL 3: TOTAL SCORE = 13 TO 18

Your Private Body Talk is neither better nor worse than that of most people. Unfortunately, average is no cause for celebration. Your body-image distress occurs frequently, can be quite uncomfortable, and can interfere with the quality of your life.

LEVEL 4: TOTAL SCORE = 20 TO 28

You often reach faulty conclusions about your looks. Your negative body-image feelings are seriously disruptive in many situations. Certain aspects of your appearance are a focus of chronic concern. About 30 percent of people score in this range.

LEVEL 5: TOTAL SCORE = 27 TO 48

As a result of regularly committing most of the cognitive errors, your Private Body Talk is extremely illogical and causes you considerable emotional pain. You experience very intense and disruptive body-image distress in many different situations. Only 10 percent fall into this category of severe and chronic loathing of their looks.

Recall that in the previous chapter I presented a graph of the evidence that Doubters of Appearance Assumptions have a much less negative body image than do Assumers. Similarly, my research confirms that people's Body-Image Error scores have a strong bearing on the nature of their body-image experiences. Based on hundreds of subjects who completed the Body-Image Tests (from Step 2), I determined the percentage of each of the five error-level groups who had a negative body image on Appearance Evaluation, Body Areas Satisfaction, and Distressing Situations tests. The bar graph on page 208 shows clearly that as one's error level increases, so do one's body-image problems. Whereas body-image dissatisfaction and distress are practically nonexistent for Level 1 scorers, a negative body image is overwhelmingly prevalent among people at Level 5.

CORRECTIVE THINKING: YOUR NEW PRIVATE BODY TALK

Your Old Inner Voice has hassled and haunted you for a long time. It will not vacate your Private Body Talk without a fight. But this is a fight that you can win. By chipping away at your Appearance Assumptions, you have already lessened the likelihood of problematic Private Body Talk. You also need to learn how to stop committing your cognitive errors—that is, how to change the erroneous, irrational, self-defeating ways of thinking about your appearance that get you into emotional trouble.

To tackle the Dirty Dozen errors, you'll add a "D" to the A-B-C Sequence of negative body-image experience. By now, you should be quite skilled at monitoring the Activators, your Beliefs, and their Consequences. This added "D" stands for *Disputing*—disputing the cognitive errors and automatic thoughts in your Private Body Talk. To dispute your faulty thinking successfully, you must make a continued and determined effort in monitoring your own mental mistakes and the

HOW DO BODY-IMAGE ERRORS AFFECT YOUR BODY IMAGE?

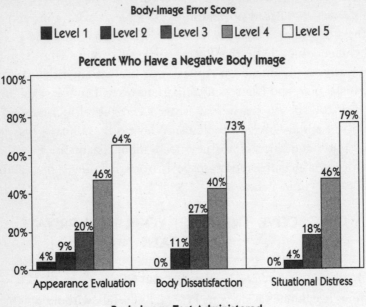

Body-Image Error Score

■ Level 1   ■ Level 2   ■ Level 3   ■ Level 4   □ Level 5

Percent Who Have a Negative Body Image

Body-Image Test Administered

distorted thinking that occurs in particular situations. In disputing your familiar "tapes," you'll develop and rehearse a number of ways to *rethink* yourself out of your unsatisfying emotional experiences. In effect, you will learn how to argue yourself out of the Body-Image Errors when they occur. You will put these arguments into practice in the Private Body Talk of your daily life, replacing faulty ways of thinking with new constructive ways of thinking.

Cognitive therapists refer to these strategies as *cognitive restructuring* or *corrective thinking*. You won't change overnight. Have you ever known anyone who has? Gradually, however, you *will* notice that you are becoming more and more successful at altering how and what you think about your appearance. And, of course, as a result, you'll begin to feel more content and more in control of your body image.

Stop, Look, and Listen

Whenever you have some negative feeling about your appearance in a real-life situation, three words should immediately pop into your mind: *Stop, Look,* and *Listen.*

First *Stop* your Private Body Talk in midsentence. You literally think "Stop!" as you flash a big, red stop sign in your mind and halt your stream of thought. Before you can change your Private Body Talk, you must first interrupt its flow.

Then *Look,* or self-monitor, the ABCs of your upsetting body-image experience. Ask yourself what the "A"—the Activating event—is that triggered your emotional reactions? Then, jump to the "C"—the Consequences—and ask yourself, "What emotions am I feeling right now?" Lastly, ask yourself about the "B"—the Beliefs. "What am I thinking here that's making me feel so bad?" What Appearance Assumption is behind your distress? What particular cognitive errors were you committing? *Look* at the situation, at your reaction, and at the likely thoughts and errors that are creating your emotions.

Finally, *Listen!* Listen to a more reasonable, rational, realistic point of view. Right then and there, talk to yourself with your New Inner Voice, using an inner dialogue to challenge, dispute, and correct your troublesome thinking. To undo your body-image distress, you must spend at least a minute or two listening to your better judgment. Talk to yourself just as you would to a good friend who's said the same critical things about himself or herself that you've privately said about yourself.

Because corrective thinking can be difficult in the midst of a distressing episode, you must prepare and rehearse corrective thinking ahead of time—*before* the activating situations occur. This is what we'll do next.

TALKING BACK

At the end of Step 4, you completed a Helpsheet called "Questioning Your Appearance Assumptions." This enabled you to begin to dispute the ten common schemas using your own New Inner Voice. On page 224, you will find the "Helpsheet for Corrective Thinking," which you will use to learn to "talk back" to your cognitive errors. You can then use your counterarguments at point "D," when you are disputing and correcting your distorted thinking in everyday life.

In the pages that follow, I am going to take aim at each Body-Image Error, providing discussion and lots of examples that will show you how to "talk back." First, read about disputing all twelve errors. Underline or take note of anything that hits home or seems potentially valuable. Afterward, it'll be *your* turn to take aim, with the aid of your Helpsheet.

Correcting the Beauty-or-Beast Error

Recall that Beauty-or-Beast thinking is "either/or" thinking: "Either I'm attractive or I'm ugly." "Either I lose five pounds or I'm fat." "Some people have it and some don't; I don't." Clearly, this is extremism. Here are several ways to dispute such black-and-white thinking:

• Force yourself to see shades of gray. Remind yourself that not being a 10 on a 10-point attractiveness scale doesn't necessarily make you a 1.

• Say to yourself: "Okay, so I'm not totally perfect; but I'm not totally imperfect either. Some things about me enhance my looks." Then, remind yourself of these assets.

• Consider how you think about other people's looks. "Do I judge other people's appearance with only two extreme categories? Or do I view them on a realistic continuum?" If the latter, ask yourself, "Why should I regard other people more realistically than I regard myself?"

• Ask yourself, "Honestly now, what *is* the evidence, other than my own thinking, that I'm seen as extremely homely?" And ask, "Is there evidence to the contrary?" Think about compliments you may receive and about times you felt less negative about your looks.

• Alter extreme "beastly" thinking by being more objective about your looks. In your thoughts, replace "I'm a horse face" with "I have a long nose." Replace "I'm a damned scarecrow" with "I have a thin physique." "I have potholes as my complexion" is, more objectively, "My complexion isn't smooth." "Hippo hips" becomes "rounded hips."

Correcting the Unreal Ideal Error

The Unreal Ideal refers to the use of a societal ideal as a standard of acceptable appearance. You feel unattractive when you judge yourself against unrealistically high standards of perfection. These are images (or ideals, if we let them be) that very few of us can match. By definition, professional models are chosen for their extreme and unusual appearance.

The truth is that beauty is relative and in the eyes of the beholder. Standards vary from time to time and culture to culture. If beauty were everything, then only good-looking people would date, marry, or get jobs. Remember, from Step 1, that research confirms that people who have the beauty or the body that we idealize do *not* necessarily have a better body image. Happiness depends not on what we have, but on how we regard what we have. Fashion models are often very critical and worried about their looks.

The Unreal Ideal often leads to thinking with words like "should," "must," or "I have to be." Here, "shoulds," "oughts," and "musts" are your enemy. You need to develop counterarguments to challenge comparison against arbitrary and unrealistic standards of appearance.

• Instead of saying, "I *should* be thinner, taller (or whatever)," correctively assert, "It might be nice if I lost a few pounds, but I look pretty good the way I am. I refuse to berate myself for not looking like a fashion plate."

• Other corrective thoughts include: "I don't have to have a perfect-looking body to have a positive and attractive appearance." Or, "Nobody's perfect; even models have their imperfections and worry about their looks." Or, "Nobody (but me) is expecting me to look different. Nobody's complaining about me but me."

• Or, "I refuse to continue to buy into this societal ideal of feminine beauty (or masculine good looks); it's sexist, and I refuse to treat myself in a sexist way."

Correcting the Unfair-to-Compare Error

You will remember that Unfair-to-Compare is similar to the Unreal Ideal error, except that here you compare yourself with people you encounter in everyday situations. Typically, you compare your appearance *only* with people you think have what you'd like to have, which leads you to spend a lot of time noticing others whom you think look better than you do.

Seldom do you notice that there are plenty of folks around who look "worse" than you do. Feelings of envy and intimidation arise from Unfair Comparisons. Examples of faulty Private Body Talk here are: "I wish I were as attractive as that person is," or "That person makes me feel so ugly."

Corrective thinking for this error is similar to that for the Unreal Ideal. The first step is to realize what you are doing: You have compared yourself with somebody and ended up feeling negative about your looks. Then, after this realization, your corrective inner dialogue might be:

• "Everybody is better looking than somebody else; everybody is less attractive than somebody else. I don't have to feel bad just because there's something about me that I don't like as much as what someone else has."

• Or, "The fact that I like the way that person looks has nothing to do with how *I* look. That person doesn't make me look bad; he (or she) doesn't *make* me do anything."

• You might also say to yourself: "If I'm going to compare, then I need to be fair. Whom am I *more* attractive than?"

• Finally, "I am going to take time now to think of something about me (a special skill, talent, or personality trait) that compares quite well with other people."

Correcting the Magnifying Glass and the Blind Mind Errors

These errors are two sides of the same coin. You overemphasize the physical features you don't like and minimize the ones that are not a problem, creating tunnel vision. When you think about your friends, do you think only about their weight or their wrinkles or their birthmarks? Of course not. You have a more balanced picture of their appearance and who they are as people. So how do you develop a more balanced view of yourself? Use these alternatives:

• First of all, ask yourself, "Am I focusing on what I don't like and forgetting about parts of me that are fine?" Think of two or three of your favorite features. Then, when you magnify, *un*blind your mind and say to yourself, "I'm magnifying here and that's not the whole picture of my appearance. I'm just dwelling on what I don't like. I do like (for example) my beautiful eyes, and my white teeth, and I'm really pleased with my hairstyle."

• Promise to follow the *Equal Time Rule:* Spend an equal amount of time on those unspoken positive features or traits you possess every time you catch yourself mentally picking on the disliked features.

• In addition, say to yourself: "I may not be crazy about my (hair, weight, nose, legs, or whatever), but there's sure a lot more to me than that. Other people see more to me than the flaw I keep criticizing myself for."

• Just as you do to correct the Beauty-or-Beast error, replace exaggerated, pejorative statements about magnified features with more objective, less derogatory descriptions. "Small-chested" is more accurate than "flat as an ironing board."

• And when criticizing yourself in front of the mirror, say "There, I caught myself at it again—picking on my looks. I'm going to stop, walk away from this mirror, and come back only after I apologize to myself, give myself a smile, and say something nice to myself."

Correcting the Ugly-by-Association Error

Remember that Ugly-by-Association happens when you critique one aspect of your appearance, then another, and another. Like a snowball rolling down a hill, the farther it goes, the bigger and more powerful it becomes. It's easier to stop it at the top of the hill than near the bottom. You can combat this mental mistake by halting your body-image criticisms before they spread too far. Realize that obsessing over what's wrong with every aspect of your body does not fix what's wrong. The obsessing *itself* is what's wrong. Try these ideas for corrective thinking:

• Put your mental stop sign up and say to yourself, "I'm going to stop this right now! I'm just multiplying my misery." Then follow the Equal Time Rule, and compliment yourself. If you are in front of the mirror, walk away. If you're not at the mirror, walk away from the mirror in your mind.

• Repeat to yourself this variant of an old saying: "If I can't say anything nice about myself, I'll not say anything at all." Then do something totally unrelated to what you look like until your negative body-image feelings subside.

• Suppose you've been chastising yourself about your weight. Then you zoom in on your hair and begin criticizing it. Catch yourself and say, "Okay, I've started doing it again. Just because I'm dissatisfied with my weight is no reason for picking on other things about my looks. I'm going to leave my hair out of this!"

Correcting the Blame Game Error

This Body-Image Error involves making the mistake of "misattribution." When you play the Blame Game, you incorrectly hold your appearance responsible for some undesirable event, whether past or present. Examples of Private Body Talk based on the Blame Game are: "I don't have a girlfriend because I'm so ugly." Or, "People aren't friendly because of my weight."

To correct thinking based on the Blame Game, you first must realize that blaming your looks for unfortunate events usually involves jumping to conclusions. You are often just guessing, and your guess is based on a bias. If you consider the facts, often the only proof you have for blaming your appearance is your own negative feeling about your appearance— hardly ironclad evidence. A sequence of corrective thinking is needed to begin to set yourself straight:

• "Just because I am feeling unattractive doesn't mean that my looks are causing anything bad to happen. Now, what real evidence do I have that my appearance is to blame for this? What other likely explanations are there?"

• "Here I go again, accusing my looks of ruining everything. Instead, I'm going to leave my appearance out of it and focus on what I can do to make things better."

• Sometimes all you need to do is catch yourself blaming your looks, see that you have no evidence for your conclusion, and tell yourself, *"Stop Blaming!"* Then, move on to more important things—like being friendly or having fun.

• Suppose you do have good evidence that your looks really are to blame for something. So what? Not everybody is going to like your looks—or your haircut, or your clothes, or (for that matter) your car or your house. One person's opinion is not everybody's opinion. And if a few people reject or mistreat you because of such things, it may be their inadequacy, their problem, and their loss! There are judgmental and bigoted people in the world. If you are overweight and somebody is prejudiced against overweight people, this person is not rejecting *you,* he or she is rejecting millions of people. Do you really need to care what such a prejudiced person thinks about you?

Correcting the Mind Misreading Error

When Mind Misreading, you project your own thoughts about your appearance into the minds of others. You incorrectly infer that other people judge your looks as you do. Your Private Body Talk dwells on negative thoughts or opinions that you suspect other people could be having about your appearance. You think, "Everybody who talks to me is thinking about my acne (or large ears, crooked teeth, big breasts, toupee, or whatever)." Or, "Anybody who walks behind me will notice my 'bubble butt.' "

Mind Misreading often occurs in tandem with the Blame Game. Suppose your Private Body Talk complains: "My partner didn't initiate sex because he (or she) hates my body." You blame your appearance for sexual rejection, but Mind Misreading set you up in the first place. Maybe your partner was simply not in the mood—was tired, preoccupied with work, or having a headache. How do you know what's going on in your partner's mind? Besides, why did you expect your partner to read *your* mind and know that you wanted to make love?

The corrective thinking to dispute the Blame Game is helpful in overcoming Mind Misreading as well. Here are some additional strategies to help you keep straight who's thinking what:

• "I may be smart, but I can't read minds. The only mind I'm reading here is my own."

• "I need to stop thinking about what others may be thinking. Instead, I need to change what *I* am thinking."

• "If it's not my looks that are bothering people, what could it be?" As you entertain alternative explanations, consider several that are frequently true. For example, people are not likely to be friendly if *you* are unfriendly. Have you been acting defensive or standoffish because of *your* fear that others won't like you or your looks? Others could be shy, preoccupied with their own problems, or simply having a bad day. Could they be unfriendly because something is wrong with *them*—not with you?

Correcting the Misfortune Telling Error

The faulty thinking of Misfortune Telling involves dire predictions about how your appearance will cause bad things to happen. When Misfortune Telling, you typically think with words like "always" or "never." For example, "I'll *always* be a second-class citizen because of my looks." Or, "I'll *never* get hired as long as I'm fat." Or, "I'm too old-looking *ever* to be asked out." Of course, Misfortune Telling can also be situationally focused, as Laurie predicted: "I'll have a terrible time wearing this bathing suit at the beach."

In correcting your distorted thinking, you should again realize that, without real evidence, you are jumping to conclusions. How do you *really know* that your worst fears will come true? You need to separate your fears from your perceptions of the future. Here are some good ideas for corrective thinking:

• Replace a thought like, "I'll never be loved because of my appearance," with what's really going on: "I am *worried* that I'll not be loved." By definition, the future hasn't happened yet; it's your anxiety or despondence that's happening. If you work on feeling better about your appearance, you will feel less apprehensive. Tackle the other worries separately.

• Review the evidence. Have your pessimistic predictions always come true? Think of times when things turned out differently than you had expected. What did you do that made the difference?

• Say to yourself, "I'm going to quit worrying about the future and focus on the present. What can I do now to prove my doom-and-gloom predictions wrong?" Instead of deciding the future will be terrible, figure out what you can *do* to make it more tolerable—perhaps even pleasant. Develop a specific plan.

Correcting the Beauty Bound Error

The Beauty Bound error involves thinking "I can't do something because of how I look." The greatest danger of this error is that it can create a self-fulfilling prophecy. For example, if you think you look too awful to go a party, you skip the party and sit at home cursing your "loathsome looks" for preventing your having fun. Some people put themselves in a Catch-22 position with edicts like "I can't go to exercise class to lose weight until I lose weight." Misfortune Telling can set you up for the Beauty Bound error. Having made false predictions, you restrict your activities to avoid what you expect.

Later, in Step 6 of the program, I will teach you some excellent behavioral strategies to overcome the ways you allow the Beauty Bound error to limit your life. But first, let's develop some cognitive solutions to Beauty-Bound thinking:

• Ask yourself, "So *why* can't I do such-and-such?" For example, "I can't go to the party unless I lose twenty pounds." Why not? Is there a rule or law that says so? The real answer is "Because I think others will notice how fat I look and won't like me." Remind yourself that this belief reflects Mind Mis-reading and Misfortune Telling. Recognize that it is your discomfort that's stopping you, not what you look like or what other people are thinking.

• Instead of saying "I can't do it," take a problem-solving perspective. Ask "*How* can I do it? What would make it easier to do?" For example, "I can't go to the grocery with this haircut" becomes "I *can* go to the grocery if I wear my new hat." Replace "I can't go to the beach until I lose more weight" with "I can go to the beach if I use my Body-and-Mind Relaxation to help me feel more comfortable."

• Think about the fact that other people with less-than-perfect looks participate in the activities that you prohibit yourself from doing. Will you *really* be the only heavy person at the party?

• Counter your pessimism with motivating experiences. I suggest you read the inspirational, not-just-for-children book *The Little Engine That Could.* "I think I can! I think I can!"

Correcting the Feeling Ugly Error

Many people reason illogically, deriving their conclusions from their emotions. When you conclude that you *are* unat-tractive because you *feel* unattractive, you are committing the cognitive error I've called Feeling Ugly. Frequently, this error occurs after you've already committed some other error in thinking that produced body-image discontent. In turn, Feel-ing Ugly thinking then increases the likelihood that other mental mistakes will follow. Feeling Ugly acts like a bridge, carrying you from one error to another in a self-defeating cycle of body-image distress.

The fundamental corrective approach here is to realize that your feelings and self-perceptions are just that—feelings and self-perceptions. When you start Feeling Ugly thinking, you lock yourself in your own little closet of an emotion-based viewpoint. How often have you heard people commit this error, criticizing something about their looks, while your impression of their looks is not as negative as theirs? A friend may say, "My new haircut is really ugly," yet objectively, you can see that it looks fine. Or another friend complains, "My hips are as big as a buffalo's," and knowing how big buffalo hips really are, you realize the gross exaggeration. Because you're *not* that person, you can objectively recognize that the person's looks aren't the real problem; the problem is what the person *believes* about his or her looks. You rightly conclude that even if your friend's hair could look better or his or her derriere could be smaller, your friend's appearance is nowhere near a total disaster.

So when you are feeling unattractive, try to think more objectively, as an unbiased observer would. Here are some more helpful strategies for corrective thinking:

• Use your mental STOP! sign to halt your thinking. Tell yourself, "I'm not feeling especially attractive now. This is not a good time to contemplate my looks. All I'm doing is making myself feel worse. So stop it!"

• Replace the "I *am*" thoughts with "I *feel*" thoughts. For example, replace "With this hairstyle I *am* stupid-looking" with "I *feel* less happy with my new hairstyle than I'd like." Then deal with your feelings by examining the other errors that caused your body-image distress to begin with.

• Fixating on your feelings usually intensifies them—the way dwelling on the sensations of a headache intensifies your pain. So *refocus your attention* to something that can create different feelings. If you are alone, read the comics in the newspaper, or watch a sitcom on television. If you are with other people, redirect the conversation to interesting things in their lives.

Correcting the Moody Mirror Error

The last of our Dirty Dozen errors is the Moody Mirror. Like the Feeling Ugly error, it too involves emotional reasoning. Moody Mirror occurs when you are in a bad mood or are upset about something other than your appearance. Your bad mood spreads to affect—or perhaps I should say "infect"—your Private Body Talk. Corrective thinking treats the infection.

• Ask yourself: "Was something else already bothering me before I started worrying about or criticizing my body?" Then say "Okay, my appearance isn't really the issue here. I've had a bad day or a disappointing experience. That's what I've got to deal with right now. I'm going to leave my looks out of this."

• Or you may say, "Here I go again, victimizing my body when it's just an innocent bystander." Then step away from the mirror or the body thoughts (after a brief apology, of course, to your body for the false accusations).

• As you do to combat the Feeling Ugly error, *refocus your attention* to something that can modify your mood. Extricate yourself from the emotional quicksand.

Disputing Your Body-Image Errors

Now it's time to use your New Inner Voice to correct the twelve cognitive errors we've discussed. Look at the Help-sheet on page 224. You'll want several copies of this, or you may wish to copy its format into your diary. For each error that distorts your Private Body Talk, you will use the Help-sheet to develop counterarguments to dispute it. Here's how:

1. Begin with the error you commit most frequently. Review entries in your Body-Image Diary to find real-life examples of your Private Body Talk that reflect this error.

2. On the Helpsheet, write down your problematic Private Body Talk. Include the self-statements, beliefs, and interpretations that reflect the error.

3. Reread my discussion of how to "talk back" and dispute this mental mistake.

4. On the Helpsheet, write down your own corrective thinking for disputing this error. You may borrow from my examples, but ultimately you must "talk back" with the New Inner Voice that's right for you. So write down two or more of the best counterarguments that work for you. (You'll find that some arguments will work against more than one error. These arguments are among the strongest weapons in your arsenal.)

5. Complete a separate Helpsheet for different instances of each error. Always select those instances that are most distressing or occur most often.

6. Carry out these five steps for each error you commit, even errors that you make only occasionally.

MAKING CORRECTIVE THINKING A NATURAL PART OF YOUR LIFE

Please don't opt for "osmosis therapy"—figuring that absorbing my words will work just as well as finding your own. It's crucial that you complete Step 4's Helpsheet for Questioning Your Appearance Assumptions and Step 5's Helpsheet for Corrective Thinking. Your New Inner Voice must speak with *your* chosen words, so I urge you to spend the small amount of time it requires to put your words on paper—for your body image's sake. If you are trying to talk yourself out of active involvement, with thoughts like, "Oh, I get the idea, this is

HELPSHEET FOR CHANGE

Corrective Thinking by "Talking Back"

Type of Body-Image Error: _____

My problematic Private Body Talk says:

_____

_____

_____

_____

_____

_____

_____

Disputing the error with corrective thinking, my New Inner Voice says:

_____

_____

_____

_____

_____

_____

_____

just positive thinking," you are wrong. This approach to changing your body-image experiences is deeper and more complex than just thinking nice thoughts. You are discovering, challenging, and disputing the very personal inner causes of your body-image distress. Neglecting to write down your counterarguments will definitely reduce your benefits. Don't settle for less than you deserve and less than you can have. So if your Old Inner Voice is coaxing you not to use your Helpsheets, don't listen to it!

Learning by Rehearsal

Changing your unhappy Private Body Talk requires careful thought, diligent effort, and practice. It's a *learned* skill, and the more you do to perfect this skill, the more effective you'll be in conquering your negative body image. The more often you use your New Inner Voice, the more effortlessly you'll be able to change your old mental "tapes." With this in mind, I'd like you to strengthen your New Inner Voice as follows:

Silently reread the corrective dialogues you wrote on the Helpsheets for handling the cognitive errors you commit. Make any additions and adjustments you need. Next, read these aloud. I want you to hear yourself say them in your own voice. Then read your corrective dialogues aloud again, but this time tape record them. Listen to your tape recording once a day for the next week. Soon you will be able to anticipate exactly what you will say next on the tape— evidence that you are really internalizing corrective thinking.

Learning by Rewards

Psychologists know that people are more likely to engage in behavior that is *rewarded* and *rewarding* than in behavior that is without incentive. It is essential that you reward yourself for applying corrective thinking. Recognize your efforts; mentally applaud your successes. For example, when Laurie successfully stopped comparing herself with her more slender best friend as they tried on clothes at the mall, she recognized she had cut short her usual sequence of negative body-image experiences, which, in the past, would have left her tearfully depressed. So she said to herself, "I really took charge of this potentially upsetting situation. Good for me!" Then, Laurie bought herself some new nail polish to reward her success.

A New Diary for a New Body Image

The most immediate benefit of corrective thinking is that you feel less anxious, despondent, frustrated, or ashamed about your appearance. Because these improvements are important to recognize explicitly, you now should add a final step to your A-B-C-D Sequence of body-image experiences. Add an "E" for the *Effects* of corrective thinking. Just as you have become aware of the negative emotional effects of cognitive errors and irrational thinking, you need to learn to spot the emotional improvements that result from changing your Private Body Talk.

You can trade your old Body-Image Diary in for a brand-new version—your *Corrective Thinking Diary*. From now on, use this version to record your Disputing of errors and the Effects of this corrective thinking in your daily life. Turn to page 230 at the end of this chapter and examine the format of your new diary. To illustrate how you will use this new format, I've included a couple of examples from the diaries that Laurie and Everett kept.

As soon as possible after you have had a body-image experience in which you countered your distressing Private Body

Talk with corrective thinking, record the sequence of events in your new diary. *Stop* the faulty Private Body Talk, *look* objectively at what your Old Inner Voice was telling you, and *listen* to the New Inner Voice of your corrective thinking. Notice the effects—you feel less upset and more in control. Give yourself a few mental kudos for your accomplishments.

How to Get There from Here

As you apply corrective thinking in your everyday life, there are some key things to keep in mind. Your initial efforts at corrective thinking may seem unnatural. That's to be expected. Because your Old Inner Voice is so familiar, your New Inner Voice may not "sound like you." In time, it will. Moreover, don't expect corrective thinking will cause your negative body-image emotions to vanish immediately and totally. At first, your corrective thinking will mostly prevent your distress from getting out of hand. Realize that "less bad" is good. Also adjust your corrective thinking as needed. New events or situations will call for new counterarguments. Be flexible. Be innovative.

Patience is an essential virtue here. I recall that Everett, after a day or two of corrective thinking, complained that despite his cognitive efforts, he still hated his body. In defeat, Everett concluded, "Either this doesn't work or, if it does, I'm a hopeless case." Eventually, he learned both were untrue, after becoming more patient with himself. Cognitive change is gradual. So celebrate your victories. Accept any tough times as expected bumps in the road. Being a perfectionist, Laurie experienced her greatest progress once she was able to give herself permission to feel bad for a while, even though she had successfully corrected her Private Body Talk in a given situation. As Laurie would advise you, "Don't give yourself a hard time whenever you have a hard time. That only makes it worse."

In the next chapter, you will develop even more ways—active, *behavioral* ways—to enhance your body image. Before we proceed to Step 6, however, I want to leave you with the personal experiences of two of my clients, Janet and Cliff.

Janet's Success

Janet was a twenty-eight-year-old single parent and nurse who was extremely dissatisfied with her body. She hated being so tall (6'1"), and she despised having freckles and red hair. She committed all of the dozen Body-Image Errors; in particular, the Mind Misreading and Moody Mirror errors tainted her Private Body Talk every day. She devoted substantial mental energy to what nasty thoughts her coworkers and her dates might be having about her appearance. Whenever life's hassles put her in a bad mood, she would immerse herself in disparaging thoughts about her body.

Janet targeted these errors and worked out specific plans and arguments to attack them. In her own words, here's what happened:

I've made major strides in defeating my tendency to wallow in ugly thoughts. Two things have helped most. First is my ability to catch myself Mind Misreading before I get really absorbed in it. All I do is mentally "change the channel" and think about more interesting things. Second is something I do to stop berating my looks when I'm in a sour mood. I got the idea from what I do when one of my kids is being temperamental and is unfairly taking it out on my other child. I separate them—each one going to a different room. So I do this when my mood picks on my body image. I take my mood into a different room and pretend to leave my body behind. I know it sounds silly, but it helps me separate my mood from my body image.

Cliff's Success

Cliff, a fifty-one-year-old teacher, is another success story. His principal Body-Image Errors were the Unreal Ideal, Unfair-to-Compare, the Magnifying Glass, and the Blind Mind. Cliff often compared himself with "muscle man" ideals (the Unreal Ideal). With despair, he noticed any guy who might have a bigger build than his own (Unfair to Compare). Also apparent in his Private Body Talk was considerable tunnel vision. Cliff obsessed that his chest and shoulders weren't broad enough, and he hated the fact that his chest hair was sparse (Magnifying Glass). There was no place in his body image for appreciation of his physical assets (Blind Mind).

Cliff was initially resistant to keeping his Corrective Thinking Diary, but ultimately, his diary was what helped him the most:

I was so invested in despising my looks that I refused to believe I could change. But I began to see a clear connection between my style of thinking about my body and how I would feel. The more I wrote down what was going on in my head and then wrote down what I wished I could think, the clearer it became. I was my own worst enemy. It wasn't easy, but I kept arguing myself out of the ridiculous ruts I'd think myself into. Instead of being the victim of my own thinking, I'm now much more the master of it.

HELPSHEET FOR CHANGE

My Corrective Thinking Diary

A-B-C-D-E Sequence

A: Activators: _____

_____

B: Beliefs: _____

_____

_____

C: Consequences: _____

_____

D: Disputing by Corrective Thinking:

_____

_____

_____

_____

_____

E: Effects of Corrective Thinking:

_____

_____

_____

Don't forget to reward yourself!

Laurie's Corrective Thinking Diary

A-B-C-D-E Sequence

A: *Activators:*   Trying on swim suits at Bikini Hut

B: *Beliefs:*   I look huge; I can't stand looking at myself. The saleslady thinks I'm fat. I'll never find a swimsuit that's okay.

C: Consequences: Depressed; want to leave the store

D: *Disputing* by Corrective Thinking:

"Huge" is an exaggeration. I <u>can</u> look at myself if I just relax and quit self-criticism. The saleslady is not focusing on my weight—I am. So STOP! I just need to pick a swimsuit that's <u>pretty</u>. I know I'll like it later.

E: *Effects* of Corrective Thinking:

I settled down. Bought a really cute suit. Everybody loves it. I'm looking forward to the summer at the beach

Don't forget to reward yourself!   Got sandals to match— on Sale!

Everett's Corrective Thinking Diary

A-B-C-D-E Sequence

A: *Activators:*   *At the Holiday Inn lounge, wishing I could ask Peggy to dance (she's 3 inches taller than I am).*

B: *Beliefs:*   *She thinks I'm goofy looking and she'll turn me down. I'll be humiliated.*

C: *Consequences:*   *Paralysis. Angry at myself.*

D: *Disputing* by Corrective Thinking:

The fact is I'm a good dancer and Peggy likes to dance. Just focus on having fun. My looks aren't on trial. If she says No—So what?! It won't end the world and doesn't indict my looks.

E: *Effects* of Corrective Thinking:

I asked & she said "Sure." Just enjoyed the music and dancing. Felt more confident. What a fun night!

Don't forget to reward yourself!

STEP 5

Progress Check: How Am I Helping Myself?

• You're continuing to use your Body-and-Mind Relaxation to manage stress in your life, including body-image distress.

• You are continuing to question the Appearance Assumptions that set you up for a negative body image.

• Reviewing your Body-Image Diary entries and using the Step 5 Helpsheets, you have detected the Body-Image Errors that are typically evident in your episodes of body-image distress.

• You are finding the words with which your New Inner Voice can effectively challenge and dispute your faulty Private Body Talk, and you're writing these counterarguments on Helpsheets. You are reviewing, rehearsing, and fine-tuning your corrective thinking. You are strengthening your New Inner Voice's power to conquer your upsetting Private Body Talk.

• You're applying Corrective Thinking in your everyday life. As you encounter a difficult situation, you are able to "Stop, Look, and Listen" and actively use corrective thinking to change how you feel. With your new Corrective Thinking Diary, you're monitoring and recording the A-B-C-D-E Sequence of your body-image experiences.

• You are being realistic in your expectations and patient with yourself. You are rewarding your efforts and enjoying your progress.

Your Own Worst Enemy

Defeating Your Self-Defeating
Behavior

EVERETT DOES IT SEVERAL times a day, especially in the morning before going to work and in the evening before going out. When he's not doing it, he's thinking about it. It consumes much of his time and his thoughts. Though it helps him feel better for a brief while, it gives him little lasting pleasure. He tries not to do it, but he cannot seem to stop himself.

What's Everett hooked on? Alcohol? Cocaine? Some weird sexual practice? Not at all. Like 30 million other men in America, Everett is balding. But Everett can't stand it. He counts the hairs lost forever as they swirl down the drain of his sink. He spritzes and sprays and carefully combs the remaining strands over his visible scalp. He inspects the result in the mirror, again and again from every possible angle. He can't seem to leave well enough alone. Everett is hooked on his looks. His fix is fixing his hair. Still, Everett achieves little satisfaction. He hates losing hair. He hates his looks.

·　·　·　·　·

Laurie is a fashion plate. Her wardrobe is extensive and always up-to-date. Whatever she wears is always stylish and well-coordinated. Her makeup is impeccably applied. Her delicate blond coiffure is flawless. From looking at her, you would assume that she must derive tremendous pleasure from being so attractive. But you'd be wrong. Laurie is constantly concerned that she doesn't look right. Preparing her appearance takes at least two hours each morning. Dressing for a party involves her changing clothes four or five times. Because she thinks that her hips are too large and worries that her tummy sticks out, she must select the outfit that won't reveal her "ugly secrets." Deathly afraid of gaining a few pounds, Laurie is always dieting and weighs herself three times a day.

DISCOVERING YOUR SENSELESS SELF-DEFENSES

In Steps 4 and 5, you saw how cognitive therapy can help you change the faulty thinking that provokes and perpetuates your negative body image. Now, in Step 6, you will learn how *behavior therapy* can help you change the behavior patterns that are tied to your body-image problems. As Everett and Laurie exemplified, people do all kinds of things to manage their appearance and cope with their disturbing body-image thoughts and feelings. You may know this personally from monitoring the A-B-C Sequence of your own body-image experiences. You've probably discovered that you try to avoid certain Activators that trigger episodes of body-image distress. It's also probable that among your Consequences are self-protective actions you take to minimize your misery once it's begun. For example, you may sulk, seek support, blame others, or try to "repair" your looks.

Any body-image misery, whether experienced or expected, is accompanied by various maneuvers for self-defense. These are patterns of behavior designed to correct, conceal, or compensate for what you *think* is wrong with your appearance. Typically, however, these same defensive actions become a part of your vicious cycle of body-image distress. Though they may offer some temporary relief from distress, they ultimately reinforce the conviction that your looks are defective.

In this chapter, you will discover your own self-defeating behavior patterns and learn how to eliminate them. Well-learned behavior patterns can develop a life of their own. Habit, pure and simple, keeps them going. Moreover, these habits stir up their own distress and, in a circular manner, are then used to cope with the discontent they have created.

As usual, your first task is to discover what needs fixing. Identifying your self-defeating behavior patterns requires that you recognize their essential, self-defensive purpose: *to avoid or escape feeling bad about your looks*. These behavior patterns are learned and persist even if they aren't wholly successful in protecting you from discomfort. We establish lots of behavior patterns, so that bad events either won't happen or, if they do, so that they won't feel nearly as unpleasant. Psychologists call this "instrumental learning by negative reinforcement." This is quite different from "instrumental learning by positive reinforcement," in which we do things because they produce purely positive outcomes and emotions. Defensive actions are motivated more by preventing discomfort than by providing pleasure.

There are two basic types of self-defense: flight or fight. Similarly, there are two kinds of defensive body-image behavior: You either can attempt to avoid (disguise, flee) the problem, or can constantly confront (obsess over) it and struggle to make it go away. I call these two forms of behavioral self-defense *Evasive Actions* and *Appearance-*

Preoccupied Rituals. Most people with a negative body image engage in both types of defense.

EVASIVE ACTIONS

People who are unhappy with their appearance may go to great lengths to avoid revealing their "flaws," not only to others but also to themselves. Let's take a look at the two types of Evasive Actions, *running* and *hiding,* and see how they may crop up in your life.

Running

If you review your Distressing Situations Test from Step 2 and review your Body-Image Diary, you will find that there are various situations and activities that you avoid. When you commit the Beauty Bound error, you tell yourself you *cannot* do certain things because of your appearance. You are not avoiding these things because they are inherently harmful or life-threatening. What you are actually avoiding are experiences that threaten your body image by eliciting feelings of self-consciousness, shame, or anxiety. These fall into four categories—The "Four Ps": *Practices, Places, People,* and *Poses.* Following are some common examples of each, but these do not exhaust the possibilities.

1. Do You Avoid Certain *Practices*?

Here are some activities commonly avoided by people who have a negative body image:

- Physical activities that might call attention to your

body—such as exercising, running, participating in recreational sports, or dancing.

• Normal activities in which somebody might see you not "fixed up"—such as going to the grocery with "sweats" on, going to your mailbox or answering your doorbell without your makeup on, or going out for a walk without perfectly fixed hair.

• Wearing clothes of a style, color, or fabric that might reveal your "flaws"—such as those that show body shape, body hair, birthmarks, scars, or other features you dislike.

• Eating in the presence of others you fear will think you are too fat—so you abstain, nibble, or order only the salad with low-calorie dressing. (Dessert may require complete privacy.)

• Getting feedback about your looks—for example, weighing yourself, looking at your reflection in a mirror, or viewing a picture of yourself—because "what you can't see can't hurt you!"

• Certain social physical contact—such as giving or receiving hugs that might disclose what your body feels like.

• Being photographed or videotaped.

• Sexual relations in which your partner can see you in the buff.

• Physical exams at the doctor's office—because they bare too much or because you don't want to find out how much you "officially" weigh.

2. DO YOU AVOID CERTAIN *PLACES*?

If you have a poor body image, chances are we won't find you in some of the following locations:

• Wherever your body is relatively exposed—such as at the beach or pool, in public showers or dressing rooms.

• Places in which appearance is stressed—such as dressy occasions, singles' gatherings, particular clothing stores.

• Places where mirrors are prominent—such as department-store dressing rooms or exercise classes held in mirrored rooms.

• Places with conditions that might make your "defects" more visible—for example, brightly lit or windy environments.

3. Do You Avoid Certain *People*?

It can be difficult for those who have a negative body image to be around these individuals:

• People who are attractive in ways you'd like to be—for example, tall, thin, tanned, or well-built.

• Good-looking members of the other sex.

• People who either do things or talk about doing things to look good, things you think *you* should be doing—for example, people who are on a diet, who exercise regularly, or who wear stylish clothes.

• People who might comment on your appearance— usually a friend or relative inclined to make unwanted comments (e.g., about your size, how much you eat, or your manner of dress).

4. Do You Avoid Certain *Poses*?

If you are self-conscious about your looks, in all likelihood you are careful about:

• Where or how you sit or stand during social inter-action—for example, stances or profiles that might accentu-ate your disliked physical characteristics (e.g., body shape, weight, height, posture, hair, or facial features).

• Particular gestures—for example, smiling (which ex-poses disliked teeth, dimples, or wrinkles) or hand gestures (which show short fingers or chipped nails).

• Certain positions during sexual relations—those that allow your partner to see clearly specific areas of your body.

WHAT ARE YOU RUNNING FROM?

On the following Self-Discovery Helpsheet, list the Practices, Places, People, and Poses that *you* avoid for the sake of self-defense. Review the examples just discussed and look again at your Body-Image Diary for evidence.

Hiding

The other way to control your negative body-image feelings involves Evasive Actions I call "grooming to hide." You use various means to conceal what you dislike about your appear-ance. Certain Appearance Assumptions that you discovered in Step 4 (such as Assumptions 2 and 5) can lead you to disguise what you despise. If you believe that your true appearance is noticeably ugly and that it will damage others' impressions of you, you probably feel you must hide what you really look like.

The tools of bodily adornment are "mood-altering sub-stances." We wear certain clothes, cosmetics, and hairstyles either to feel attractive ("positive reinforcement") or to feel less unattractive and conceal our shortcomings from others ("negative reinforcement"). The latter is self-defensive grooming—grooming to hide what we look like.

SELF-DISCOVERY HELPSHEET

What Am I Running From?

List the activities and situations you avoid in attempts to spare
yourself negative body-image feelings.

Practices:

    1. _____

    2. _____

    3. _____

Places:

    1. _____

    2. _____

    3. _____

People:

    1. _____

    2. _____

    3. _____

Poses:

    1. _____

    2. _____

    3. _____

The balding man hides beneath his hat. The heavy-hipped lady hides her shape with dark, loose garments. The older woman hides her wrinkled complexion with layers of makeup. She also uses tinted glasses to camouflage the bags beneath her eyes. The thin guy wearing long-sleeved shirts throughout the summer hides his skinny arms. The teenager with a scar on her throat hides it with high-collared blouses. The man with protruding ears hides them with his long hair. The person with skinny (or fat) legs always wears long pants, never shorts. Each of these people grooms to hide.

How Are You Grooming to Hide?

Think about the physical characteristics that bother you. What do you do to conceal them from view? What do you do to camouflage them so they'll be less visible to others? List these behavior patterns on the Self-Discovery Helpsheet on page 243.

APPEARANCE-PREOCCUPIED RITUALS

The second type of self-defeating behavior pattern is Appearance-Preoccupied Rituals—incessant, obsessive-compulsive efforts at damage control. People trapped in such rituals spend excessive time and money to make themselves look right. Unlike the mirror avoiders, these individuals practically live in front of their mirrors, fussing over and fixing their myriad flaws. They are "shop-aholics" for any product promising a perfect appearance. And they insatiably seek social support: "Do you think I look okay? Are you sure? Are you *really* sure?"

Appearance-Preoccupied Rituals show up in two versions of compulsive behaviors: *Fixing* and *Checking*.

SELF-DISCOVERY HELPSHEET

How Am I Grooming to Hide?

List the ways in which you use clothes, cosmetics, or hairstyles to conceal or disguise what you consider to be your physical flaws.

1. _____
2. _____
3. _____
4. _____
5. _____
6. _____
7. _____
8. _____
9. _____
10. _____
11. _____
12. _____

Fixing

Fixing Rituals involve elaborate and time-consuming efforts to manage, adjust, or alter your appearance. These rituals occur in various forms, but three are most common.

With *Maintenance Fixing*, meticulous management of your appearance each day is quite an ordeal. You must do dozens of things, with considerable precision, to be satisfied that you look okay. Special occasions demand even more time and perfection.

Circular Fixing occurs when you regroom several times while getting ready to go out. You fix and refix your hair. You change clothes repeatedly. Each time, something doesn't look (or feel) quite right, so you start over. What a frustrating experience!

Fantasy Fixing applies to you if you want to overhaul your appearance dramatically. Efforts at fine-tuning aren't sufficient because you wish for a "total new look"—a radical transformation. As a result, you devote lots of mental energy, behavioral effort, and expense to "make yourself over."

These are some tell-tale signs of compulsive Fixing Rituals:

• Getting out of the bathroom and getting dressed on time is a rare accomplishment.

• You primp and preen more than you want. Intellectually, you know you look fine, but emotionally and behaviorally, you cannot leave well enough alone.

• Every situation requires that you change what you are wearing. Otherwise, you worry that your looks might be inappropriate.

• If other people are in your household, they've probably commented on how much time you spend on your appearance. Their comments may range from benign kidding to expressed irritation at having to wait for you to get ready.

• You buy lots of clothes or grooming products that you seldom wear or use. At first, you were sure they were what you needed. Ultimately, they didn't achieve what you had hoped.

• When you see your reflection in a mirror, you automatically adjust some aspect of your appearance—like your hair, your tie, or your dress—even though nothing was really amiss.

• You regularly make major changes in your appearance— for example, with different hairstyles, different hair colors, or cosmetic makeovers.

• You often entertain the idea of having cosmetic surgery.

Checking

Checking Rituals usually go hand in hand with Fixing Rituals. Put simply, the thought that something *might* be awry in your grooming makes you nervous and preoccupied. God forbid that you might not look okay. Better check it out! So you do.

To illustrate, let me present an analogy. As you are dozing off for a good night's sleep, the question crosses your mind, "I wonder if I locked the door?" You feel sure that you did. Still, the question lingers. You cannot lay the matter to rest and go to sleep. So what do you do? You get up and check that the door is locked. Safe at last, you're ready for sweet dreams!

The purpose of Checking Rituals is to obtain relief from the nagging preoccupation and worry about your looks. Over time, such actions can become learned habits. Thus, Checking Rituals may sometimes be conscious, deliberate attempts to avoid worrying; other times, they may be mindless, automatic actions. This is true whether the rituals entail checking on locked doors or checking on your appearance. While we're at it, check out the following signs of this Appearance-Preoccupied pattern:

• You have intrusive thoughts that you need to inspect your appearance. These thoughts are hard to push aside until you've acted on them.

• Whenever you pass by a mirror (or other reflecting surface), you look to see that your appearance is okay.

• Several times daily, you visit the restroom with the chief purpose of inspecting your looks, though you have no good reason to believe that anything is wrong.

• If worried about your weight, you compulsively weigh yourself to determine if you have gained or lost any small amount.

• You routinely check others' opinions about your appearance, seeking reassurance that you look okay. Trusted friends and loved ones are the ones most often asked.

• In social situations, you repeatedly check how your appearance compares with that of other people in order to reassure yourself that you are acceptable.

What Are Your Appearance-Preoccupied Rituals?

To discover what defensive behavior patterns you have cultivated into Appearance-Preoccupied Rituals, think about how you spend a typical day, as well as how you behave on a special evening out or before an important meeting. Think about repetitive Fixing Rituals you engage in. Think about the Checking Rituals that seem hard to resist. List your Appearance-Preoccupied Rituals on the Helpsheet on the next page.

SELF-DISCOVERY HELPSHEET

What Are My Appearance-Preoccupied Rituals?

My "Fixing Rituals"

1. _____
2. _____
3. _____
4. _____
5. _____
6. _____

My "Checking Rituals"

1. _____
2. _____
3. _____
4. _____
5. _____
6. _____

AVOIDING AVOIDANCE

Having discovered your particular patterns of self-defeating body-image behavior, you are now ready for the second phase of Step 6: changing these patterns. It's time for you to control them, instead of letting them control you. Let's begin by tackling your Evasive Actions.

The best way to cure avoidance is to "avoid avoiding"—to confront what you have been trying to escape. I call this challenge *Facing It*. Scientific study after study has proven that people can overcome their fears by gradually exposing themselves to what they are afraid of, whether it is a fear of snakes, flying in airplanes, giving a speech, or a fear of looking bad or feeling bad about one's looks.

You already possess most of the skills you need to face down your body-image fears. In Step 3, you learned Body-and-Mind Relaxation, you learned how to construct hierarchies, and you carried out Body-Image Desensitization. In Steps 4 and 5, you developed your New Inner Voice—an important ally for Facing It. Your command of all these skills gives you a distinct advantage in the battle against Evasive Actions.

Priorities for Action: Your "Facing It" Hierarchy

Go back to your Self-Discovery Helpsheet, "What Am I Running From?" on page 241. Reread the Practices, Places, People, and Poses that you avoid because they are associated with the experience or expectation of negative body-image emotions.

Now you will make a simple judgment about each situation or activity you avoid, a judgment that psychologists term *self-efficacy*. Self-efficacy is your degree of confidence that you could actually enter the situation or engage in the activity. For example, suppose you've listed that you avoid "trying on clothes at Wilbur's Boutique." Ask yourself, "How confident am I that I could actually go and try on a few outfits at Wilbur's?" Your answer reflects your self-efficacy for this activity. Give each entry on your list a self-efficacy rating from

0 to 100. A rating of 0 means "No way. Never in a million years would I be able to do that." A rating of 100 says, "I'm 100 percent sure I can do that." A 50 means you give yourself a 50-50 chance that you could face it. Jot down your self-efficacy rating for each item on your list, directly on the Helpsheet, to the left of the item.

Be sure your list contains a reasonable range of self-efficacy ratings, though most should be under 50 (that is, fairly difficult). Locate any items having the same numerical rating. Decide which is really a little harder and rerate them. If all ratings are below 50, yours is a "hard-to-do list." If all are above 50, it's an "easy-to-do list." To balance a lopsided list, simply add a few more Evasive Actions, either easy or hard.

If any item isn't feasible for practical reasons—like eating Thanksgiving dinner with your weight-critical in-laws in Phoenix when it's July and you're in New Jersey—replace it with a doable item that's comparable in self-efficacy. If an activity or situation is too general, pick a representative instance. For example, "going to singles' bars with a friend" becomes "going to Lefty's Lounge with Bob."

Now, having fine-tuned your list, transcribe the items and their ratings to the new Helpsheet on the next page, your "Facing It" Hierarchy. Put the most difficult situations and activities (with the lowest self-efficacy ratings) at the top of the hierarchy and the easiest ones (with the highest ratings) at the bottom.

Getting Basic Training to PACE Yourself

As you've probably guessed, next you'll begin to face each of the situations and activities in your hierarchy. You engage in the Practices you avoid, go to the Places you avoid, be with the People you avoid, and strike the Poses you avoid. Do this a

HELPSHEET FOR CHANGING EVASIVE ACTIONS

My "Facing It" Hierarchy

Self-Efficacy Rating*		What I Am Going to Face
_____ (lowest)	12.	_____
_____	11.	_____
_____	10.	_____
_____	9.	_____
_____	8.	_____
_____	7.	_____
_____	6.	_____
_____	5.	_____
_____	4.	_____
_____	3.	_____
_____	2.	_____
_____ (highest)	1.	_____

* Self-efficacy ratings are from 0 for no confidence to 100 for complete confidence.

step at a time, starting with number 1—the easiest thing at the bottom of your hierarchy—and working your way up through the toughest.

I'm sure you are feeling pretty apprehensive about facing these uncomfortable situations. You may already be thinking about what you're *not* going to do. Don't let yourself retreat! I am not going to ask you to march unarmed into enemy territory. Together, we will develop a systematic plan of action. All you have to do is follow your plan. It will lead you to victory over avoidance.

Facing It always consists of four basic steps: *Prepare, Act, Cope,* and *Enjoy*. The first letters of these steps conveniently remind you to *PACE* yourself. Let me explain each step.

1. *Prepare:* You are about to face a situation deliberately that is guaranteed to be uncomfortable for you. Rather than charging in unprepared, write down your strategy ahead of time. This step is very important, because it involves planning and rehearsing the remaining three steps. In making your preparations, decide precisely what you are going to do and when you are going to do it. Figure out how you will answer that Old Inner Voice of procrastination that says, "I can't. Not now. I'll do it tomorrow." Anticipate what pessimistic Private Body Talk will likely pop into your head and how you might feel. Decide exactly how you are going to handle these negative thoughts and emotions if they do occur. Finally, promise to reward your efforts at Facing It. Decide in advance what your reward will be. Having spelled out this detailed plan in writing (see the special Helpsheet on page 253), review it and rehearse it in your mind.

2. *Act:* The time has come. It's time to Face It and execute your plan! You already anticipated that you might get cold feet at this point, so give yourself the pep talk, the moment of Body-and-Mind Relaxation, or whatever else you need to

follow through with what you've so often avoided. As you begin confronting it, hold up your mental applause sign. Good for you!

3. *Cope:* Uptight thoughts and feelings come as no surprise. You expected them, so accept them. Use the coping skills you've learned to roll with the discomfort. As planned, use corrective thinking or aspects of Body-and-Mind Relaxation, like calming imagery or breathing techniques. Remind yourself that you *can* handle it—that you *are* handling it.

4. *Enjoy:* It's over—you did it! Now don't forget the bargain you made with yourself. Facing It deserves a reward. Celebrate the fact that you followed through. Don't criticize or undervalue your accomplishment. Don't say to yourself, "Yes, I did it, *but* . . ." No buts are allowed. Just enjoy your success. Give yourself a special treat—some affordable trinket, a cone of tasty frozen yogurt, or a relaxing moment with your favorite music—and relish it. You earned it.

Preparing Your Plans: "Ready, Set, Go"

The Helpsheet on the following page, entitled "Preparing My Plan for Facing It," will aid in developing your plan of action for each item in your hierarchy according to the PACE format. Make copies and fill them out as you move up your Facing It hierarchy. Take a look at the illustrative Helpsheet on page 254 that Everett used in confronting one of his Evasive Actions—his avoiding giving others a profile view of his nose during conversations.

Start at the bottom of your hierarchy, with the activity or situation that you are reasonably confident you can face. *Prepare* by drafting your plans for Facing It.

HELPSHEET FOR CHANGING EVASIVE ACTIONS

Preparing My Plan for Facing It

Practice, Place, Person, or Pose Avoided:

_____

Step-by-Step Plan for Facing It:
Prepare: Exactly what will I do?

_____
_____
_____
_____

Act: Where? When? For how long? What will I do if I get cold feet?

_____
_____

Cope: What uncomfortable thoughts and feelings do I expect and how will I cope with them?

_____
_____
_____

Enjoy: How will I reward my efforts?

_____
_____

What were the *results* of Facing It?

_____
_____

HELPSHEET FOR CHANGING EVASIVE ACTIONS

Everett's Plan for Facing It

Practice, Place, Person, or Pose Avoided:

A pose in which people look at my nose profile.

Step-by-Step Plan for Facing It:
Prepare: Exactly what will I do?

Purposefully engage in conversations in which I briefly and repeatedly turn my head to the side and expose my profile to the other person.

Act: Where? When? For how long? What will I do if I get cold feet?

At work: once in a.m., twice in p.m. /5 minutes each for 1 week. Use my relaxation if I get cold feet.

Cope: What uncomfortable thoughts and feelings do I expect and how will I cope with them?

"Mind-Misreading" thoughts (i.e., "they think my nose is stupid looking") → nervous, self-conscious. Use corrective thinking to combat error in thought. Use breathing/smiling to handle discomfort.

Enjoy: How will I reward my efforts?

Enjoy sitting in hot tub at end of day. Compliment myself in my own mind.

What were the *results* of Facing It?

Uncomfortable for 1st 2 days but it got easier. Making a game of it helped!

Now decide how you will *Act.* Specify the place, date, time, duration, and frequency of your action. For example, suppose your item reads, "I avoid standing anywhere that people are behind me and can see the shape of my rear." Your action plan might be: "Each day at work for the next three days, at ten A.M. and four P.M., I am going to spend five minutes at the file cabinets where my coworkers can see me from behind."

What are your plans to *Cope?* Write them down. Remember, your goal is *not* that you be free from any discomfort while facing what you avoid. Your goal is to carry out the activity and cope with any discomfort you experience. So, in my example, know that when you stand at the file cabinet, you will use pleasant imagery and particular corrective thinking to combat errors in your probable Private Body Talk.

What reward will you *Enjoy* afterward? Be specific. Be generous.

Having scripted your plans, now rehearse them. Mentally review what you will do to Act, Cope, and Enjoy. Visualize each step. Picture yourself carrying out your plan.

Now that you are prepared, execute your plan. Act . . . Cope . . . Enjoy!

Follow these same steps for each item as you proceed up

your hierarchy—succeeding all the way to the top. If an item seems too difficult, break it down into simpler steps. For example, the situation "having my partner see me naked" might begin with his or her seeing you in your underwear. Save complete nudity for later, when you've worked up to it. Keep your focus on wherever you are in your hierarchy. Don't worry about items you haven't prepared for yet. You'll deal with them when you get there.

As you move up your hierarchy, you'll accumulate plans of attack for defeating your various Evasive Actions. After each victory (no matter how small), make a note of what worked and what didn't. Always take a moment to record the results of your Facing It on the Helpsheet.

COMING OUT OF HIDING

With the second type of Evasive Action, you "groom to hide." The Facing It exercises to change these behaviors are just like those to confront the situations and activities you avoid.

Developing Your Facing It Hierarchy for "Grooming to Hide"

Earlier, on page 243, you listed your tricks for hiding what you dislike about your looks. You know what to do next: Use this list to develop your next Facing It hierarchy (on page 258). Here, rate your confidence in being able to *refrain* from using each particular action to conceal your looks. Again, organize and fine-tune your hierarchy from easiest (highest self-efficacy) to hardest (lowest self-efficacy).

Because you probably engage in avoidant grooming behaviors in many situations, you'll need to pick specific contexts in which to work on them. For example, let's suppose that you listed, "I always wear heavy makeup to hide my freckles," or, "I wear long, baggy sweaters to hide my stomach." For each, think of a couple of situations in which you could conceivably *not* do these things. My clients often select practical, everyday situations like going to class, walking around at the mall, or shopping at the grocery store. Don't pick an infrequent situation, like going on your summer vacation, unless it'll happen soon. Also, don't choose situations in which your *not* engaging in the particular behavior would make you quite out of place. I am asking you to "blow your cover," but nobody's asking you to go to a wedding in your bathing suit.

Preparing Your Plans for Coming Out of Hiding

Start with the bottom item and PACE yourself. Use the Helpsheet format on page 259 to put down on paper how you will Prepare, Act, Cope, and Enjoy the success. Check out the Helpsheet (on page 260) that Laurie used to stop avoiding wearing form-fitting slacks that "made her feel fat." After rehearsing and carrying out your plan, note the results. Then, march onward, proceeding up the hierarchy as usual!

ABOUT FACE

As they set about reversing their troublesome Evasive Actions, most of my clients find it efficient to work on both Facing It hierarchies at the same time. You too might prefer this. Do a few items that involve facing avoided activities or situations, and then do a few that involve coming out of hiding. Once you've got a few victories under your belt, you will realize that your self-efficacy is growing, and your ability to PACE

HELPSHEET FOR CHANGING EVASIVE ACTIONS

My "Facing It" Hierarchy

Self-Efficacy Rating*	How I "Groom to Hide" (Behaviors in Specific Situations)
_____ (lowest)	12. _____
_____	11. _____
_____	10. _____
_____	9. _____
_____	8. _____
_____	7. _____
_____	6. _____
_____	5. _____
_____	4. _____
_____	3. _____
_____	2. _____
_____ (highest)	1. _____

* Self-efficacy ratings are from 0 for no confidence (in refraining from the behavior) to 100 for complete confidence (in refraining).

HELPSHEET FOR CHANGING EVASIVE ACTIONS

Preparing My Plan for Facing It

How I "Groom to Hide":

_____

Step-by-Step Plan for Facing It:
Prepare: Exactly what will I do?

_____
_____
_____
_____
_____

Act: Where? When? For how long? What will I do if I get cold feet?

_____
_____

Cope: What uncomfortable thoughts and feelings do I expect and how will I cope with them?

_____
_____
_____

Enjoy: How will I reward my efforts?

_____
_____

What were the *results* of Facing It?

_____
_____

HELPSHEET FOR CHANGING EVASIVE ACTIONS

Laurie's Plan for Facing It

How I "Groom to Hide":

Avoid "snug" pants, or wear long oversized shirt/sweater over them (to hide my hips and rear).

Step-by-Step Plan for Facing It:
Prepare: Exactly what will I do?

1) Start with less tight slacks—wear them with tucked-in blouse to grocery and bank. 2) Graduate to tighter jeans worn to grocery, bank, and Saturday picnics.

Act: Where? When? For how long? What will I do if I get cold feet?

Above places 2-3 times a week for 4 weeks (1–2 hours each time). If I "chicken out" I'll ask husband for encouragement.

Cope: What uncomfortable thoughts and feelings do I expect and how will I cope with them?

Accept the discomfort as temporary. Use corrective thinking and imagery (picturing success). I keep saying "I can do this."

Enjoy: How will I reward my efforts?

With a tall glass of cold herbal tea. Plus
my husband's "Great, Laurie!"

What were the *results* of Facing It?

Though I prefer wearing other things, I can wear
snug slacks/jeans now without "feeling fat"
and self-conscious.

---

yourself is greatly improved. You are avoiding and hiding less and less. What was once a chore now seems more like a game. And you are winning!

You've seen from their Helpsheets how Everett and Laurie tackled some of their Evasive Actions. With determination and persistence, both proceeded up their hierarchies with increasing confidence. Instead of "running" or "hiding," they were able to face things they had anxiously avoided. Before we move on to the next phase of Step 6, I'd like to share with you the successes of two other people, Earl and Chelsea.

Earl

Earl was intensely self-conscious about his penis size. Convinced that it was too small, he took great pains to ensure that no one would see it. When undressing or showering at the gym, he always faced a wall or wrapped a towel around his waist. Earl worked out his plan gradually to "avoid avoiding." He began by turning naturally in the direction of others during his shower. Soon, he could dress and undress in the locker room without having to shield himself with his towel. To cope with self-consciousness, Earl reminded himself that nobody really cared how big or small he was. He simply focused on how soothing the shower felt or on how well-toned his stomach muscles were. Later, he celebrated his courage with a frosted mug of his favorite imported beer.

Chelsea

Chelsea would never go out in public without layers of makeup. She was terrified at the thought that someone would see her and think she looked homely because of her large pores and less-than-peachy complexion. So she developed her plan for Facing It. Chelsea first journeyed, without makeup, to the mailbox to retrieve her mail. Next, she went to a nearby convenience store with less makeup than usual. Then, on three occasions, she went to the grocery, each time cutting down on the cosmetics.

Did Chelsea feel nervous each time? Of course she did, because she was Facing It, instead of avoiding it. Did her discomfort decline? Absolutely, because she had prepared herself! She used her calming relaxation skills and her New Inner Voice to control her Private Body Talk while she was "taking on" her avoidance. Her corrective thinking countered thoughts that stemmed from mental mistakes like Feeling Ugly, Mind Misreading, and Misfortune Telling. After each trip, she rewarded herself by listening to jazz tapes. Ultimately, Chelsea felt less trapped by her avoidance and was glad to be facing her body-image anxiety.

RIDDING RITUALS

Now that you know how to vanquish Evasive Actions by using the techniques for Facing It, let's consider the other self-defeating behavior pattern: Appearance-Preoccupied Rituals. Repeatedly fixing and checking your appearance is needlessly time consuming. Worse, these worrisome actions do not alleviate, but rather fuel, your discontent by reinforcing your belief that something is wrong with your looks. Your rituals also sustain the assumptions that if you don't look perfect all the time, bad things will happen or people won't like you.

To defeat these defensive behaviors, you either prevent them from starting or interrupt them once they've begun. I call this challenge *Erasing It*.

Delaying Your Rituals

The first strategy for Erasing It is very simple. You learn to wait a while before enacting your ritual. This strategy works especially well for Checking Rituals.

Typically, appearance-checking activities are preceded by an inner urge to check. You have a gnawing feeling that you *need* to inspect your hair, survey your makeup, weigh yourself, or seek reassurance about your looks. In many instances, your uneasiness is accompanied by automatic "What if" thoughts in your Private Body Talk that, because of faulty thinking, invariably conjure up horrible scenarios. "What if my hair is out of place and looks really stupid?" "What if my makeup is wearing thin and my bad complexion is showing?" "What if I've gained weight and I look fat?" "What if my wife thinks this hat looks dumb and she's embarrassed to be with me?"

Your Checking Rituals serve several defensive purposes. They interrupt your obsessive thinking and discomfort. They directly answer your "What if" questions. If you learn that you look fine, you'll feel relief. If you find that indeed something was slightly amiss, you will feel relief after you've fixed it.

By postponing your checking behaviors for a short period, you usurp the power of your urge. You are no longer a slave to your anxiety. Instead of permitting the urge to control your immediate actions, *you* take charge of the decision about when to check on your looks. This undermines both the urge that initiates the ritual as well as the ritual itself.

Wanda is a sales agent for a large real-estate company. She's on the road a lot, showing property to prospective buyers. During the course of a typical day, she used to check her appearance often. Each time she stopped at a traffic light, she checked her hair and makeup in the rearview mirror. While at the office, she would check her appearance two or three times per hour, using the small mirror in her desk drawer or the mirror in the ladies' room. When Wanda decided to delay her rituals, she deferred inspecting her reflection in the rearview mirror until she'd arrived at her destination. Each time she had an urge to look in the mirror at the office, she delayed checking for thirty minutes. At first, the wait made her feel anxious—what if she looked goofy all that time?—but by using Body-and-Mind Relaxation, she was able to turn her attention back to her work. Eventually, Wanda's urge to check became less insistent.

Restricting Your Rituals

Fixing Rituals may be even more self-defeating than Checking Rituals. Maintenance Fixing may take hours and cause you and others considerable inconvenience. Circular Fixing is exasperating as well as time consuming. And Fantasy Fixing can be terribly expensive.

The next Erasing It strategy requires that you restrict your ritualistic pattern. Each episode of a Fixing Ritual usually continues until one of two events occurs. Either you are sufficiently satisfied with the results of your fixing, or you run out of time. Instead of allowing the ritual to run its course, you can weaken it by placing specific limits on it. Following are three ways to do this.

"BEAT THE CLOCK"

Let's focus on Maintenance Fixing, although you can use the "Beat the Clock" strategy to overcome other types of rituals as well. First determine how long your Maintenance Fixing usually takes. Then make an objective estimate of how long would be reasonable for you to take. For example, suppose your morning maintenance ritual takes two hours. You figure that you should be able to get ready in one hour. Set your initial goal generously at being ready in one hour and fifty minutes. Set an alarm clock or kitchen timer to this limit and play "Beat the Clock." After several days of success, set the limit lower, say to one hour and forty minutes, and Beat the Clock for a few more days. Continue restricting your Maintenance Fixing in this fashion, shaving off ten minutes at a time until you've reached the reasonable amount of time. Reward your progress by using a portion of the total time saved for something you really enjoy.

Laurie basically likes her hair, but she insists that it always look perfect. It's the saving grace that she relies on to compensate for the physical features she dislikes. She dreads having a "bad hair day." Each morning, Laurie would fuss with her hair, styling it and restyling it until her ride for work arrived. Often, she spent over an hour on her hair, instead of the fifteen minutes that would have been sufficient. Each morning for two weeks, Laurie set her timer for a gradually declining interval (forty-five minutes, then thirty, then twenty, and finally fifteen minutes), and she played Beat the Clock. She required herself to be finished with her hair, out of the bathroom, and into her favorite chair for her morning juice *before* the timer alarm went off. By making this commitment and making a challenging game of it, Laurie eliminated her morning preoccupation with her hair. Her hair never actually looked less attractive than it used to, back in the days of one-hour fixing sessions. When occasionally Laurie had a "bad hair day," she stuck to her new abbreviated schedule anyway—and the world did not come to an end.

RATIONING RITUALS

This method of restricting rituals sets a limit on the number of times you engage in a particular type of behavior within a certain period. Let's suppose that whenever you go out to dinner with a friend or loved one, your requests for reassurance that you look okay begin to sound like a broken record. The more you ask, the more insecure you feel, especially as you begin to sense your companion's annoyance. So you set a quota. You allow yourself only two requests for reassurance during an entire evening. You may use your allotted queries whenever you wish, but having used your ration, you're through. Of course, over time, the goal is to set your ration progressively lower until it reaches zero.

Bradley's most frustrating ritual consisted of Circular Fixing. Every Thursday night, he attended a Sierra Club meeting to discuss environmental issues. Before going, he would change shirts and slacks several times. Nothing ever seemed to look right. Most Thursdays, his ritual caused him to be late for the meeting. Bradley was fed up with this pattern, so he developed and implemented a plan for Erasing It. He set aside one shirt-and-pants combination he liked, then he followed the "Second Choice Rule." If he got dressed and had the urge to change clothes, the requirement was that he *must* wear his second choice, the preselected outfit. Over time, Bradley reduced his redressing ritual. Now he usually wears whatever he first puts on.

"BY APPOINTMENT ONLY"

An urge often dictates when your rituals occur. So instead, schedule them! In effect, you will be making an appointment with yourself to carry out your ritual. Like any normal appointment, the one for your ritual begins and ends on time. And because you are permitted to have the ritual "by appointment only," it cannot occur at unscheduled times. If you miss your appointment, you must wait for the next scheduled occasion.

Charles has had complexion problems since his teen years. His face readily develops blackheads. Three or four times each day, Charles would sit in front of his magnifying mirror and peruse his pores in search of blackheads, squeezing them and picking at them. Not only did these frequent search-and-destroy missions take a lot of time, they took their abrasive toll on his complexion. To gain control over this pattern, Charles scheduled it. It was allowed only during ten-minute visits to the mirror at seven A.M., one P.M., and seven P.M. Thus, he restricted both the duration and the frequency of his ritual. Much to his own benefit as well as his dermatologist's relief, Charles gradually reduced his unhealthy practice to once a week.

Obstructing Your Rituals

Most habitual behavior patterns occur whenever an opportunity presents itself. Given certain cues in the environment, you carry out the behavior before you know it. For the person trying to quit smoking, the availability of cigarettes and being with others who are smoking are powerful behavioral instigators. That's why experts advise ridding the house of cigarettes and socializing with nonsmokers. For bulimics, access to certain foods can trigger a binge-purge episode. Accordingly, their therapists will insist that they clear their cupboards of such tempting foods.

Because checking or fixing can be extremely hard to resist, you may need to obstruct any opportunity it may have to occur. You "block its path." This is only a stopgap measure to improve your chances of short-term success. The long-term goal is to control your actions no matter what the circumstances. Otherwise, you have merely exchanged one form of avoidance for another.

Think about one Appearance-Preoccupied Ritual for which you need certain "tools" or conditions. For example, rituals in which you repeatedly scrutinize your appearance require a mirror. Even if a mirror is present, you cannot see your reflection if the room is dark or if the mirror is covered with a sheet or towel. Compulsive weighing would be impossible without a scale. How could you "make trouble" for your ritual by altering the environment? Developing this strategy is a challenge to your creativity.

With a receding hairline and thinning hair at the crown, Everett was desperately worried about going bald. Whenever he brushed his hair in his bathroom, he would use a hand-held mirror to inspect the back of his head in the larger mirror over his sink. Without the hand-held mirror, of course, he could not see his bald spot, obsess about it, and compulsively brush and rebrush in an attempt to conceal it. To rid himself of this ritual, Everett relocated the little mirror to the shed in his backyard. If he really wanted to "fix" his bald spot, he could. But he had to be dressed, go out to the shed, retrieve the mirror, and return to the bathroom. Then, the deal was that he had to restore the mirror to its place in the shed. Guess what? Everett soon found that the effort wasn't worth it. He was able to get ready regardless of the "readiness" of his bald spot.

Paige felt compelled to weigh herself almost every time she ate or drank anything and was nervous and distracted until she confirmed that she had not gained several pounds. So she put several layers of masking tape on the weight-displaying window of her scale. Paige weakened her compulsion to weigh herself because she had blocked her ritual's path. She combined this technique with the "By Appointment Only" tactic, weighing herself only on Saturdays when she changed the tape.

Resisting by Rebellion

Although this final strategy for Erasing It can be the most difficult, it is often the most effective. You rebel against the ritual, resisting it cold turkey. You may want to try it first on weaker rituals. For stronger compulsions, you will probably graduate to this approach after the successful use of other methods of delaying, restricting, and obstructing your behavior.

Being in complete control of a ritual (instead of vice versa) by refraining from doing it despite the fact that all the conditions are ripe for its occurrence can greatly boost your self-confidence. When "Resisting by Rebellion," you face the temptation and exercise restraint. Your New Inner Voice both commands and commends your rebellion. Body-and-Mind Relaxation and corrective thinking are your allies. You force yourself to remain in the situation without performing the ritual—the longer the better. If you try this and don't succeed, give yourself the deserved credit for trying. As you've heard me say before, never give yourself a hard time for having a hard time!

Often, a gradual approach is most helpful. Schedule your rebellions for progressively longer durations, building up your resistance. In other instances, it may be effective for you to remain in the situation until the urge to act upon your compulsive pattern has subsided. Like a former smoker who chews gum, occupy yourself with other activities. In either case, winning the battle will definitely require a series of skirmishes. Habits die hard.

Adrienne used strategies of resistance to combat two self-defeating behavior patterns. Whenever she went out with a friend or on a date, she used to spend almost as much time in the restroom checking and fixing her appearance as she spent with her companion. As Adrienne described the experience, "I would end up stuck to the mirror like a magnet. I kept freshening my makeup, messing with my hair, adjusting my clothes. I couldn't seem to pull myself away." So Adrienne planned her resistance. On several occasions when at a restaurant, she allowed herself to visit the restroom only three times per evening, each time for just a few minutes. If she had to wash her hands, she made a point of staring down at the sink instead of up at the mirror. The next step required that, on each visit, she look at herself in the mirror but refrain from touching her body to fix anything. Next she graduated to longer intervals between "checkups." Relying on her coping skills to get through her initial discomfort, Adrienne was ultimately able to break her obsessive-compulsive pattern of checking and fixing.

At the end of the chapter, I'll tell you about Adrienne's other remarkable success.

Constructing Your "Erasing It" Hierarchy

Now it's your turn to defeat your Appearance-Preoccupied Rituals. Once again, you approach this challenge systematically. Erasing It requires planning and ingenuity on your part to devise a strategy appropriate for your particular behavior pattern. You then assign yourself the corrective action and execute it often to erase the old pattern.

Go back to the Helpsheet on page 247, where you listed your Checking and Fixing Rituals. Read through your list and evaluate your confidence that you could refrain from engaging in the behavior if you were in the situation where it normally would occur. As you've done before, assign each entry on your list a self-efficacy rating from 0 to 100. Next, arrange these rituals in order of self-efficacy in your Erasing It hierarchy on page 272, going from the highest rating at the bottom to the lowest rating at the top.

Preparing and Executing Your Plans for Erasing It

Start with the ritual at the bottom—the easiest one to eliminate. Write down your plan for Erasing It, following the Helpsheet format on page 273. PACE yourself, just as you do in facing your Evasive Actions. As you plan, anticipate and specify each step—Prepare, Act, Cope, Enjoy. Visualize yourself confronting the situation, carrying out

HELPSHEET FOR CHANGING APPEARANCE-PREOCCUPIED RITUALS

My "Erasing It" Hierarchy

Self-Efficacy Rating*	Checking and Fixing Rituals I Am Going to Erase (Behaviors in Specific Situations)
_____ (lowest)	12. _____
_____	11. _____
_____	10. _____
_____	9. _____
_____	8. _____
_____	7. _____
_____	6. _____
_____	5. _____
_____	4. _____
_____	3. _____
_____	2. _____
_____ (highest)	1. _____

* Self-efficacy ratings are from 0 for no confidence (in refraining from performing the ritual) to 100 for complete confidence (in refraining).

HELPSHEET FOR CHANGING APPEARANCE-PREOCCUPIED RITUALS

Preparing My Plan for Erasing It

My Appearance-Preoccupied Pattern:

_____

Step-by-Step Plan for Erasing It:
Prepare: Exactly what will I do?

_____

_____

_____

_____

Act: Where? When? For how long?

_____

_____

Cope: What uncomfortable thoughts and feelings do I expect and how will I cope with them?

_____

_____

_____

Enjoy: How will I reward my efforts?

_____

_____

What were the *results* of Erasing It?

_____

_____

your plan, coping effectively with any troubling thoughts or feelings, and celebrating your achievement.

With your plan in hand, let the battle begin. With each success behind you, keep moving up the hierarchy. Working through your hierarchies for Facing It and Erasing It will take time—probably several weeks at least. As soon as you have made reasonable headway in Step 6, you may begin Step 7. Be strengthened by each victory. Make a note of your results to remind yourself of what's working and how far you have come. And above all, never surrender!

A FINAL SUCCESS STORY

Adrienne had another ritual—a very costly one. She went on frequent shopping sprees in the hope of transforming her looks. After only fifteen minutes in a clothing store, she would be well on her way to a brand-new wardrobe. The clerks at the cosmetics counters could see her coming from a mile away. "The devil made me do it," she'd joke after each spree. Adrienne's basic problem wasn't that she was financially irresponsible. Her problem was that she was driven by attempts to buy a better body image.

Her plan for behavioral change combined several strategies. First, during several trips to her favorite stores, she blocked the path of her ritual by leaving her credit cards, checkbook, and cash at home. Layaways were not allowed. Adrienne didn't even try anything on. Her well-rehearsed reply to the saleswomen was, "Just let me browse. I'm not buying today." After succeeding on ten spend-free trips in a row, she graduated to trying on one outfit and then, as planned, leaving the store without buying it. Eventually, she allowed herself to go shopping and make one planned, affordable purchase.

Before implementing her plan, Adrienne would sit in her car in the parking lot outside the store, do some Body-and-Mind Relaxation, and picture herself taking action, coping, and savoring her success. After carrying out her plan, she rewarded herself by choosing an interesting movie at the video store to enjoy that evening. Adrienne's husband supported her efforts to change. After her first month of restraint, he prepared a candlelight dinner for her. What a great way to celebrate!

Ultimately, Adrienne successfully rationed her purchases of clothing and cosmetics. She estimated her savings to be over $200 a month. Her greatest savings, however, were not monetary. She saved herself from the self-defeating actions that controlled her. She saved herself from further damage to her body image and self-esteem. Her husband was delighted by her change, and Adrienne felt proud and in control of her behavior for the first time in many years.

STEP 6

Progress Check: How Am I Helping Myself?

• Body-and-Mind Relaxation is second nature by now. You are using it successfully to prepare for and handle difficult situations in your daily life.

• From time to time, you're repeating aspects of Body-Image Desensitization. For example, you stand nude in front of your mirror, relax away discomfort, and hear your New Inner Voice.

• You are keeping up your Corrective Thinking Diary, documenting how you actively apply corrective thinking in your daily life. With your New Inner Voice, you are making progress in anticipating and altering your faulty Private Body Talk.

• You are identifying your Evasive Actions and Appearance-Preoccupied Rituals and are constructing hierarchies of these patterns. On Helpsheets, you are drawing up the battle plans to face and erase these troublesome patterns, one at a time.

• To combat and conquer each pattern, you are learning to PACE yourself—to Prepare, Act, Cope, and Enjoy. You are patient with yourself, accepting that these important changes take time. So you're taking the time, working through the hierarchies, and recording your progress!

More Than Skin Deep

Treating Your Body Right

". . . 'tis in ourselves that we are thus, or thus.
Our bodies are our gardens,
to the which our wills are gardeners."
—William Shakespeare, *Othello*

TINA WAS A CLIENT whom I counseled several years ago. She had low self-esteem and was depressed much of the time. Tina's negative body image contributed greatly to her unhappiness. Tina regarded herself as a "stump"—short and fat. Whenever she thought about or described her body, the spotlight was always on her stumpiness. I asked Tina to make a list of positive things she did for her body and positive things her body did for her. A week later, she returned with her list of only two items. "What do I do for my body? I feed it." (Then she added, "probably too much.") "What positive things does my body do for me? It sleeps." (And she added, "At least when I'm asleep, I don't have to think about how stumpy I look!")

Tina could think about her body along only one dimension—its "awful" appearance. Over the course of therapy, we worked together to expand her viewpoint and create more satisfying body-image experiences. Tina started swimming, which she had loved as a child before deciding she was too stumpy to go to the pool. A monthly professional massage left her loving the way her body felt tingling and alive. Tina discovered that she felt especially perky when wearing certain bright shades of blue. Previously, she'd always hidden herself in grays and browns. As Tina altered her behavior to defy her narrow, negative conception of her body, she found new, positive things to do for her body and gratifying things it could do for her.

Like Tina, you are going to learn how to treat your body right. Before we launch into Step 7's specifics for change, however, I want to give you an important perspective on your body image.

YOUR INTIMATE RELATIONS WITH YOUR BODY

Whether romantic or platonic, any relationship consists of an exchange of actions and reactions between partners—both positive and negative "gives and gets." In successful, satisfying relationships, partners feel that the giving and getting is balanced fairly and that the positive, rewarding exchanges exceed the negative, punitive ones. In dysfunctional relationships, this balance of giving and receiving is skewed, and negative exchanges far outweigh positive ones. As a result, partners feel varying degrees of unhappiness, ranging from resigned discontent to raging resentment or numbing depression. Whether in self-protection or protest, each partner usually reacts in ways that make the relationship even worse. For example, quietly withdrawing and trying to avoid or ignore the other partner is not going to strengthen a troubled relationship. Angrily demanding better treatment—and retaliating against the partner for not providing it—will only escalate the tension.

Your body image involves a relationship, and your self-defeating actions and conflictual mental conversations are signs that it's a dysfunctional one. The "gives and gets" seem unfair, and the exchanges are frustrating and demeaning. You then react in ways that make things worse rather than better. Recognizing how you mistreat your "body-partner" is crucial to the development of a satisfying relationship.

Much of our focus so far in the program has been on changing the *negative* interactions in your relationship with your body. In correcting your Private Body Talk, you are eliminating the critical attacks and wrongful accusations you hurl at your body-partner. You are learning to be less demanding of perfection and to be more tolerant of your body-partner's shortcomings. In Facing and Erasing your self-defeating behaviors, you are beginning to act less defensively toward your body-partner. Although you are still sometimes bothered about your appearance, you are handling your distress better. You are less absorbed in frustrating and angry efforts to control or fix your body-partner. You realize you cannot divorce yourself from the body you live in, "until death do you part."

As in human relationships, however, a satisfying body-partnership requires something more. How often have you felt fulfilled by a friendship only because the friend *didn't* criticize or tease you? How many people do you know who attribute their happy marriages to the fact that their spouses *don't* beat them? The fact is that good things happen in good relationships. There are supportive, affirming, and rewarding experiences, not merely a lack of upsetting ones. Marital and family therapists help people improve their relationships by increasing the occurrence of shared, positive experiences, which fortify the partners' bond and help offset their history of negative interactions. The aim of Step 7 is to add good times—like bonus points—to your relationship with your body.

BODY-IMAGE ENHANCEMENT: ACHIEVING AND PLEASING

Body-image enhancing activities fall into three categories, based on what aspect of bodily experience is involved: (1) physical health and fitness, (2) sensate experiences, and (3) physical appearance. Much of what we've done thus far in the program concerns physical appearance, because this is the focus of your dissatisfaction. But if appearance were the only thing the human body had to offer, we'd all be mannequins in department store windows. Our bodies aren't just looks, they're instruments of action and sensation. As we interact with our environments, our bodies receive and create powerful sensory experiences. Appearance-preoccupied people often minimize or ignore ways to derive satisfaction from their bodies that have nothing to do with appearance. (Can you recognize this as a variant of the Blind Mind error?) Moreover, some people get so caught up in loathing their looks that they fail to act in ways that would allow them to enjoy their appearance.

Two types of experiences can enhance your relationship with your body: *mastery* and *pleasure*. Mastery brings satisfying feelings of accomplishment that result from reaching a set goal. For example, setting and achieving the goal of running two miles can produce a fulfilling sense of mastery. You did it! Pleasure simply means having fun. Pleasure does not require achieving a goal, only enjoying an activity because it inherently feels good. For example, soaking in a hot tub generates terrific, soothing sensations. Of course, some activities provide both mastery and pleasure. Aerobic dance involves mastering new steps and achieving greater fitness, and it also provides a pleasant, invigorating sense of bodily freedom.

Discovering Your Potential for Positive Physical Activities

On pages 282–285 is a self-discovery questionnaire called the "Survey of Positive Physical Activities," which contains a sample of activities that can engender experiences of physical mastery and pleasure. Filling out this survey will help you discover specific activities to enhance your relationship with your body. Basically, you should rate how often you engaged in each activity during the past year and how much mastery and pleasure you derived. Notice that at the end of the questionnaire you may add other activities that might give you feelings of physical mastery or pleasure, even if you engaged in them seldomly.

Using Your Survey Results

Now I want you to review your answers. Regardless of how often you engaged in the activities, circle the ones that you rated as a 2 or 3 on either pleasure or mastery.

To see what *types* of activities promise or already provide you with the most mastery or pleasure, categorize the activities you just circled as relating either to physical appearance, to health/fitness, or to sensate experience. You may wonder why I didn't already do this for you. The reason is that each activity has the potential to yield different experiences for different people. For example, one person might regard "put-

SELF-DISCOVERY HELPSHEET

Survey of Positive Physical Activities

For each activity listed in this survey, rate how often you engaged in the activity during the past year. Then rate how much mastery you experienced and how much pleasure you felt. If you did not engage in the activity, rate the mastery and pleasure you would expect.

Frequency During the Past Year (Freq):
> 0 = I never did this.
> 1 = I did this once or only a few times.
> 2 = I did this fairly often.
> 3 = I did this often.

The Experience of Mastery (M) refers to your sense of accomplishment or achievement felt from engaging in the activity.
> 0 = None
> 1 = Somewhat
> 2 = Moderate
> 3 = A lot

The Experience of Pleasure (P) refers to feeling enjoyment or having fun when engaging in the activity.
> 0 = None
> 1 = Somewhat
> 2 = Moderate
> 3 = A lot

Freq	*M*	*P*	
___	___	___	1. Taking a long or brisk walk
___	___	___	2. Waterskiing or surfing
___	___	___	3. Wearing expensive or formal clothes
___	___	___	4. Playing a team sport (baseball, softball, football, soccer, volleyball, basketball, etc.)
___	___	___	5. Hiking or rock climbing
___	___	___	6. Playing golf
___	___	___	7. Playing tennis or racquetball
___	___	___	8. Taking a relaxing shower or bath
___	___	___	9. Downhill skiing
___	___	___	10. Crosscountry skiing
___	___	___	11. Wearing favorite casual clothes
___	___	___	12. Brushing hair in a soothing manner
___	___	___	13. Sitting in a Jacuzzi or hot tub
___	___	___	14. Playing pool or table tennis
___	___	___	15. Putting on makeup
___	___	___	16. Having sexual relations
___	___	___	17. Bowling
___	___	___	18. Gardening or doing lawn work
___	___	___	19. Wearing new or colorful clothes
___	___	___	20. Social dancing
___	___	___	21. Scuba diving
___	___	___	22. Sunbathing

Freq   *M*   *P*

—— —— ——   23. Riding a bicycle

—— —— ——   24. Having a manicure

—— —— ——   25. Getting a body massage or backrub

—— —— ——   26. Canoeing or rowing

—— —— ——   27. Getting a facial or a cosmetic makeover

—— —— ——   28. Lifting weights or using exercise machines

—— —— ——   29. Masturbating

—— —— ——   30. Horseback riding

—— —— ——   31. Playing lawn sports (badminton, croquet, etc.)

—— —— ——   32. Wearing favorite jewelry

—— —— ——   33. Wearing cologne or perfume

—— —— ——   34. Wearing your hair in a different style

—— —— ——   35. Doing aerobic dance exercise

—— —— ——   36. Giving massages or backrubs

—— —— ——   37. Doing yoga or Body-and-Mind Relaxation

—— —— ——   38. Roller-skating or ice-skating

—— —— ——   39. Doing heavy outdoor work

—— —— ——   40. Having a scalp massage

—— —— ——   41. Brushing your teeth

—— —— ——   42. Swimming

—— —— ——   43. Running or jogging

Freq   M   P

___ ___ ___   44. Doing calisthenics (push-ups,
                   sit-ups, etc.)

___ ___ ___   45. Being naked at home

___ ___ ___   46. Rubbing your own body with
                   lotion

___ ___ ___   47. Individual dancing (ballet,
                   expressive)

___ ___ ___   48. Performing martial arts

              Other Health/Fitness Activities:

___ ___ ___   _____

___ ___ ___   _____

              Other Sensate Experiences:

___ ___ ___   _____

___ ___ ___   _____

              Other Appearance-Related Activities:

___ ___ ___   _____

___ ___ ___   _____

ting on makeup" as an appearance activity, because it gives her a sense of artistic competence or pleasure about her looks. Somebody else might regard the activity as sensate, because she enjoys the tactile pleasure of applying the makeup on her skin. Similarly, an activity like lifting weights can enhance feelings about appearance, the experience of feeling fit, or bodily sensations during the activity.

Beside each, write an "A" for appearance, "H" for health/ fitness, or "S" for sensate experience. If some fall into more than one category, you may mark them more than once, but think about which category that activity satisfies most.

Okay, let's tabulate your results. Count the number of activities in each category, excluding those that are not feasible in the next month. For example, don't count "sexual relations" if you are not in a sexual relationship. Don't count "sunbathing" if you are knee deep in snow. You can forget about "bowling" if your arm is in a cast. How many health/ fitness activities are there? How many sensate experiences did you circle? And how many were appearance-related activities? For activities falling into more than one category, only count them once in the category to which they contribute the most.

To carry out Step 7 of the program, you will need at least four activities in each of the three categories, but the more activities the merrier. If you have fewer than four per category, you'll need to come up with more activities that could foster feelings of physical mastery or pleasure. Here are some tips:

The easiest way to generate additional activities is to look for circled items that you can break down into more specific activities. Some items already contain multiple activities. For example, the item "playing team sports" lists six sports. The item "wearing favorite casual clothes" could become "wearing my favorite sweater" and "wearing my red cowboy boots."

Look at activities that you initially classified into multiple categories but counted only in the primary category of the experience. You may be able to shift a few of these to a secondary category that needs more activities.

If you still come up short, do some brainstorming. Think of additional, unlisted activities that fall into the needed category. Ask yourself, "What have I done or considered doing that would lead to my feeling physical pleasure or competence?" If you still need more, review the activities you rated as a 1 on mastery or pleasure to see if you underrated them. Maybe some offer more positive experiences than you originally thought.

Having identified at least four activities in each category, now turn to the three Helpsheets on the following pages. At the top of each, list your selected activities for that category. These will help you build a cooperative, fulfilling relationship with your body that will increase your feelings of competence and contentment. But to give this positive relationship a chance to develop, you must commit some quality time and effort to nurturing it.

MAKING POSITIVE CHANGES WITH HEALTH/ FITNESS ENHANCEMENT

Health/Fitness Enhancement refers to all the things your body can do that promote your experience of physical competence and well-being. Regular involvement in exercise can benefit mental health in general and body image in particular. Compared to "couch potatoes," people who are active in recreational sports or regular exercise feel better, not only about their fitness and health but about their appearance as well.

The most serious psychological roadblocks to Health/ Fitness Enhancement are related to motivation. In researching motivations for exercise, I found that people exercise for four basic reasons: (1) To be more attractive or lose weight; (2) To promote physical competence, fitness, and health; (3) To improve mood and manage stress; and (4) To meet, socialize, and have fun with other people.

Reflecting the first motive, many people exercise only to

HELPSHEET FOR BODY-IMAGE ENHANCEMENT

Scheduling Positive Physical Activities

List at least four *Health/Fitness Activities* in which you will participate in the near future:

1. _____
2. _____
3. _____
4. _____
5. _____

SCHEDULE

Date	Activity Number	Mastery Rating	Pleasure Rating	Date	Activity Number	Mastery Rating	Pleasure Rating

Ratings of mastery and pleasure are:
0 = None; 1 = Somewhat; 2 = Moderate; 3 = A Lot

HELPSHEET FOR BODY-IMAGE ENHANCEMENT

Scheduling Positive Physical Activities

List at least four *Sensate Activities* in which you will participate in the near future:

1. _____
2. _____
3. _____
4. _____
5. _____

SCHEDULE

Date	Activity Number	Pleasure Rating	Date	Activity Number	Pleasure Rating
___	___	___	___	___	___
___	___	___	___	___	___
___	___	___	___	___	___
___	___	___	___	___	___
___	___	___	___	___	___
___	___	___	___	___	___
___	___	___	___	___	___
___	___	___	___	___	___
___	___	___	___	___	___
___	___	___	___	___	___
___	___	___	___	___	___

Ratings of pleasure are:
0 = None; 1 = Somewhat; 2 = Moderate; 3 = A Lot

HELPSHEET FOR BODY-IMAGE ENHANCEMENT

Scheduling Positive Physical Activities

List at least four *Appearance Activities* in which you will participate in the near future:

1. _____
2. _____
3. _____
4. _____
5. _____

SCHEDULE

Date	Activity Number	Mastery Rating	Pleasure Rating	Date	Activity Number	Mastery Rating	Pleasure Rating

Ratings of mastery and pleasure are:
0 = None; 1 = Somewhat; 2 = Moderate; 3 = A Lot

produce a certain look—as in "My, you *look* fit." They focus on managing their appearance through exercise. Good health is not really their goal. Women are somewhat more likely than men to give appearance and weight management as their primary reason for exercise. Research that psychology student Pam Novy and I conducted has shown that people who exercise for this reason are more likely to have a negative body image. They exercise, then get on the scale, exercise, and get on the scale. However, the scale doesn't measure what your body can do or how it can feel.

Regular physical exercise is most beneficial if done for the right reasons. Fitness is an inner experience of what your body can *do*—its dexterity, strength, agility, endurance, and stamina. This mastery aspect of exercise reflects the second motive. Although this is a healthy reason for exercise, some people take it to an extreme and become trapped in a relentless, competitive struggle with their bodies. Psychiatrist Dr. Alayne Yates has studied these "compulsive exercisers" extensively, many of whom have eating disorders. As they push themselves harder and harder, their pursuit of physical mastery knows no bounds. Driven to achieve total control over their body, they end up feeling that their body controls them. Exercise for them becomes an "addictive" behavior that increasingly consumes their life and ultimately offers little pleasure. As time goes on, they are exercising more but enjoying it less. In fact, the research of Wisconsin sports psychologist Dr. William P. Morgan has indicated that mood disturbances like depression are often a product of "overtraining."

Regular exercise in moderation, on the other hand, can produce benefits to your emotional health *and* your body image. Psychologists Erik Fisher and Kevin Thompson at the University of South Florida discovered that "exercise therapy"—a combination of aerobic activities and weight training—led to significant improvements in people's feelings about their appearance. At Old Dominion University, doctoral student Sherri Hensley and I also evaluated the effects of regular participation in an aerobic dance class. Not only did the exercisers improve their physical fitness, they emerged with a more positive body image than that of their peers who had remained sedentary. Moreover, body-image benefits that accrued were *not* the result of changes in weight.

The pleasure aspect of exercise derives from the third and fourth motives—to improve mood and to enjoy socializing. Exercise can aid in our management of stress and can provide opportunities to make new friends and have fun in the company of others. These are great reasons to be physically active!

As you carry out activities for Health/Fitness Enhancement, I want you to highlight the mastery and pleasure experiences that are *not* related to appearance or weight control. When you took the Body-Image Tests in Step 2 of the program, you discovered your Appearance Orientation and your Fitness/Health Orientation. Take a moment now to look up your scores. If your Appearance Orientation is higher than average, you probably exercise in order to manage your appearance or weight. You need to work on shifting your attention to your experiences of physical mastery and pleasure during exercise. This will make physical activity a more satisfying experience for you.

If your Fitness/Health Orientation score is below average, you may be reluctant to exercise regularly, if at all. Please understand that I'm not asking you to become an Olympic athlete. I'm simply asking that you give yourself a chance to feel good. If your Fitness/Health Orientation score is quite high, check your motives for exercise. Do you push so hard or evaluate your physical competence so harshly that you take the fun out of exercise? If so, ease off and focus on enjoying yourself!

Beginning this week, set aside the necessary time for two of the health/fitness activities listed on your Helpsheet. Schedule these as you would any appointment. When you engage in these positive activities, be especially aware of the feelings of mastery and pleasure that dominate your experience. Afterward, on the lower portion of the Helpsheet, rate the mastery and the pleasure that you derived from the activities. Each week, carry out at least two fitness/health activities. Don't always do the same ones. Branch out and try new activities.

A final healthy reminder: If you have been sedentary for some time or have health problems, do the smart thing. Consult your physician about your exercise plans.

MAKING POSITIVE CHANGES WITH SENSATE ENHANCEMENT

Each of our bodies is equipped with millions of specialized cells that permit us to experience the world around us. We can experience the visual beauty of a multicolored sunset or a child's smile. We can experience the awesome sounds of Beethoven or the song of a distant meadowlark. With our sense of smell, we can enjoy the essence of fragrant flowers. We can take gustatory delight in our favorite flavor. We can feel our bodies move rhythmically to music. Our sense of touch permits us to enjoy feeling our skin being gently warmed by the sun, cooled by a soft breeze, and soothed by the caring embrace of a loved one. If you are like most people, you have never given your body credit for these wonderful sensory experiences. With all that our body gives us, why should we dwell ungratefully on what our body looks like?

Over the next week, create opportunities to enjoy two of the sensate activities you listed on the Helpsheet. Schedule these and carry them out. During each sensate activity, immerse yourself in the experience. As you do when carrying out Body-and-Mind Relaxation, concentrate on the pleasurable feelings. Let them grow and fill your consciousness. Each week from now on, explicitly treat yourself to two sensate activities. As enjoyable as they may be, don't stick to the same ones (like having sex!) over and over. Keep trying different ones, especially activities that you have never done or haven't done recently. Use your Helpsheet to record how much pleasure you reap each time. You need not rate mastery, because the purpose of sensate activities is pleasure, not achievement.

MAKING POSITIVE CHANGES WITH APPEARANCE ENHANCEMENT

In Step 6 of the program, you began changing the self-defeating behavior you use to manage your physical appearance. Evasive Actions (running and hiding) and Appearance-Preoccupied Rituals (fixing and checking) create problems because they are time-consuming, negatively motivated defenses against feelings like shame and anxiety. As you've learned, these grooming patterns ultimately reinforce your negative body image.

Grooming doesn't have to be a problem. It can be a positive activity that enhances your experiences of mastery and pleasure. Whether your grooming affirms a good body image or reinforces a negative one depends in large part on how much grooming you do.

In the previous chapter, I described the person who "grooms to hide" and is constantly checking and fixing. This

Insatiable Groomer spends an excessive amount of time and money procuring goods and services in pursuit of physical perfection or in an attempt to conceal or eradicate flaws. Satisfaction is short-lived; primping, preening, fussing, and fretting are chronic.

A second grooming pattern is exhibited by the *Gloomy Groomer*. Unlike Insatiable Groomers, Gloomy Groomers have given up. They neglect or avoid their appearance, believing either that nothing could improve their looks or that they lack the skill or knowledge or money they would need to make improvements. Most Gloomy Groomers don't want to do anything to call attention to their body, as that would make them feel more self-conscious, so they restrict themselves to a narrow range of "safe" ways to look. Some rationalize their avoidance with a belief that grooming is somehow bad— vain, narcissistic, or provocative. Gloomy Groomers have concluded, "What's the use? I'm just fated to look this way. I'd really rather not think about it."

Take Hank, for example. He almost always wears a plain white shirt, a rumpled brown suit, and he combs his few long strands of hair around his balding head in a fruitless attempt to conceal his hair loss. Hank's wife, Adelle, has worn the same swimming-pool-blue eye shadow and thick black mascara for twenty years. She wears only sack-like dresses, usually solid black or navy blue. Although neither Hank nor Adelle likes his or her own appearance, neither tries to make even simple changes in grooming in order to enjoy his or her appearance more. To them that would seem vain and, besides, they really wouldn't know what to do anyway.

Obviously, Insatiable Groomers and Gloomy Groomers are locked into appearance-management patterns that provide little lasting satisfaction. Insatiable Groomers keep fueling their discontent. Gloomy Groomers don't do anything to rock the already sinking boat. Whether focusing on "damage control" or on hopeless defeat, both kinds of groomers have developed an extreme and rigid relationship with their body's appearance.

The third type of groomer, the *Flexible Groomer,* has the healthiest attitude. Neither preoccupied by compulsive grooming nor neglectful or avoidant of appearance, the Flexible Groomer has found the happy medium between the unhappy extremes. Results of my own published research confirm that people who are flexible in how they manage their appearance feel more confident and in control of their lives. For example, in my studies of women's cosmetics use, I found that women who are versatile in the amount and type of cosmetics they wear feel more in control in social situations than those who are more rigid in their use of makeup. Moreover, those who wear loads of cosmetics no matter what the situation greatly underestimate their unadorned attractiveness. For them, makeup is more a mask than an adornment. Flexible grooming gives you choices, control, and the healthy experience that you are acceptable with a variety of looks.

Lilian's goal is to enhance her appearance in a way that reflects her individuality. She uses a moderate amount of cosmetics, but she isn't reluctant to try a new look from time to time. In choosing clothing styles and colors, Lilian wears what pleases *her* eye—not merely what fashion dictates or what hides the hips she's not so crazy about. Every year or so, Lilian modifies her hairstyle somewhat, as long as it is easy to care for, simply because she knows this will be a nice change and make her feel refreshed. She grooms to create positive, pleasurable experiences. She doesn't strive to become a flawless beauty queen, nor does she try to hide herself and fade into the woodwork. A Flexible Groomer like Lilian isn't afraid to look less than perfect and isn't afraid to experiment.

Becoming a Flexible Groomer requires a two-pronged approach. First, continue to use the techniques of Step 6 to weaken your negative grooming behaviors. Keep Facing It and Erasing It! Second, build on positive activities for Appearance Enhancement that you've identified in the current Step. You must learn to use the mood-altering tools of adornment— like clothes, cosmetics, hair care, jewelry, and fragrances—to *enjoy* your physical appearance. Play up your assets rather than obsess over disguising your imperfections! Your appearance can give you feelings of mastery and pleasure, much as health/ fitness and sensate activities can.

Here, the experience of mastery might entail figuring out how to put clothing together to create a certain look you desire. It might involve learning how to apply makeup more simply or how to wear your hair in an easier-to-manage style. However, you need to tread very carefully here and to be aware of your motives. Mastery at concealing or camouflaging "defects" or at emulating the Hollywood star of your choice (your "Unreal Ideal") is not a healthy kind of mastery.

Flexible grooming should be more *play* than work, an enjoyable activity rather than a chore. Deriving pleasure from your grooming activities doesn't make you vain or self-centered. It means you appreciate the body that's yours. What could be wrong with that?

So examine the appearance-related activities that you listed on your Helpsheet. Schedule and carry out at least two of these each week. Keep your motives and your perfectionism in check. Just enjoy! And afterward, don't forget to record your experiences on the Helpsheet.

TAKING AFFIRMATIVE ACTIONS

If you wanted to improve a troubled relationship with a friend or partner, I would advise you to create new shared experiences in which you put aside the past and concentrate on the present; otherwise, history will keep repeating itself. You both must make a commitment to do what you know, intellectually, you need to do to improve the relationship. You take *Affirmative Actions*—even if you don't feel like it. For example, each person takes responsibility for having contributed to an unsatisfying relationship by saying to the other, "I'm really sorry. I have not treated you as well as I'd like to. I want to start fresh. I want to be as good to you as I can." Then each person affirms, "There are lots of things about you that I truly like. Instead of being so critical of you, each day I'm going to remind you (and myself) of what I value about you."

If you were in an unfulfilling relationship and your partner or friend said these things to you, you might be a bit skeptical at first. In view of the past, that's understandable. But if you sincerely wanted the relationship to work, you would welcome the person's words. And what if the words were followed by actions? What if your partner or friend started to behave in caring and affirming ways toward you? You would begin to let go of the past, enjoy the present, and have more optimism about the future.

Now let's turn to Affirmative Actions for improving your relationship with your body. Like Body-Image Enhancement activities, Affirmative Actions involve doing special things to foster *positive* body-image feelings. Affirmative Actions for a better body image are the deliberate and explicit efforts you will make to counteract the inertia of your past negative experiences and start anew. Following are four types of Affirmative Actions for body-image improvement.

Writing Wrongs

If you think of your body as you would a friend, you must know by now that you have mistreated your friend. In this affirmative exercise, you are to write your "body-friend" a letter to try to get the relationship on the right track. In your letter, apologize to your body-friend for previous mistreatment, give your body-friend assurances that you want to change, and compliment your body-friend for the good things it has given you. Keep your letter nearby (perhaps taped to your bathroom mirror) to remind you of the new relationship that you and your body can have.

Your reaction to this assignment will probably be the same as the incredulous response of many of my clients. "You want me to do *what*, Dr. Cash? Write a letter to my body? That's nuts. I'd feel like an idiot!" Yes, it does seem pretty odd. But that's okay. Do it anyway. Don't judge it now.

To help you draft your letter, here's an example of a terrific one written by Laurie:

Dear Body of Mine,

I want to begin by saying I'm sorry. I've owed you an apology for a long time. I've been unfairly critical of you over the years. I've said some unbelievably nasty things about you. I've put you through a lot. I apologize!

With all you've done for me and all the happy times we've had together, I've never given you the credit you deserve. If it weren't for you, I wouldn't have been captain of my high school basketball team. I wouldn't have been able to enjoy my first kiss (and more!). Despite my lack of appreciation, you've managed to get me nice compliments. People are always saying how great your eyes are and how nice your hair looks. Instead of recognizing your assets, I've dwelled on how much you weigh. I know that it's not fair for me to eat the french fries, the cheesecake, and all the other stuff, and then to blame you for the consequences. Frankly, Body of Mine, you're not that fat. I exaggerate sometimes. Sorry!

I'm in therapy now to change how I relate to you. I'm working on being less critical of you and on our doing more fun things together. I'm beginning to appreciate the good times you give me. I'm feeling better about *me* by being nicer to *you*. Thanks! See you in the mirror soon!

Love,
Laurie

Now it's your turn for "Writing Wrongs." Use the Help-sheet on the next page to compose a letter to your body. Remember, write it as you would to an estranged friend with whom you wish to renew and improve your relationship.

Mirror Affirmations

How often have you stood in front of the mirror, stared at what you dislike, and belittled your looks in your Private Body Talk? In Step 3 of your program, you began taking control of these reflexive reactions with Body-Image Desensitization. Now that you are better able to keep your cool when you view your reflection, it's time to create some decidedly positive experiences as you look in the mirror.

"Mirror Affirmations" are basically compliments or morale boosters that you give yourself. In my professional experience, I have found that people who have a negative body image

HELPSHEET FOR AFFIRMATIVE ACTIONS

"Writing Wrongs"

Dear Body of Mine,

_____

_____

_____

_____

_____

_____

_____

_____

_____

_____

_____

_____

_____

_____

_____

_____

_____

Love,

_____

have trouble handling compliments from others about their appearance. They secretly desire compliments to bolster their insecure view of their appearance; yet, when compliments are offered, they question or dismiss them rather than accept them with: "Thanks. That was nice of you to say." If your New Inner Voice is able to speak affirmatively about your body, your body image will be less dependent on other people's compliments and you will be able to accept them more graciously when they do occur.

You can create affirmations from the compliments that others have given you or you can make up your own compliments—ones that you *wish* others would give you. Your affirmations can celebrate your efforts to change your body image. Affirmations also can take the form of rational revisions of your own negative body-image thoughts (for example, "My nose is unique and gives me character"). Other examples can be found in the Positive Thoughts section of the Body-Image Thoughts Test you completed during Step 2 of the program. If you didn't endorse these thoughts then, begin to endorse them now. Affirmations may also be declarations of your New Inner Voice that challenge the Appearance Assumptions that you discovered in Step 4 (for example, "I don't have to be thin to be happy").

Each day, stand in front of your mirror, make eye contact with your reflection, and make a positive statement about your body or about your new attitude toward your body. Say your affirmation aloud and repeat it confidently and convincingly three or four times. Affirmations are statements that you *want* to believe and to feel, even though you may not be completely sold on them just yet.

Here are examples of some of the Mirror Affirmations that my clients have used:

- "I really like my bright eyes. I like how they sparkle."
- "What a great smile! People love to see me smile."
- "I don't have to have a perfect complexion to like myself."
- "Being tall feels wonderful!"
- "I look so energetic in red. I really like wearing this outfit."
- "I'm so glad to be working on my body image. I'm really making changes!"
- "There's much more to me than meets the eye."
- "I love the free and alive feeling in my body when I exercise."
- "I don't need to be perfect; I can accept myself as I am."
- "I'm looking good. I'm feeling good. Go get 'em!"

Begin every day with a Mirror Affirmation. Prepare ahead of time by writing them down on the Helpsheet on page 304. Eventually, you can be more spontaneous and create your affirmation at the spur of the moment. Will you feel a little silly talking to yourself in front of the mirror? Probably, but you've survived feeling silly before. After a few days, this feeling will pass and will be replaced by increased confidence. This is your New Inner Voice talking!

Feature Attractions

The third Affirmative Action is a celebration, held in honor of what you like about your body. I call this exercise "Feature Attractions." One day each week is Feature Attractions Day, during which you give special treatment to a specific aspect of your body. This aspect may be some physical attribute, such as your hair, your complexion, or your physique. It may relate to your physical capabilities, like being a

HELPSHEET FOR AFFIRMATIVE ACTIONS

Mirror Affirmations

List 10 morale-boosting statements that you want to believe and feel about your body and about your new and improved body image.

1. _____
   _____

2. _____
   _____

3. _____
   _____

4. _____
   _____

5. _____
   _____

6. _____
   _____

7. _____
   _____

8. _____
   _____

9. _____
   _____

10. _____
    _____

good dancer or having muscular strength. You decide. Then, on Feature Attractions Day, give special recognition to this asset with your Mirror Affirmations and your Body-Image Enhancement activities.

The point of Feature Attractions is to make a concerted effort to experience a positive, affirming attitude toward your body. You are not taking your assets for granted. Nor are you giving them only minor recognition with fleeting Blind-Mind thoughts like "Yeah, I suppose my hairstyle usually looks nice," or, "Being able to run three miles is okay, I guess." A satisfying relationship with your body requires that you give credit where credit is due. And face it, credit is due!

Lynne was a client whose Feature Attractions Day celebrated her hands. Her Mirror Affirmations complimented how smooth they are. She had her nails manicured, including application of her favorite raspberry-colored polish, and she enjoyed the "cared for" feeling it gave her. Later, she "handily" played the piano for an hour. In the evening, Lynne invited her boyfriend to come over—just to hold hands!

Before a Feature Attractions Day, jot down your plans for celebration on the Helpsheet on the next page. At the day's end, note the results of the exercise. How did it feel to treat your body right?

I Am Becoming

Are you tired of not looking the way you want? Do you often imagine your physical ideals, only to remind yourself of how far you fall short of them? In Step 2, you took the Wishing Well Test and discovered how much you differ from your ideals. In Step 5, you learned that there are two Body-Image Errors, the Unreal Ideal and Unfair to Compare, in which you

HELPSHEET FOR AFFIRMATIVE ACTIONS

Feature Attractions

Date	Featured Asset	Activity

_____ _____ Plans: _____

_____

Results: _____

_____ _____ Plans: _____

_____

Results: _____

_____ _____ Plans: _____

_____

Results: _____

_____ _____ Plans: _____

_____

Results: _____

_____ _____ Plans: _____

_____

Results: _____

compare yourself to some unattainable standard or to another person and end up feeling inferior. Of course, you remember the Beauty Bound error as well, in which not measuring up to some ideal leads you to restrict your life: "I don't look good enough to . . ."

The fourth Affirmative Action is an imaginative exercise I call "I Am Becoming." Instead of denigrating yourself for not living up to your ideals, I want you to *become* them. Review your answers to the Wishing Well Test from Step 2. If you could magically transform yourself to match your physical aspirations, how would you think, feel, and act differently than you do now? On your Helpsheet on page 308, write down exactly how you expect things would be.

On Everett's "I Am Becoming" day, he imagined being taller and having a full head of hair. This mental image gave him the freedom to act more assertively, make more eye contact, and smile more often. What began as a game of pretend gradually became very real. He felt better about himself. People responded to him in a way that felt good. Everett realized that his old image of himself was holding him back. He did not have to *look* different to *be* different.

Every week or two, pick a day and live the day as if you embodied your ideals. Read your description and imagine very clearly that this is how you look. Use the visualization skill you learned in Body-and-Mind Relaxation to help you experience this. How will you think in your Private Body Talk? How will you feel about your body and yourself? How will you act? Carrying out your "I Am Becoming" exercise can be emotionally and behaviorally liberating. And fun too! Be sure to record your results on the Helpsheet.

HELPSHEET FOR AFFIRMATIVE ACTIONS

I Am Becoming

Description of My Body Ideal:

_____

_____

_____

_____

_____

How I Expect to Think, Feel, and Act:

_____

_____

_____

_____

_____

_____

How Did I Think, Feel, and Act?

_____

_____

_____

_____

_____

_____

Your Turn

My final assignment is a challenge to your creativity. I want you to design *your own* Affirmative Action, beyond the four I have designed for you. You see, improving your relationship with your body is ultimately up to you. What innovative activity can you think of that would serve to affirm your physical being? What else could you do to give your body image a lift? Sorry, no hints from me. This time you are on your own. Do some brainstorming. Put your final ideas in writing on the Helpsheet on page 310, and then translate your ideas into action. Write down the results of your do-it-yourself Affirmative Action.

Step 7 has required you to shift gears and accentuate ways that you and your body can get along. Many of my clients dramatically accelerate their body-image improvements at this stage. You can learn what they have learned: A positive body image is more than the absence of a negative body image. Treat your body right! Then you'll be ready for Step 8, the final, forward-looking step of the program.

HELPSHEET FOR AFFIRMATIVE ACTIONS

Being Affirmative on My Own

My Affirmative Action Plans:

_____
_____
_____
_____
_____
_____
_____
_____
_____

My Results:

_____
_____
_____
_____
_____

STEP 7

Progress Check: How Am I Helping Myself?

• You have incorporated your relaxation and corrective thinking skills into your everyday life. You're recording your experiences in your Body-Image Diary.

• You continue to work on strengthening your New Inner Voice, which steers you in the right direction and supports your efforts to change.

• You are finishing up carrying out your Facing It plans to combat Evasive Actions and your Erasing It strategies for ridding your life of Appearance-Preoccupied Rituals.

• You are discovering effective, active ways to improve your relationship with your body—to infuse your body image with experiences of mastery and pleasure. You are regularly scheduling all three types of positive Body-Image Enhancement activities: Health/Fitness Enhancement, Sensate Enhancement, and Appearance Enhancement.

• You are learning to be a Flexible Groomer, instead of an Insatiable Groomer or a Gloomy Groomer.

• You are taking Affirmative Actions by creating special, explicit experiences to accept, compliment, and celebrate your physical being. You are making concerted efforts to treat your body right!

Happily Ever After

Maintaining Your Positive Body Image for Life

"We are bound to our bodies like an oyster is to its shell."

—Plato

EVERETT DECIDED IT HAD been long enough. He hadn't had a date for nearly a year. But now, feeling greater comfort with his looks and more confidence in himself, Everett was ready to put a little romance in his life. So, with a spirit of adventure, he joined a dating service, where he made a videotape in which he introduced himself and described his interests and lifestyle to prospective dates. Being videotaped would have been unimaginable only a few months ago; the anxiety and self-consciousness would have been too much for him to handle. Everett felt proud of himself for taking the plunge. He fantasized phone calls from women who had seen his tape and wanted to get to know him better. "It's a whole new ball game," he reveled.

Then four days after making the tape, the curve ball came—when he called the dating service to ask about his viewing tapes of the women interested in going out with him. "Sorry, Everett, but we have nothing for you yet" was the reply. "It may take a while, maybe a few weeks. We'll call you if anyone expresses interest." The words echoed loudly in his head: "*IF* ANYONE EXPRESSES INTEREST. *IF* ANYONE . . ." Everett was devastated. His Old Inner Voice returned and ridiculed him for thinking that anyone would want to date him. It convinced him that women had seen his tape and were turned off by his looks. He became angry with himself for getting his hopes up. "Nothing has really changed," Everett brooded. "I'm the same stupid-looking fool I've always been."

Everett was in a funk for a couple of days, but he grew tired of his nonstop "pity party" and gradually pulled himself out of it. The dating service did call a week later with the reassuring news of date prospects. After dating several women, Everett met Missy through a mutual friend, and they've been seeing each other ever since.

What happened to Everett—an experience he calls his "negative body-image flashback"—isn't uncommon. However, these unsettling experiences need not unravel the progress you've made. The main purpose of Step 8 is to help you look toward the future. You want to ensure having a positive body image next month, next year, and forever. How can you continue to progress and to solidify your positive body-image changes? How can you prevent significant relapses of body-image dissatisfaction or distress? How will you deal with any tough times for your body image? Let's not leave your future to fate. By looking ahead to anticipate what tomorrow might bring and by planning how you want tomorrow to be, your future body image is within your control.

TAKING STOCK OF YOUR BODY-IMAGE PROGRESS

First you need to evaluate how far you have come. Let's discover what actual changes you have made, and let's find out what aspects of your body image might need some additional work. You can discover these things with great precision by retaking the body-image tests you took in Step 2. This is the same approach I take with my clients, who are often amazed when they compare their "before" and "after" scores. They had grown so accustomed to their positive changes, they hadn't realized just how much they'd improved.

Because seeing your earlier test responses might influence your judgment, I recommend that you cover your previous answers. You'll need six sheets of lined paper, one for each of the tests. Title each sheet with the name of the test, and write down your answers as you go along, following the instructions for taking each test just as you did before. Remember, you will need about ninety minutes to complete, score, and interpret all the tests. Choose an occasion when you have privacy and won't be interrupted, and a time when you feel as you typically do, not when you are in a lousy mood (your taxes are due) or are feeling unusually good (you just won the lottery). It's okay if you are unable to complete all six tests at one sitting, but don't stop in the middle of a test. For each test question, think about your experiences and respond as candidly as possible.

Go ahead and take all the tests before scoring them; then follow the scoring instructions given in Step 2. For your convenience, new Personal Body-Image Profile forms for recording and classifying your posttest results are on the following pages. Be sure to use the form that contains norms for persons of your sex.

THE PERSONAL BODY-IMAGE PROFILE FOR WOMEN

My Posttest Profile

Score the tests as explained in Step 2. Enter each score in the blank provided below. Then, to classify your score from "Very Low" to "Very High," mark an X in the proper box on the grid.

BODY-IMAGE TEST	Score	Very Low	Low	Average	High	Very High
1. Body Areas Satisfaction Test	____	8–22	23–25	26–27	28–32	33–40
2. Mirror Image Test						
A. Mirror Discomfort	____	1–10	11–25	26–35	36–69	70–100
B. Mirror Image Satisfaction	____	8–22	23–25	26–27	28–32	33–40
3. Wishing Well Test	____	0–8	9–17	18–26	27–50	51–90
4. Distressing Situations Test	____	0–50	51–72	73–80	81–110	111–192
5. Body-Image Thoughts Test						
A. Negative Thoughts	____	0–8	9–17	18–21	22–39	40–120
B. Positive Thoughts	____	0–16	17–26	27–32	33–39	40–60
6. Body/Self Relationship Test						
A. Appearance Evaluation	____	7–17	18–23	24–25	26–29	30–35
B. Appearance Orientation	____	12–40	41–46	47–48	49–53	54–60
C. Fitness/Health Evaluation	____	11–33	34–40	41–42	43–47	48–55
D. Fitness/Health Orientation	____	14–41	42–49	50–52	53–59	60–70

THE PERSONAL BODY-IMAGE PROFILE FOR MEN

My Posttest Profile

Score the tests as explained in Step 2. Enter each score in the blank provided below. Then, to classify your score from "Very Low" to "Very High," mark an X in the proper box on the grid.

BODY-IMAGE TEST	Score	Very Low	Low	Average	High	Very High
1. Body Areas Satisfaction Test	___	8–25	26–28	29–30	31–33	34–40
2. Mirror Image Test						
A. Mirror Discomfort	___	1–10	11–20	21–30	31–65	66–100
B. Mirror Image Satisfaction	___	8–25	26–28	29–30	31–33	34–40
3. Wishing Well Test	___	0–8	9–17	18–26	27–50	51–90
4. Distressing Situations Test	___	0–24	25–43	44–49	50–65	66–192
5. Body-Image Thoughts Test						
A. Negative Thoughts	___	0–7	8–15	15–17	18–32	33–120
B. Positive Thoughts	___	0–13	14–21	22–25	26–34	35–60
6. Body/Self Relationship Test						
A. Appearance Evaluation	___	7–19	20–24	25–26	27–29	30–35
B. Appearance Orientation	___	12–36	37–42	43–44	45–50	51–60
C. Fitness/Health Evaluation	___	11–36	37–42	43–44	45–50	51–55
D. Fitness/Health Orientation	___	14–41	42–49	50–52	53–59	60–70

SELF-DISCOVERY HELPSHEET

Taking Stock of My Changes

Enter your pretest scores (from Step 2) and current posttest scores (from Step 8). Beside each score, indicate how it was classified on your Body-Image Profile:

Very Low = VL, Low = L, Average = A, High = H,
Very High = VH

BODY-IMAGE TEST	*PRETEST*		*POSTTEST*	
	Score	Category	Score	Category
1. Body Areas Satisfaction Test	____	_____	____	_____
2. Mirror Image Test				
A. Mirror Discomfort	____	_____	____	_____
B. Mirror Image Satisfaction	____	_____	____	_____
3. Wishing Well Test	____	_____	____	_____
4. Distressing Situations Test	____	_____	____	_____
5. Body-Image Thoughts Test				
A. Negative Thoughts	____	_____	____	_____
B. Positive Thoughts	____	_____	____	_____
6. Body/Self Relationship Test				
A. Appearance Evaluation	____	_____	____	_____
B. Appearance Orientation	____	_____	____	_____
C. Fitness/Health Evaluation	____	_____	____	_____
D. Fitness/Health Orientation	____	_____	____	_____

Discovering Your Gains

It's time for the grand unveiling! Let's discover how much progress you've made by comparing your current test results with those you obtained before beginning this program. To make this easier, I've provided a special Helpsheet, "Taking Stock of My Changes," located on page 318. Transfer *all* your "before" and "after" scores to this Helpsheet, as well as the category into which each score falls, from "Very Low" to "Very High."

In the pages that follow, we'll examine your scores, one at a time, so that you will see the specific gains you have made in overcoming your negative body-image experiences. But first I want to congratulate you on your accomplishments. You have worked hard to earn these improvements. The gains that you made are cause for celebration. So, as you review your progress, decide how you are going to celebrate!

What about scores that you find didn't change very much? Don't expect that you will have shown huge improvements in *every* aspect of your body image; that would be unrealistic. You've made some important advances, so please don't short-change yourself by "making your glass half empty." Another caveat: Don't assume that any scores showing little or no change are the final verdict on your ability to overcome body-image difficulties. Instead, look at these scores as directions for future work and improvement. I'll help you get on the track that heads you in the right direction.

GETTING SATISFACTION

My research has proven that most people who complete th program feel much more satisfied with various areas of the body—especially the areas that they had previously dislik the most. Did your score on the Body Areas Satisfaction Test increase? If so, did it improve enough to place your score in a higher category—for example, shifting from "Low" or "Very Low" to "Average" or better? Go back and compare your satisfaction ratings of the specific body areas. What happened for those areas you had disliked most before the program?

COMFORT WITH YOUR MIRROR IMAGE

How do you feel now when you look in the mirror? Has your Mirror Distress score decreased, compared to what it was before the program? Has your Mirror Image Satisfaction score gone up? Are you able to look in the mirror and feel greater satisfaction with various areas of your body? Are there areas that are still uncomfortable for you to look at? Having a "tough spot" isn't uncommon—it's an opportunity for future change.

WISHING WELL . . . WISHING BETTER

The Wishing Well Test reveals the extent to which you feel you match your physical ideals. On this test, an improved body image would mean that your score is *lower* than it was before the program. Did your Wishing Well score decrease? If so, by how much? Three factors can contribute to improvements here: First, you may see your physical attributes more objectively, rather than in an exaggerated or distorted manner. Second, you may have altered your ideals to become less extreme in what you expect of your appearance. Finally, you may emphasize your ideals less. They are, after all, only preferences, *not* necessities.

BODY-IMAGE DISTRESS IN YOUR EVERYDAY LIFE

One of the goals you've been working hardest to achieve has been to reduce your body-image distress in response to various activating events and situations. My most recent research on the effectiveness of this program indicated that most people significantly lowered their scores on the Distressing Situations Test. They became freer from upsetting body-image emotions in many situations that had previously triggered distress. Use your test results to pinpoint the specific situations you have mastered and the situations that may require some further attention.

THINKING ABOUT YOUR THINKING

On the Body-Image Thoughts Test, have negative thoughts in your Private Body Talk become less frequent? Have your positive thoughts increased? Once again, even if your test results verify that you have cleaned up your Private Body Talk appreciably, you will probably find that some negative thoughts linger. Identify what they are, and we'll work on them!

YOUR RELATIONSHIP WITH YOUR APPEARANCE

On the Body/Self Relationship Test, the first score, Appearance Evaluation, reveals how you feel about your overall appearance. Improvements here mean that your "big picture" of your looks is better than it used to be. If this hasn't improved as much as you'd like, it is probably because there is some physical characteristic—a tough spot, as I mentioned above—that you may still believe ruins everything. Identifying why and how you allow this one thing to spoil your overall view of your looks can provide the catalyst you need to bring about substantial positive change in your opinion of your appearance.

The second score, Appearance Orientation, is an indicator of the degree to which you are invested in your looks. Most people with a negative body image place excessive importance on their appearance. So, if you started the program with a very high Appearance Orientation score, I hope that your score has declined and you've become less of an Insatiable Groomer. Some of you, particularly the Gloomy Groomers, began with low scores. For you, an increase in your Appearance Orientation would be a nice change, showing that you have learned to derive positive experiences from your relationship with your looks. Whichever your case may be, a score that puts you around the middle of the range for the "Average" category is a good place to be.

YOUR RELATIONSHIP WITH YOUR BODY'S FITNESS AND HEALTH

The second pair of scores on the Body/Self Relationship Test are Fitness/Health Evaluation and Fitness/Health Orientation. Because you've just started working on Health/Fitness Enhancement activities in Step 7, these scores may not have changed much. Be patient—greater change will occur as you spend more time involved in physical activities. If your score didn't change because it was fairly high to begin with, keep up the healthful work!

Rediscovering Your Goals

The most gratifying aspect of my work is seeing my clients learn to feel better about themselves. I hope that your test scores show that you've made terrific improvements in lots of areas. As you reviewed your scores, you probably realized that some changes didn't occur because you were already doing fine in that aspect of your body image and weren't trying to fix what wasn't broken. Other scores may not have changed much simply because they require more time and effort. People change at different paces.

Changes in your scores are one way to measure your progress, but not the only way. Another way takes your *personal goals* into account. In Step 2, you identified these goals on your "Body-Image Needs" Helpsheet (on pages 95–96). Go back and look at each goal ("need") you listed on the Helpsheet and decide how much progress you feel you have made. Then decide what changes you feel you still need to make. Turn to your new Helpsheet, "My Future Body-Image Needs," on pages 323–324, and record your gains and your updated goals.

In the weeks to come, apply the knowledge and skills you've acquired in this program to further your body-image progress where you need it most. Take aim at each goal and develop your plans to work toward it—one day at a time. All the while, affirm and applaud the positive changes you have made. Sustained growth requires continued nourishment.

PREPARING TODAY FOR TOMORROW

If you have taken the lessons of this program to heart and mind and put them into action, you have accomplished some wonderful body-image changes. Step 8 helps you make sure that you sustain these changes and continue to make beneficial new ones. But why wouldn't you? The answer is quite simple. People neglect to think ahead—to anticipate obstacles and plan how to overcome them successfully. Unfortunately, as a result, you can be ambushed by adversities. By understanding

HELPSHEET FOR CHANGE

My Future Body-Image Needs

Physical characteristics I need to feel better about:

How I have improved _____

_____.

I still need to _____

_____.

Feelings I need to control or eliminate:

How I have improved _____

_____.

I still need to _____

_____.

Physical ideals I need to emphasize less:

How I have improved _____

_____.

I still need to _____

_____.

Negative thoughts I need to get rid of:

How I have improved _____

_____.

I still need to _____

_____.

Positive thoughts I need to have more of:

How I have improved _____

_____ .

I still need to _____

_____ .

Situations I need to learn to handle better:

How I have improved _____

_____ .

I still need to _____

_____ .

Appearance-oriented behaviors I need to change:

How I have improved _____

_____ .

I still need to _____

_____ .

Fitness/health-oriented behaviors I need to change:

How I have improved _____

_____ .

I still need to _____

_____ .

Other things I still need to change to improve my body image:

I need to _____ .

I need to _____ .

your particular body-image vulnerabilities, you can plan ahead and prepare yourself to handle the people and situations that place you at risk.

Beware of Your Stagnating Attitudes

First, you need to recognize certain attitudes that can threaten your ability to maintain the gains you have achieved and can interfere with your further improvement. Do you have any of the following "Stagnating Attitudes?"

The "Now Is Forever" attitude reflects the flawed view that this program is like a magic wand: Once you've waved the wand, all your woes will disappear forever. You must resist thinking, "Now that I've read the book and completed the program, I've got a great body image. Terrific! I'll never need to work on my body image again." This is like the attitude of some college students I've taught, who decide, "Now that I've finished the final exam, I can forget everything I've learned." What you have learned in this program will continue to be useful only if you *use* it and nurture initial, small changes—day by day.

The "Good Things Never Last" attitude is at the opposite extreme. Have you ever had mixed feelings when good things happen, because you fear that they won't last? This attitude leads to "success anxiety," which can then become a self-fulfilling prophecy. For example, some people become apprehensive if they are promoted at work or if they find themselves falling in love. They worry because now they have something to lose, and they begin to look for signs that their job or their romance is not really secure. They behave in ways that sabotage their success, undermine their happiness, and lead them to conclude that they were right all along—that good things never last.

Rather than worrying that your improved body image won't last, channel that energy into taking the necessary steps to sustain it. With deliberate care, good things certainly do last.

Do I expect that you now have a completely positive body image and that you never have any negative thoughts or feelings about your appearance? No, I don't. And I don't want *you* to think everything should be perfect now either. It is not reasonable to expect yourself always to be happy or always to have a positive body image. You may think, "I've read the book, done most of the exercises, and I feel a lot better. But because I still have some body-image problems, there's no point in my continuing this work."

Such thoughts may reflect the attitude that "My Best Isn't Good Enough." Nonsense! Faulting yourself for unattained changes is profitless. For most people, the greatest changes come later on. For one thing, it takes time to learn and practice new skills so that they become a natural part of your life. For another, change is a healing process that can't be rushed. (Would you expect someone who had a badly broken leg to run the Boston Marathon after only a few weeks of recovery? Certainly not.) Because improvement builds on itself, you can be optimistic that with continued effort, your best *will* be good enough.

Related to this attitude that is the notion that "Some Things Will Never Change." Either perspective can lead to what psychologists call *learned helplessness,* which occurs when people believe that their actions to control events are futile. If you believe that aspects of your negative body image are irreparable, then you'll do nothing to try to change them. Obviously, if you do nothing, nothing will change. However, if you suspend your doubts and work on the problem anyway, change has a chance. Have you ever accomplished something you had previously thought you couldn't do? Think about it!

A final Stagnating Attitude is that "Tough Times Mean Failure." I remember receiving a phone call from Laurie about four months after she had completed the program. Laurie was bothered that she had gained about five pounds as the result of her indulgences over the Christmas holidays. More troubling to her than her weight gain, however, were her ensuing body-image emotions. Laurie was upset that she was upset. "I should be able to handle this better," she moaned. "I know I shouldn't be bothered by a few pounds. I'm sorry. I know you're disappointed in me. I guess I didn't improve as much as I had thought."

I wasn't disappointed in Laurie. She was. Her disappointment resulted from expecting too much of herself under difficult circumstances. Once Laurie accepted that a "lapse" is not a "relapse" and that she needed to be patient with herself, she was fine. Tough times mean tough times, and that's all. Though they certainly challenge our coping skills, they're not a test—some huge moral, litmus test—of our strength of character.

Troubleshooting Difficult Situations

You don't want to slip back into your old negative body image. So how do you keep your winnings? The answer is "prevention power." Most problems can be anticipated. By now, you have already identified some of the situations that are likely to prompt negative body-image emotions. Thinking about what these situations have in common can yield important information that you can use to your advantage. For example, do the troublesome situations involve others seeing more of your body than you'd like? Do they entail how your clothes look or fit? Are they situations that accentuate your weight?

Whenever you anticipate entering one of these high-risk situations, there are two ways to ready yourself and steady yourself. Both rely on skills you have already developed.

First, schedule a session of Body-Image Desensitization. As you learned to do in Step 3, practice melting away your anticipated anxiety while visualizing progressively more difficult events taking place.

Second, use your skills from Step 6 to *PACE* yourself. *Prepare* for the situation. Picture yourself being in the situation. Mentally rehearse how you would deal with the "worst-case scenario." Picture yourself successfully handling potentially troublesome events. *Act* on your plan for confronting the situation. *Cope* effectively by using relaxation and corrective thinking, just as you had planned. Your New Inner Voice can talk you through a difficult time by telling you to take it easy, to slow everything down, and to keep your mental mistakes to a minimum. Remember to Stop (your distressing Private Body Talk), Look (at what's causing you to become upset), and Listen (to your rational New Inner Voice). Your goal here is just to make it through the situation, not to feel absolutely great. *Enjoy* the fact that you've taken control and done your best to manage adversity.

Everett knows that he usually dislikes how his hair looks after getting it cut and that he can end up feeling upset and self-conscious about his appearance for days. By preparing for the experience ahead of time, actively using the PACE techniques, and controlling the urge to inspect his hair in the mirror, Everett can now successfully prevent himself from going off the deep end after a haircut.

Dealing with Difficult People

Many of your "at risk" situations probably pertain to other people. There are three different ways that people can threaten your body image. Let me show you how to deal with them.

"TOO PERFECT" PEOPLE

Some people don't have to *do* anything to set off your body-image distress. Their mere presence is enough to make you think that you are unattractive. These are the people whose appearance can be intimidating—as in "Nobody has a right to look so good." Their looks match your personal physical ideals and remind you that you don't measure up.

To deal with these all-too-perfect specimens, stop committing the Unfair-to-Compare error. Comparing yourself to them is unfair to both of you. Interact with them instead. Focus on what they say and do, not on how they look. Treat them like ordinary people, not like gods or goddesses. Neither you nor they deserve to be victims of their good looks. If they are really nice people, enjoy them. If they are insensitive jerks, move on!

INATTENTIVE PEOPLE

Your romantic partner or spouse may sometimes be inattentive to your looks—not necessarily critical, but not complimentary either. "Wow, you really look great today!" are words that rarely if ever cross their lips. As a result, you may feel insecure about what your partner privately thinks about your appearance. You believe that the lack of compliments must mean that your looks don't merit praise.

Before you can address these inattentive people, you must

recognize your own mental mistakes. You're probably Mind Misreading, projecting your own negative thoughts into someone else's head. What solid evidence do you have that the person dislikes your looks? What else could account for the person's inattentiveness? Several possibilities should come to mind:

• Some people are lousy at giving compliments about anything. Not only do they fail to give you strokes about your appearance, but they neglect to give you positive feedback about your accomplishments either. Obviously, the deficiency is with them, not with you.

• Some people are "appearance blind." They don't pay much attention to how others look—including themselves. If they were to take the body-image tests in this book, their Appearance Orientation score would be low. While these people may compliment your actions, they don't compliment your appearance simply because it never occurs to them to do so. No news isn't bad news. No news is no news! Again, the problem is theirs, not yours.

• Another rational explanation for people being inattentive to how nice you look has to do with familiarity. They've grown accustomed to your face (and your body and your style of grooming). They've come to expect you to look nice, so they take your appearance for granted. If their silence and your insecurity force you to ask, "Do you really find me attractive?," they reply, "Of course I do. You know that. Why would you ask me such a silly question?" Keep in mind that familiarity doesn't breed contempt; it breeds laxity.

• An additional reason people are quiet about your looks may have to do with how you respond to compliments. Imagine a friend says to you, "That's a sharp outfit you're wearing. You look terrific today!" Would you smile and graciously thank your friend for the nice comment? Or would you react with something like, "Oh, I can't believe how out of shape I'm getting. I've got to work out more"? No doubt your friend would be reluctant to reopen that can of worms.

Once you've realized that there are plenty of reasons that certain friends or loved ones may seldom compliment your appearance, you'll see that their silences need not be an indictment of how you look. Most often, the problem belongs to the other person or is intrinsic to the relationship. But if you still feel you need some positive strokes from these people, how can you inspire kind words from time to time?

The best way is to give what you wish to receive, to heed the Golden Rule and "do unto others." Psychologists call this principle the *norm of reciprocity*. In human relations, inattentiveness begets inattentiveness, and compliments beget compliments. Sincerely compliment your inattentive friends or loved ones. Let them know what you like about *their* looks. Make positive comments when they look especially nice. When they return the compliment or offer one spontaneously, let them know you appreciate it. Tell them that because *they* are important to you, their words and opinions are important to you. Don't question or contradict the compliment. Accept it. If you don't reward the person's efforts, the efforts won't last.

Don't expect miracles. People change slowly. Some folks are not going to change at all. Don't let their inattentiveness fuel an Appearance-Preoccupied Ritual in which you constantly seek reassurance. With Mirror Affirmations, recognize your assets and give *yourself* the compliments you want. Punch your own ticket!

INSENSITIVE PEOPLE

Certain people—a parent, a spouse, a romantic partner, a friend, or an employer—may seem intent on saying to you what you don't want to hear. They make critical or insensitive remarks that churn up your body-image distress. Their comments may take various forms. There is "friendly" teasing: "You know I only kid you about your 'honker' of a nose because we're good buddies!" There are "caring" concerns: "It's because I love you that I can be honest about how stupid you look in that hat. I wouldn't want you to embarrass yourself." Of course, there is also "helpful" advice: "I don't mean to nag you about how pudgy you've become. I'm just worried about your being so out of shape. I only want what's good for you."

I once had a client, Francine, whose mother took every opportunity to pester her to lose weight. Her mother had become an ever-present calorie counter, reminding Francine what to eat and what not to eat. Francine was constantly subjected to her mother's know-it-all advice on what to wear to hide her shape. "Now Francine," she'd nag, "nobody will like you if they have to look at your flab." In addition to carrying around a few extra pounds, Francine had to bear the weight of her hypercritical mother.

Before I tell you how Francine effectively handled dear old Mom, let me briefly describe three common but ineffective approaches for dealing with such insensitive people. See if any of these reflect how you handle things. With a *passive* or unassertive approach, you silently sustain the insults—perhaps even thinking you deserve them. Not wanting to cause trouble, you try to conceal your hurt or anger. Alternatively, you may take an *aggressive* approach with the offending person. You lose your cool and issue threats or retaliatory insults. A third unproductive ploy is the *passive-aggressive* response. You express your anger indirectly by sulking or becoming uncooperative or grouchy.

The most effective way to handle insensitive people is to take *assertive* action. Assertiveness is the rational middle ground between the extremes of passivity and aggressiveness. You need to figure out how to neutralize their troublesome remarks—how to take the sting out of their comments. Perhaps they really are trying to be friendly, or caring, or helpful. Perhaps they've got their own ax to grind. After getting some perspective on their motives, you carry out thoughtful, direct communication that has six specific elements—steps that you can recall with the acronym "RIGHTS":

1. *Review* the situation ahead of time. Decide what the problem is, how you feel about it, and how you're going to approach the offending person about it. Decide what you want to accomplish. The unassertive person has trouble planning ahead and wants to sweep the problem under the rug. The aggressive person doesn't think ahead either, but reacts angrily and impulsively to each situation as it arises. With the assertive approach, first think about what you want to communicate, decide what words you will use, and write them down and practice them aloud ahead of time. This way, you will be equipped and more confident when you talk with insensitive persons about their unacceptable behavior.

2. *Initiate* discussion at a time and place that's convenient for you and the other person. It's better to be proactive than to wait around until you are offended again. You want to be able to talk without the pressure of time or the interference from other ongoing events. The unassertive individual has

trouble creating these circumstances, preferring instead to avoid discussion. The aggressive person relishes using a hit-and-run tactic.

3. *Get specific* about the problem. Calmly and confidently tell the person exactly what remarks or behavior you object to. Stay focused and stick to the facts. Be descriptive, not accusatory. For example, you might say something like what Francine said to her mother: "On several occasions recently, you've mentioned that you think I should lose weight. I want to talk with you about your comments and how I feel about them." Don't take the passive path, saying, "I'm really sorry to bring this up. It's really no big deal. It's probably my fault for being so sensitive, but . . ." On the other hand, don't exaggerate or use aggressive, inflammatory words—for example, "Every time I'm with you, you are always bitching at me about being fat!" Don't get sidetracked and start to throw in the kitchen sink when you describe what's bothering you— like, "I'm tired of your snide remarks about my weight. I'm fed up with your complete lack of consideration of me. You've never really listened or cared."

4. *How you feel* is essential to express. Tell the person how his or her remarks affect you. Explain your feelings with "I" statements. For example, "When you make jokes about my being bald, *I* feel hurt. *I* also feel disappointed that you wouldn't realize I would be hurt by your kidding." Blaming the person about how he or she makes you feel will put him or her on the defensive, and then you won't feel that the person is really hearing you. Keep your description focused on your feelings, and don't interject opinionated conclusions. The statement, "I felt embarrassed when we were at the picnic and you criticized how I look in shorts," accurately expresses a feeling. The statement, "I feel you are an inconsiderate person

and take great pleasure in embarrassing me," is an opinion. The other person could simply dismiss your opinion with "You're wrong!" It's harder for him or her to dismiss your feelings.

5. *Target the change* you are requesting. You propose the specific solution, stating clearly and firmly what you want. You say, "I'm asking that from now on you stop calling me 'Jelly Belly' in front of your friends." That's a more effective request than "I wish you'd stop being so rude."

6. *Solicit an agreement* from the offending person. Point out the natural benefits to *each* of you if the person cooperates with your request. Specify a win-win proposition. "If you stop asking me whether I've gained weight, I'll spend less time getting dressed before we go out, and I know I'll be more pleasant to be with." You may offer to provide certain positive consequences in order to negotiate change. "If you promise to refrain from criticizing my appearance today, I'll give you a back rub tonight." Particularly when the offensive behavior is longstanding or when the offender is callous to previous requests, you may need to state specific negative consequences for noncompliance. "I do want you to know in advance that if you make jokes about my hair tonight, I will leave the party without you."

You can use these six steps—your RIGHTS—to change assertively how people influence your body-image experiences. Francine followed these steps and got her mother to stop hounding her about her weight. Assertiveness is made even easier if you keep in mind that the reason some people act insensitively is that they have their own body-image problems. For example, as Francine came to realize, parents who have struggled to lose weight not uncommonly shift the focus of their weight watching to their children. It's easier to pick on you and say, "Why don't *you* lose weight?" or, "As big as you are, I can't believe you're going to have dessert."

Although I've used weight as an example here, this "pass the misery" dynamic can pertain to any aspect of appearance. Furthermore, critical people may actually be envious of you or your looks. Perhaps you are the focus of their Unfair-to-Compare thinking, so something about your appearance makes them feel unattractive. Similarly, they may be threatened by your opinion of them, so they try to feel more secure by finding something wrong with you.

One of my friends, Cheryl, is a tall, slender woman who is physically fit. She told me that it's not unusual for certain other women in her aerobics class to ask her if she's lost weight lately or to tell her that she'd surely look a lot better if she gained five pounds. These comments used to be crushing to Cheryl. Even though her weight is actually fine for her height and bone structure, the remarks reactivated old body-image wounds—she had been teased as a skinny child and teenager. Eventually, Cheryl realized that her critics—heavier women who were prone to gain weight and were very competitive in their aerobic exercise—were probably threatened by her looks and athletic competence. This insight helped her neutralize the remarks and behave more assertively whenever a critical comment was directed at her.

Are there other possible motives for insensitivity? Jealous romantic partners (or "best" friends) may be concerned that if you look too good, you'll have opportunities for other relationships. Their barbs and insults about your looks may be unconscious attempts to undermine your self-confidence in order to prevent losing you to the competition. Although you value their companionship, you should calmly let them know that you don't appreciate their comments and ask them to make a real effort to change so that conflicts don't continue.

If your assertive strategy doesn't work the first time, then try again. I'm sure if you try a variety of approaches, you'll develop the one that's most effective for you and for your critics. Sometimes people have to be told not once, but twice, or even three times, that you don't appreciate their nagging, or teasing, or critical comments. So don't give up and don't be intimidated. You have the right to assert yourself!

In Your Unforeseeable Future

We've just discussed how to plan strategies for dealing with your "known enemies"—the people or situations that are your vulnerabilities for negative body-image experiences. Sometimes, however, you may be hit by a surprise attack of negative body-image feelings. How can you possibly plan for the unexpected? You can't anticipate what these surprise situations will be, but you can plan for setbacks in general. The answer to the question "What if things get worse?" is very simple. If you experience a temporary setback, you keep on keeping on. Let me remind you of some of your options.

You've learned a marvelous method of relaxation—of slowing things down, melting away stress, and feeling better whenever you want to. So when the hassles hit, call a time out. Pause for a few minutes, close your eyes, release tension, visualize pleasant images, repeat calming self-instructions, and produce a body-and-mind experience of contentment. Just relax and focus on modifying your mood. Leave your looks out of it.

During these unforeseen tougher times, don't fall prey to the Moody Mirror, Feeling Ugly, and Blame Game errors.

Have a little chat with yourself, in which your New Inner Voice says something like, "Okay, right now I'm feeling negative and critical, but I know I won't always feel this way. This isn't the best time for me to be making judgments about my appearance, so I'm just going to back off of myself and think about this later when I can make fairer, more rational judgments." Give yourself a break.

There *will* be times when you'll not feel positive about your appearance—you are not perfect and cannot always feel wonderful. Everybody experiences rough patches, bad days, and disappointing events. Most important is that you not give *yourself* a hard time for having a hard time! Instead, accept that you are having difficulties and decide what you can do to make things better.

Keep in mind that if you sometimes feel negatively about your appearance, it doesn't mean that this program didn't work. Nor does it mean that you have failed or are completely hopeless. It merely means that you feel good some of the time, and less good at other times. It means that you're just as human as everyone else.

WHEN YOUR BODY CHANGES

Not long ago, I attended my twenty-fifth high-school reunion. Many of us hadn't seen one another since graduation. Our first evening together was a casual cookout. Most of the reacquainting conversations focused at some point on how our current looks matched our memories of each other (assisted by several circulating copies of our high-school yearbook). The discussions seemed to fall fairly equally into a few categories: (1) "My God, you look just the same!" (usually reserved for average- or better-looking classmates); (2) "You *really* look great, you *really* do!" (to those whose attractiveness had increased); and finally, (3) "So how have you been?" (which seems to have been the socially sensitive equivalent of "The aging process hasn't been kind, has it?" or "Who the hell are you?").

Sadly, the most changed was the prettiest cheerleader. She had been disfigured by a life-threatening illness and its medical treatment, and she felt compelled to explain the change in her appearance repeatedly throughout the evening. The former basketball team captain and heartthrob of most girls in the class was paraplegic—destined by the Vietnam War to spend his life in a wheelchair. Several classmates who had put on substantially more than a few pounds joked about how they had "grown" over the years. One woman's gray locks prompted her broken-record insistence that we not call her "Grandma." A sizable percentage of the guys had a lot more scalp to show for the passage of time. "Oh well, hair today, gone tomorrow," they bantered. Some of the women came equipped with pictures of themselves when they had been pregnant, seeking confirmation that they were no longer "as big as a barn." A few youthful faces were lost to wrinkles— the result of genetics and too much sun worshiping.

The clock never stops. Time changes us—psychologically *and* physically. One certainty of life is that our bodies continue to change, for better or worse. Through nutrition, exercise, and other healthful practices, we can exert some control over the magnitude and rate of these changes. But we can never look like kids again.

That fact doesn't seem to keep many of us from trying, however. We search for lotions, potions, and other fountain-of-youth products. We sign up for "take it off now and forever" diets. We look for plastic surgeons who can cut away time with a scalpel. I believe that if we devoted to physical self-acceptance half of the emotional and behavioral energy we invest in trying to turn back the clock or in trying to have the perfect body, we would live happier lives.

This final Step of the program can help you plan for the future and face the challenges of a changing body. Your success will depend upon your using the skills you've acquired thus far. I need not review them for every possible physical change that might occur in your life. Rather, I want to put some of these changes into perspective, shedding light so that you can view your changing body with self-acceptance.

Weight Just a Minute!

As the world's tabloids tattled, Elizabeth Taylor's weight has risen and fallen. We watched singer Karen Carpenter become thinner and thinner until she lost her life to anorexia. In seldom-granted interviews, Marlon Brando shrugs off the inevitable question about his physical transformation from "hunk" to "heavy." Talk-show queen Oprah Winfrey lost pound after pound on the commercial diet she publicly endorsed. Then, as readily as she had lost the weight, Oprah put it back on and resolved to accept herself as a "big, beautiful woman." At this writing, Oprah has become thin again.

Concerns about weight are the number-one complaint of people with a negative body image. You saw in Step 1 that 41 percent of men and 55 percent of women are dissatisfied with their weight. Men who dislike their weight are fairly equally split between those who wish to gain weight (usually muscle mass) and those who aspire to lose weight. Among weight-discontent women, however, 95 percent believe they are too fat. On average, they want to lose about ten pounds. *Glamour* magazine once asked its readers what would make them happiest: losing weight, succeeding at work, dating an admired man, or hearing from an old friend. Over 40 percent chose weight loss; none of the other options came close. Perhaps the women believed that if they lost weight, all the other elements of happiness would then fall into place.

Estimates vary, but some surveys indicate that, at any given time, about two-thirds of adult women say they are on a diet. For many, women and men alike, dieting is a way of life. These yo-yo dieters lose weight and regain it in a neverending cycle. Paralleling their weight changes are dramatic body-image fluctuations. In a 1993 study, I found that after an average weight reduction of fifty pounds, dieters did experience substantial body-image improvements. However, after regaining a mere five pounds, their body image took a nose dive.

Some dieters experience "phantom fat." Despite losing weight, their feelings of being fat linger. These dieters aren't even satisfied when they are slim. They know how often they've struggled unsuccessfully to produce lasting weight loss. They expect the ups and downs will never end, and they despise their body for being so uncooperative.

Researchers who have studied the effectiveness of weight-loss programs tell us that most dieters regain the majority of their lost weight after a year or two. For this reason, many experts are now beginning to question the "dieting solution." Dr. Kelly Brownell, a leading obesity researcher at Yale, has urged that professionals develop sensible alternatives to unhealthy dieting rather than continue to encourage diets as *the* only option. Psychologist Judith Rodin has recently written a book, *Body Traps,* in which she talks about the "dieting-rituals trap." The bottom line is that our weight is strongly controlled by genetics, and chronic dieting can cause health problems, eating binges, emotional distress, and a change in metabolic efficiency that actually *increases* one's propensity to *gain* weight. A Toronto psychologist, Dr. Janet

Polivy, has even created an educational program to help people *stop* dieting.

If you are hooked on dieting, I'm not going to pretend that I can easily talk you out of it. Our culture screams at you to lose weight and promises lifelong health and happiness to the slim. Your friends and family probably *expect* you to diet. They reinforce your efforts and may chastise you if you are not on a diet. In some social situations, you may be the oddball if you aren't dieting: If everyone at lunch declares what type of diet they are on, how much weight they've lost so far, and how much they want to lose before ordering the "rabbit salad" with low-cal dressing and a no-cal drink, it's not easy to say "I like my weight the way it is" and then order the pasta with cream sauce and garlic bread.

Effective weight control is part of a healthy lifestyle. It cannot be measured by the number on your bathroom scale. It is *not* a matter of being on or off a diet, as both can be unhealthy, unnatural extremes. The key is in knowing what your body needs—your *energy balance* of nutrition, caloric intake, and caloric expenditure. Prohibitions like "I can never again eat a chocolate chip cookie" serve as self-imprisonment from which the only escape is to consume the whole bag of cookies. Good nutrition, spreading your daily food intake out over time, and regular exercise are sensible solutions to weight control.

Breaking a self-defeating dieting habit can be accomplished by applying everything you've learned in this program. Dieting rituals *are* Appearance-Preoccupied Rituals. You can use the Erasing-It techniques from Step 6 to break them. Applying what you learned in Step 5, you can correct the Private Body Talk that pressures you to diet in order to be "acceptable." You can challenge the Appearance Assumption (from Step 4) that maintains "The only way I could ever like my looks would be to change how I look." Your New Inner Voice accepts you as you are—unconditionally!

Several organizations provide information and support to help people accept their body rather than chronically engage in unhealthy, self-defeating patterns of eating and dieting:

The National Association to Advance Fat Acceptance
P.O. Box 188620
Sacramento, CA 95818
Phone: 1-800-442-1214

The American Anorexia/Bulimia Association
c/o Regent Hospital
425 East 61st Street
6th Floor
New York, NY 10021
Phone: (212) 891-8686

National Eating Disorders Organization
445 East Granville Road
Worthington, OH 43085
Phone: (614) 436-1112
Fax: (614) 785-7471

A Pregnant Pause (Not for Women Only)

For some women, pregnancy delivers a mixed blessing. Beyond her delight (or apprehension) about becoming a mother, a woman labors to cope with her changing body. Of course, early on, she may be dealing with the nausea of morning sickness, and later on with back pain from the extra cargo she must carry. Sometimes, however, she bears the greatest burden in her body image. "God, I'm big—and I'm going to get even bigger before this is over! I look so fat. Am I even remotely attractive anymore? After the baby comes, will I ever look the same? What if my stomach stays out of shape? Will my stretch marks show? What if my breasts sag?"

With pregnancy comes the challenge of accepting body change. Comparing your pregnant body with how you used to look or how other nonpregnant women appear is an Unfair-to-Compare mistake. It makes no sense. Moreover, being pregnant does *not* mean that you are fat. Being pregnant means being pregnant! Nobody will look at you and exclaim in amazement, "I know you're going to have a baby, but how come your belly sticks out?" If someone *were* to say this, I trust you would refer them to a remedial sex education class!

Pregnancy provides the perfect opportunity to develop a new appreciation of your body and its life-giving capability. In the grand scheme of things, swollen legs and feet are unimportant. Now is an ideal time to cultivate a new relationship with your body. There are sensate experiences—heightened erogenous sensitivities and awareness of your baby's movements—that you can enjoy. There are activities you can do to enhance your health and fitness, both now and after the baby comes. Rather than abandon your appearance as "too pregnant to look halfway decent," your grooming activities can help you take special pride in your special body. For example, many women enjoy the fact that their hair and nails have become lustrous and strong during pregnancy.

Now, let me have a word with my male readers. We know that our gender entails the unfortunate limitation that we'll never be pregnant. Nevertheless, if you are a prospective papa, this is a time to appreciate your partner's body and the miracle it represents. Refuse to play into any of her "bigger than a beached whale" or "nothing but a milk truck" proclamations. Enjoy her changing body. Adore it with your eyes. Caress it with your hands. Tell her how beautiful her body is to you.

Being Mature About Aging

Unlike some other cultures in the world, Western societies seem to cherish youth and regard aging as a necessary but dreaded evil. Moreover, a double standard exists for the sexes. In our culture, older men are distinguished; older women are over the hill. His graying hair gives him authority; she is expected to run to the hair-coloring salon. His facial lines give him character; she is urged to consider dermabrasion, collagen injections, or a facelift.

We can hope that these cultural biases will change. Perhaps the large number of aging baby boomers will foster a greater appreciation for the "second half" of life. Perhaps as women continue to gain economic and political power, their social value will expand beyond the mate-seeking and child-bearing years. On the other hand, as long as there is money to be made on youth-preserving products and services, the "youth is beauty" message will continue to permeate the media.

There is surprisingly little research on how aging affects body image. In my 1985 national body-image survey, I administered many of the same body-image tests you have taken in this program and compared the results from men and women in various age groups, from fifteen to seventy-five years old. I discovered that during the teen years and early twenties, people have the greatest investment in their looks. Unhappily, this is also the time of greatest body-image discontent, especially for women. Among the older groups, there was a steady decline in preoccupation with looks, and body satisfaction did *not* decline with age.

These results are both perplexing and encouraging. Paradoxically, the worst body-image years are the youthful years. When our looks are truly youthful, we don't seem to appreciate them. Fortunately, aging seems to bring a perspective that is more self-accepting. Perhaps as we get older we shift our standards appropriately, and maturity enhances our capacity to appreciate inner beauty—of others and of ourselves.

Despite the lack of scientific evidence, you and I both know that for some of us, aging does pose a serious threat to a positive body image. The anticipation of turning thirty, forty, fifty, or sixty can be laden with body-image worries. Of course, our "just kidding" friends don't really help matters with their gifts of black balloons, walking canes, reading glasses, wrinkle creams, hair-loss remedies, and those not-so-funny cards suggesting we warn the local fire department before lighting all the candles on our birthday cake!

Short of changing society (or changing friends), what can you do? You can challenge your standards. Refuse to buy into the youth-is-beauty, age-is-ugly standard—you deserve better. One of the guiding philosophies behind this program is that you should be in charge of your own body-image standards. It's important to feel good about your physical self. So, no matter what its shape, size, or features—and no matter what its age—it's essential that you accept your body. People who love you don't love you less because you are older, grayer, wrinklier, or saggier than you used to be. If you think of the people you know of various ages, you will recognize the truth that age is more an attitude than a number. Time has given you the experiences to develop the strengths of the person you are—your wisdom, your integrity, your friendliness, your sense of humor. Time offers you the continued opportunity to become the best that you can be.

In her autobiographical work *Revolution from Within: A Book of Self-Esteem,* feminist leader and author Gloria Steinem offers insights that can foster new perspectives for men as well as for women. Ms. Steinem candidly reveals her own efforts to come to terms with aging:

Looking in the mirror, I see the lines between nose and mouth that now remain, even without a smile, and I am reminded of a chipmunk storing nuts for the winter. This is the updated version of my plump-faced child. When I ask what they have to say for themselves, nothing comes back. They know I don't like them, so until I stop with the chipmunk imagery and learn to value them as the result of many smiles, they're not communicating. I'll have to work on this—and many other adjustments of aging yet to come.

A Special Word About Special People

In late 1992, I was invited to New York City to speak about my body-image therapy program at a conference called "Special Faces," sponsored by the National Foundation for Facial Reconstruction, an organization devoted to helping people with facial disfigurements. The audience was filled with individuals (and their families) whose lives had been profoundly affected by a disfiguring physical condition. Some disfigurements were the result of birth defects, including cleft lip and palate and rarer conditions such as craniofacial malformations like Crouzon Syndrome and hemifacial microsomia. Other disfigurements resulted from the ravages of disease, like facial cancer. Still others were due to severe burns. Whether caused by congenital or traumatic events, disfigurements produce a shared consequence to persons who must endure them. These people look different—different from others, and in some cases different from how they themselves once looked.

Physical disfigurement represents a significant challenge to the development of a positive body image. If you have a severe disfigurement, you are all too familiar with the pointing fingers and shocked stares of the nondisfigured public. In the grocery store, small children may call out, "Look Mommy, it's a monster!" Children with disfigurements are sometimes subjected to cruel taunts from their peers. If your appearance suddenly has been transformed by trauma, you are faced with the overwhelming tasks of resolving your loss and rediscovering yourself. You must come to terms with the reality that, even with all the surgical procedures you may endure, you may never look the same again.

These challenges should put things into perspective for those of us who worry about our skinny legs or our flabby stomach. We should all be inspired by the fact that most people with disfigurements find the inner resources and the social support to cope with their condition and discover new horizons of self-acceptance.

Following my speech at the "Special Faces" conference was a profound and provocative address by Alan Breslau, Executive Director of the Phoenix Society for Burn Survivors. Mr. Breslau described his own experiences with physical disfigurement that resulted from his being trapped in the flames of a crashed commercial airliner in 1963. The slides that accompanied his presentation graphically told his story. The fire had destroyed his nose, an ear, an eyelid, and two fingers. Half of his body had suffered third- and fourth-degree burns. He spent years in and out of the hospital, eventually undergoing fifty-two surgical operations. He talked of his struggles to accept his tragedy and deal with the aghast reactions of the public. Mr. Breslau titled his remarks to us "The Beauty of Disfigurement" and concluded with an inspiring observation:

> The disfigured need not let their scars affect their lives in a negative way. Since I cannot change the way I look, I must accept it. If others are uncomfortable with my appearance, it is not my problem, it is theirs. I will live

my life to the fullest and enjoy every moment I can. My scars are on the outside. Many people have theirs on the inside. They have the larger problem.

If you or someone you love has a disfiguring physical condition, there are plenty of resources—organizations, support groups, books, and films—that offer help. Please contact Let's Face It, an international network for "people with a facial difference." Let's Face It is located at Box 711, Concord, Massachusetts 01742-0711. You can telephone them at (508) 371-3186 and order an inexpensive booklet that lists lots of valuable resources.

CHANGING YOUR BODY IMAGE BY CHANGING YOUR BODY: SURGICAL SOLUTIONS

Throughout this program, I have tried to empower you to achieve satisfying and lasting body-image change by taking control of your experiences, *not* by changing your body. You enhance your body image by changing how you think, how you handle your emotions, and how you act in relation to your appearance. No Step in your program preaches that you should lose weight, build muscles, get a makeover, or "dress for success." In Step 7, when I spoke of "treating your body right" and showed you how to bolster your body image behaviorally with exercise and grooming, my prescription was for sensible and playful experiences of mastery and pleasure. The goal was *not* to change your body-image by "correcting" your appearance. My message to you earlier in the current chapter, when I spoke of the dieting dilemma and the inevitabilities of aging, similarly encourages self-acceptance.

The reality is, however, that millions of people around the world seek a surgical solution to their body dissatisfaction. In growing numbers, men and women—now even boys and girls—seek cosmetic surgery to change what they look like. According to the American Society of Plastic and Reconstructive Surgeons (ASPRS), the top three cosmetic procedures that women obtained in 1992 were eyelid surgery, liposuction, and collagen injections. Men represent 13 percent of the cosmetic surgery patients in the United States—double the percentage a decade ago. Among men, the top three procedures in 1992 were nose reshaping, eyelid surgery, and liposuction. Cosmetic surgery is especially popular in certain regions of the country—47 percent of the surgeries are performed in California, Florida, New York, and Texas. New Englanders, by contrast, are more likely to leave well enough alone, as they receive only 3 percent of the surgeries performed. On page 351 is a summary of how often various cosmetic procedures have been performed in the United States since 1981. These figures may be underestimates, because they don't count procedures performed by non–ASPRS physicians.

The numbers in the table make the point. Despite an apparent decline in the number of surgeries performed recently in the United States, cosmetic surgery flourishes as a means to change body dissatisfaction. Does it really help? Can changing your body improve your body image? Research indicates that the answer is a *qualified* yes. In my earlier book, *Body Images,* my colleague, Dr. Tom Pruzinsky, and a world-renowned surgeon, Dr. Milton Edgerton, reached the conclusion that for many people, cosmetic surgery does provide satisfying relief from their inability to accept their appearance. However, any experienced cosmetic surgeon will attest to the fact that the surgical solution is no panacea. Drs. Pruzinsky and Edgerton stated, "Surgery is mostly a catalyst for changing one's relationship with one's self."

TABLE 1
Estimated Number of Cosmetic Surgical Procedures Performed in the United States by Members of the American Society of Plastic and Reconstructive Surgeons

Procedure	1992	1990	1988	1981
Liposuction	47,212	109,080	101,000	55,900
Breast Augmentation	32,607	89,402	71,720	72,000
Collagen Injections	41,623	80,602	68,880	N/A
Eyelid Surgery	59,461	79,110	78,490	56,500
Nose Reshaping	50,175	68,320	73,250	54,500
Face-lift	40,077	48,743	48,480	39,000
Breast Reduction	39,639	40,258	35,500	32,000
"Tummy Tuck"	16,810	20,213	48,230	15,300
Dermabrasion	13,457	16,969	20,250	17,000
Forehead Lift	13,501	15,376	14,800	N/A
Breast Lift	7,963	14,323	12,440	12,800
Estimated Totals of these and other cosmetic procedures	394,911	643,910	681,070	380,400

Source: Information provided by the American Society of Plastic and Reconstructive Surgeons (ASPRS). According to the ASPRS, changes in survey methods likely improved the accuracy of the 1992 data compared to cruder estimates from previous years.

I do wish we lived in a world that promoted self-acceptance so successfully that no one desired cosmetic surgery. That's a world to hope and strive for. My position on cosmetic surgery is that I neither recommend nor reject it. Surgery carries potential risks as well as potential benefits. The risks and benefits depend upon the physical and psychological characteristics of the person receiving the surgery, the type of surgery performed, and the competence of the surgeon. Deciding to have surgery is not like deciding to get a new pair of shoes. The decision about surgery should never be made impulsively. It must be made *only* after careful information gathering and deliberation. In reaching a decision, you must have satisfactory answers to the important questions discussed on the following pages:

What Do You Want (and What Don't You Want) from Surgery?

It takes some honest soul searching to get in touch with your motives for surgery. Ask yourself, "What do I really hope to accomplish by changing my appearance?" The answer, "My nose (or butt, or face, or whatever) will look better" isn't enough. The motivation that leads to the most satisfying outcome has to do with your feelings about yourself. You are more likely to benefit from the surgery if your goal is to improve your self-confidence and diminish your self-consciousness.

Then you must ask, "How will I know if surgery will give me what I want?" If a happy outcome for you depends on other people's reactions—saving a marriage or having more friends, more dates, more compliments, or better career opportunities—this indicates that your aspirations are misguided. Achieving these goals will require behavioral changes, not surgical ones. Surgery cannot give you social or occupational skills. Stopping your mother-in-law from hassling you about your fat thighs is not a good reason for liposuction. Try assertiveness instead. Similarly off base are desires to resemble Madonna, Sharon Stone, Sylvester Stallone, or your good-looking best friend. Surgery cannot change your identity.

In addition to discovering what you want from surgery, think about what you *don't* want. Do you not want others to know you've had cosmetic surgery? How will you feel if they find out? If you would feel ashamed, this may suggest you have an underlying disapproval of *yourself* for having the surgery.

Some surgeries, like face-lifts, may prompt others to say you look different or to ask if you've lost weight. Given enough private recovery time, the secret remains with you. However, when you return to work or to your social life with a much fuller head of hair, a more finely sculpted nose, or noticeably larger breasts, you should expect that somebody will figure out what's happened. How will you deal with others' knowing you've had cosmetic surgery?

One thing you don't want after surgery is disapproval. Research has found that the psychological benefits of surgery can be undermined by nonsupportive friends and family members. Are there people in your life who may criticize you as vain, frivolous, or extravagant for having the surgery? How would you handle such criticisms? How would you feel if a loved one were to survey your new look and say to you, "I liked the way you used to look so much better"?

How Do You Choose a Surgeon?

Selecting a surgeon isn't like picking a plumber. Don't simply search the *Yellow Pages*. Be a smart consumer. Get several referrals from people you know and respect. Although your surgeon should be board certified, that credential alone is not sufficient. The surgeon you choose should be certified by the American Board of Plastic Surgery, which has extremely rigorous requirements. You can contact the American Board of Medical Specialties (at 1-800-776-2378) to check on your surgeon's certification. Some cosmetic procedures can be performed by physicians in other medical specialties. The American Society of Plastic and Reconstructive Surgeons has a roster of the properly certified practitioners. Give them a call (at 1-800-635-0635) to get informed.

You should have confidence in your surgeon. He or she

should have extensive experience in the particular procedure you are considering. You should also feel comfortable with your surgeon. He or she should give you information, answer your questions, ask you questions, and listen to you. The surgeon bent on "selling" the operation and getting you out of the office quickly isn't a good choice. Avoid the surgeon who readily agrees to do the procedure and then lists several other cosmetic procedures "we should do while we're at it." If you leave the office feeling worse about your appearance than you felt before the consultation, keep on walking.

Are There Any Risks to Cosmetic Surgery?

Cosmetic surgery *is* surgery. No surgery is free of risks to your health and well-being. There may also be particular risks for you, depending on your medical history and condition. You should have a thorough knowledge of all risks and their likelihood before making a decision. A surgeon is ethically and legally obligated to communicate possible complications as a part of your informed consent to receive the surgery. Before making a decision, you should have this information in writing. Review the risks on your own, then discuss them with your surgeon. Although, understandably, surgeons don't wish to scare their patients about improbable risks, honesty is essential. If your surgeon dismisses your questions with, "Trust me, nothing at all could go wrong," consult a different surgeon.

What Does the Surgery Itself Involve?

Ask your surgeon about what will happen at each stage of the process. How is the surgical procedure done? Will it be inpatient or outpatient surgery? What type of anesthetic will be used? How much postoperative pain can you expect? How much scarring, bruising, or bleeding can you expect? Will you need a friend or family member to take care of you during recovery? How long will it be before you will be sufficiently healed to return to your normal routine?

Ask to talk with other people who've had the same surgical procedure. Ask them about their experiences from start to finish. Although surgeons are prohibited by rules of confidentiality from revealing patients' names without permission, most surgeons do have patients who have agreed to serve as resources. Of course, they will be self-selected, satisfied customers. Still, they can be informative.

Most cosmetic surgeries are not inexpensive. Costs vary considerably depending on geographical location and, of course, on the specific procedure. (The ASPRS has information on typical fees for various procedures.) The cost is seldom covered by insurance, unless there is a medical reason for the surgery—like a deviated nasal septum that impairs breathing and can be corrected by a nose job. So be a good financial consumer as well. Get *all* the costs and the payment plan itemized up front (including fees for the surgeon, anesthesiologist, operating room, recovery room, etc.).

How Long Will the Cosmetic Changes Last?

Understand that few cosmetic procedures produce changes that last forever. The body continues to age, and surgery cannot stop the clock. For example, the results from collagen injections are short-lived, usually only several months. Nonsurgical chemical peels to remove fine wrinkles generally last for several years; surgical face-lifts endure a little longer. Hair transplants are relatively permanent—for the transplanted hair itself—but they don't prevent thinning of the remaining hair. So, in considering any cosmetic procedure, be informed about the degree of permanence of the physical change you seek.

What Can Be Done to Maximize Body-Image Changes from Surgery?

Surgery can be a catalyst for body-image change. I firmly believe that this book's program is valuable even to people who have thoughtfully arrived at their decision to obtain cosmetic surgery. Outer change does not remove the need for inner change. A surgeon's scalpel cannot eradicate a history of preoccupation with and hatred of one's looks. Nor can it completely eliminate habitual patterns of faulty thinking and acting in relation to one's body. If left unchallenged, history will repeat itself. Even though discontent with the "corrected" feature may subside, discontent with other less-than-perfect features can begin to emerge. If surgery has enhanced your self-acceptance, that's great. If it has diminished your self-acceptance by leading you to feel you have to change any physical characteristic that's not ideal, then surgery has done you a great disservice.

THE SELF-ESTEEM CONNECTION

In Step 1, I explained that about one-fourth of how we feel about ourselves is tied to our body image. It's difficult to like yourself if you dislike your body. Moreover, research on the effectiveness of body-image therapy has confirmed that as people learn to like their looks, they come to like themselves better. Before ending this final Step of your program, I want to discuss the corollary to this finding, as I also did in the first Step of the program: People who don't like themselves have a hard time accepting what they look like. Poor self-esteem causes people to find fault with much of what they do, with most of who they are, and with much of what they see when they look in the mirror. The Countess of Blessington once observed, "There is no cosmetic for beauty like happiness." Her maxim is even truer of body image than of actual beauty.

To become the best that you can be and to feel the best that you can feel about yourself, you must realize that your body image is only a part of you. There are other aspects of yourself and your life that you may need to work on. The insights you have gained in this program, as well as the strategies you've applied and the exercises you've carried out, are all useful in the enhancement of self-esteem. By redirecting the focus of what you have learned, you can increase your *self*-acceptance just as you increased your acceptance of your body.

Self-Help for Self-Acceptance

If you are reading these words, you obviously recognize the value of self-help as an opportunity for personal growth. To help you apply what you have learned in this program to developing even more favorable self-esteem, I've suggested a number of other excellent books and resources in the appendix. Look over the list and note the ones that apply to your needs. Don't waste precious time. Head to your library or bookstore and get started today.

Professional Help for Self-Acceptance

Because I'm a therapist and a researcher of the effectiveness of professional therapy, I understand its power to help people make positive changes in their lives. I also understand that many of you may need further assistance that transcends the capacity of my written words—the self-discoveries and prescriptive experiences that I have offered you.

If you suffer from more than your share of anxiety, depression, relationship problems, or other difficulties that diminish the quality of your life, do not hesitate to pursue the help you need. You are entitled to a happy life. Seeking professional help does not mean that you are weak or that you have failed. It means that you are taking control of your life.

SAYING GOOD-BYE

Everything you've learned in this program represents a new body lifestyle—a new relationship between you and your body. To ensure that this relationship continues to grow and produce positive experiences as well as diminish unpleasant ones, I strongly recommend that you remain active in your efforts. Continue to keep a personal Body-Image Diary for scheduling what you do and recording what happens. This diary is an excellent way for you to communicate with yourself about your struggles and victories, your plans and progress. From time to time, you can sit down and read the story of your experiences and see just how far you've come. Every couple of months, retake the body-image tests as you did in Step 8, and compare your new answers with earlier results. This is a valuable way to monitor specific areas of improvement as well as the areas that need more work.

What I have tried to give you in this book is the result of

over twenty years of professional involvement in studying and caring about the embodied reality of the human condition. Having served as your guide in this program to enhance your body-image experiences, I wish I could personally witness your journey and your successes. You've heard so much from me, I'd love to hear from you. Below is my address. I would welcome a note summarizing your reactions to and results from this program.

My very best wishes to you for a happy, satisfying body image for the rest of your life.

Thomas F. Cash, Ph.D.
Professor of Psychology
The Physical Appearance Laboratory
Old Dominion University
Norfolk, Virginia 23529-0267

STEP 8

Progress Check: How Am I Helping Myself?

• By retaking the body-image tests, you have evaluated the gains you've made in this program. This has enabled you to identify your future body-image needs, which assures your continued progress.

• In preparing today for tomorrow, you are aware of any stagnating attitudes that could interfere with your making additional body-image improvements.

• Using the techniques and skills you've learned in this program, you are preparing to deal with potentially difficult situations and thinking about how to handle the unexpected.

• You are developing assertive strategies, like the RIGHTS approach, for dealing with people who may be troublesome for your body image.

• You are working on having a healthy attitude about the changes in your appearance that will occur over time.

• If you are considering cosmetic surgery, you are asking the right questions in order to make a careful, informed decision.

• To maintain your positive body image for life, you are examining other aspects of your self-acceptance. Whether by self-help or professional help, you are planning to work on the enhancement of your self-esteem.

APPENDIX

Self-Help Resources

IMPROVING YOUR BODY IMAGE

The following list contains informative books and articles to help you further your understanding of the psychology of physical appearance and continue your body-image improvement.

Baker, N.C. *The Beauty Trap*. New York: Franklin Watts, 1984. (Exposes the pitfalls of women's pursuit of beauty.)

Banner, L.W. *American Beauty*. New York: Knopf, 1983. (One of the earliest works to chronicle the meaning and influences of beauty on women.)

Brownmiller, S. *Femininity*. New York: Linden Press, 1984. (Critically documents the physical symbols of "femininity"—including body, hair, clothes, voice, skin.)

Bull, R., and N. Rumsey. *The Social Psychology of Facial Appearance*. New York: Springer-Verlag, 1988. (Written for a scientifically astute audience, this is one of the most detailed reviews of how appearance affects human behavior.)

Cash, T.F. "Body images and body weight: What is there to gain or lose?" *Weight Control Digest,* vol. 2, no. 4 (1992), pp. 169 ff. (Explains the importance of body-image issues for people who are trying to lose weight.)

———. *Body-Image Therapy: A Program for Self-Directed Change*. New

York: Guilford Publications, 1991. (This audiocassette series is a briefer version of the program presented in the current book. It also includes a workbook for clients and a manual for professionals.)

——, and T. Pruzinsky. eds. *Body Images: Development, Deviance, and Change.* New York: Guilford Publications, 1990. (For the "advanced" reader, this volume reviews scientific and clinical knowledge regarding the development and treatments of body-image problems.)

——, and L.H. Janda. "Eye of the beholder." *Psychology Today,* vol. 18, no. 12 (1984), pp. 46–52. (A very readable explanation of some of the liabilities as well as the benefits of physical attractiveness.)

——, et al. "The great American shape-up: Body-image survey report." *Psychology Today*, vol. 20, no. 4 (1986), pp. 30–37. (Presents the results of a national survey on body image.)

Freedman, R. *Beauty Bound.* Lexington, MA: Lexington Books, 1986. (A thought-provoking, feminist perspective on the dangers of women's pursuit of beauty.)

Freedman, R. *Bodylove.* New York: Harper & Row, 1988. (Provides information on cognitive-behavioral strategies for women's management of body-image discontent.)

Hatfield, E., and S. Sprecher. *Mirror, Mirror . . . : The Importance of Looks in Everyday Life.* Albany, NY: SUNY Press, 1986. (A very readable summary of psychological research findings on the influences of human appearance throughout the lifespan.)

Hutchinson, M.G. *Transforming Body Image.* Trumansburg, New York: The Crossing Press, 1985. (One of the first books to try to help women overcome a negative body image offers a series of exercises, especially body-movement techniques.)

Jackson, L.A. *Physical Appearance and Gender: Sociobiological and sociocultural perspectives.* Albany: New York: SUNY Press, 1992. (Written mostly for professionals, this scholarly book details how physical attractiveness and body image affect the lives of both sexes.)

Morris, D. *Bodywatching.* New York: Crown, 1985. (This fascinating volume depicts, in words and photographs, the multiple meanings of physical attributes in different cultures and at different historical times.)

Orbach, S. *Fat Is a Feminist Issue II: A Program to Conquer Compulsive Eating.* New York: Berkley, 1982. (A classic offering insights and exercises for women who struggle with eating binges.)

Polivy, J., and P. Herman. *Breaking the Diet Habit.* New York: Basic Books, 1983. (Psychologists help the reader gain control over chronic and unhealthy dieting rituals.)

Prussin, R., P. Harvey, and T.F. DiGeronimo. *Hooked on Exercise: How to Understand and Manage Exercise Addiction.* New York: Fireside/Parkside Books, 1992. (Shows how addictive exercise differs from normal exercise and teaches the reader how to be free of excessive exercise.)

Rodin, J. *Body Traps.* New York: William Morrow, 1992. (Pinpoints the pitfalls of bodily pursuits—the traps of vanity, shame, competition, food, dieting, exercise, and success.)

Russell, K., et al. *The Color Complex: The Politics of Skin Color Among African Americans.* New York: Harcourt, Brace, Jovanovich, 1992. (A fascinating look at the controversial topic of how the lightness/darkness of skin color affects the lives of Black Americans.)

Wolf, N. *The Beauty Myth: How Images of Beauty Are Used Against Women.* New York: William Morrow, 1991. (A feminist perspective on the tyranny of women's pursuit of beauty.)

IMPROVING YOUR SELF-ESTEEM

Here are some excellent guides to help you learn to like yourself better and improve your emotional life:

Branden, N. *How to Raise Your Self-Esteem.* New York: Bantam, 1987. (A well-known self-help book to enhance self-respect and self-confidence.)

Burns, D. *Feeling Good: The New Mood Therapy.* New York: Morrow,

1980. (Details the tenets and techniques of cognitive therapy, especially for managing depression.)

———. *The Feeling Good Handbook: Using the New Mood Therapy in Everyday Life*. New York: Morrow, 1989. (An even more extensive volume than Burns's above book for applying cognitive therapy to a range of problems in living.)

———. *Ten Days to Self-Esteem*. New York: Morrow, 1993. (His latest self-help book lays out a ten-step program.)

Butler, P.E. *Talking to Yourself: Learning the Language of Self-Affirmation*. San Francisco, CA: HarperCollins, 1991. (Shows how changing one's inner "self-talk" can change one's life.)

Emery, G. *Own Your Own Life: How the New Cognitive Therapy Can Make You Feel Wonderful*. New York: New American Library, 1982. (Teaches the use of cognitive therapy for everyday life emotional difficulties.)

———. *Overcoming Anxiety: A Program for Self-Management*. New York: Guilford Publications, 1987. (In this audiotape series, cognitive therapy techniques are taught for the self-directed management of various forms of anxiety.)

McKay, M., and P. Fanning. *Self-Esteem*. Oakland, CA: New Harbinger Publications, 1987. (Cognitive therapy is applied to the improvement of self-esteem in men and women.)

———. *Prisoners of Belief: Exposing & Changing Beliefs that Control Your Life*. Oakland, CA: New Harbinger Publications, 1991. (Cognitive therapy is applied to help people rid themselves of core assumptions and beliefs that interfere with self-acceptance and happiness.)

Sanford, L., and M.E. Donovan. *Women and Self-Esteem*. New York: Anchor/Doubleday, 1984. (Insights into the obstacles and opportunities in women's development of self-esteem.)

Steinem, G. *Revolution from Within: A Book of Self-Esteem*. Boston, MA: Little, Brown and Company, 1992. (This famous feminist and founder of *Ms* magazine reveals her personal views on how the roots of self-esteem are created in childhood but "relearning" can occur throughout one's life.)

BIBLIOGRAPHY

INTRODUCTION

Creating a New Body Image
One Step at a Time

American Psychiatric Association. *Diagnostic and Statistical Manual of Mental Disorders,* 3rd ed. rev., Washington, D.C.: American Psychiatric Association, 1987.

American Psychiatric Association. *Diagnostic and Statistical Manual of Mental Disorders,* 4th ed., Washington, D.C.: American Psychiatric Association, 1994.

Butters, J.W., and T.F. Cash. "Cognitive-behavioral treatment of women's body-image dissatisfaction." *Journal of Consulting and Clinical Psychology,* vol. 55 (1987), pp. 889–97.

Cash, T.F. *Body-Image Therapy: A Program for Self-Directed Change.* New York: Guilford Publications, 1991.

———. "Understanding and changing body images: A cognitive-behavioral approach." Symposium presentation at the annual convention of the American Psychological Association, Washington, D.C., 1992.

———. "Body images and body weight: What is there to gain or lose?" *Weight Control Digest,* vol. 2, no. 4 (1992), pp. 169 ff.

———, and J.W. Butters. "Poor body image: Helping the patient to change." *Medical Aspects of Human Sexuality,* vol. 22, no. 6 (1988), pp. 67–70.

———, and T. Pruzinsky., eds. *Body Images: Development, Deviance, and Change.* New York: Guilford Press, 1990.

Dworkin, S.H., and B.A. Kerr. "Comparison of interventions for women experiencing body image problems." *Journal of Counseling Psychology,* vol. 34 (1987), pp. 136–40.

Fisher, E., and J.K. Thompson. "A comparison of cognitive-behavioral therapy versus exercise therapy for the treatment of body-image disturbance: Preliminary findings." *Behavior Modification,* vol. 18 (1994), pp. 171–85.

Freedman, R. "Cognitive-behavioral perspectives on body-image change." In T.F. Cash & T. Pruzinsky, eds. *Body Images: Development, Deviance, and Change.* New York: Guilford, 1990.

Grant, J., and T.F. Cash. "Cognitive-behavioral body-image therapy: Comparative efficacy of group and modest-contact treatments." *Behavior Therapy,* in press.

Noles, S.W., T.F. Cash, and B.A. Winstead. "Body image, physical attractiveness, and depression." *Journal of Consulting and Clinical Psychology,* vol. 53 (1985), pp. 88–94.

Phillips, K.A. "Body dysmorphic disorder: The distress of imagined ugliness." *American Journal of Psychiatry,* vol. 148 (1991), pp. 1138–49.

Pruzinsky, T. "Psychopathology of body experience: Expanded perspectives." In T.F. Cash & T. Pruzinsky, eds. *Body Images: Development, Deviance, and Change.* New York: Guilford, 1990.

Rosen, J.C. "Body-image disturbance in eating disorders." In T.F. Cash & T. Pruzinsky, eds. *Body Images: Development, Deviance, and Change.* New York: Guilford, 1990.

Rosen, J.C., et al. "Cognitive behavior therapy with and without size perception training for women with body image disturbance." *Behavior Therapy,* vol. 21 (1990), pp. 481–98.

——, E. Saltzberg, and D. Srebnik. "Cognitive behavior therapy for negative body image." *Behavior Therapy,* vol. 20 (1989), pp. 393–404.

——. "Cognitive-behavioral body-image therapy in the treatment of body dysmorphic and obese clients." Symposium paper presented at the annual meeting of the Association for Advancement of Behavior Therapy, Atlanta, GA, Oct. 1993.

Scogin, F., et al. "Efficacy of self-administered treatment programs: Meta-analytic review." *Professional Psychology: Research and Practice,* vol. 21 (1990), pp. 42–47.

STEP ONE: IN THE EYE OF THE BEHOLDER

Understanding the Psychology of Physical Appearance

Alley, T.R., ed. *Social and Applied Aspects of Perceiving Faces.* Hillsdale, NJ: Erlbaum, 1988.

Bar-Tal, D., and L. Saxe. "Physical attractiveness and its relationship to sex-role stereotyping." *Sex Roles,* vol. 2 (1976), pp. 123–33.

Beck, A.T. *Cognitive Therapy and the Emotional Disorders.* New York: International Universities Press, 1976.

Bernstein, N.R. "Objective bodily damage: Disfigurement and dignity." In T.F. Cash & T. Pruzinsky, eds. *Body Images: Development, Deviance, and Change.* New York: Guilford, 1990.

Berscheid, E., et al. "Physical attractiveness and dating choice: A test of the matching hypothesis." *Journal of Experimental Social Psychology,* vol. 7 (1971), pp. 173–89.

———, E. Walster, and G. Bohrnstedt. "Body image. The happy American body: A survey report." *Psychology Today,* vol. 7 (1973), pp. 119–31.

Brooks-Gunn, J., and M.P. Warren. "Effects of delayed menarche in different contexts: Dance and nondance students." *Journal of Youth and Adolescence,* vol. 14 (1985), pp. 285–300.

———. "The psychological significance of secondary sexual characteristics in nine- to eleven-year-old girls. *Child Development,* vol. 59 (1988), pp. 1061–69.

Brown, T.A., T.F. Cash, and R.J. Lewis. "Body-image disturbances in adolescent female binge-purgers: A brief report of the results of a national survey in the U.S.A." *Journal of Child Psychology and Psychiatry,* vol. 30 (1989), pp. 605–13.

Brownmiller, S. *Femininity.* New York: Linden Press, 1984.

Bull, R., and N. Rumsey. *The Social Psychology of Facial Appearance.* New York: Springer-Verlag, 1988.

Cash, T.F. "Physical attractiveness: An annotated bibliography of theory and research in the behavioral sciences." *Social & Behavioral Sciences Documents,* vol. 11 (1981), p. 83, MS# 2370.

———. "Physical appearance and mental health." In J.A. Graham & A. Kligman, eds. *Psychology of Cosmetic Treatments.* New York: Praeger Scientific, 1985.

———. "The psychology of physical appearance: Aesthetics, attributes, and images." In T.F. Cash & T. Pruzinsky, eds. *Body Images: Development, Deviance, and Change.* New York: Guilford, 1990.

———. "Binge-eating and body images among the obese: A further evaluation." *Journal of Social Behavior and Personality,* vol. 6 (1991), pp. 367–76.

———. *Body-Image Therapy: A Program for Self-Directed Change.* New York: Guilford Publications, 1991.

———. "Body images and body weight: What is there to gain or lose?" *Weight Control Digest,* vol. 2, no. 4 (1992), pp. 169 ff.

———. "Psychological effects of androgenetic alopecia among men." *Journal of the American Academy of Dermatology,* vol. 26 (1992), pp. 926–31.

———. "Understanding and changing body images: A cognitive-behavioral approach." Symposium presentation at the annual convention of the American Psychological Association, Washington, D.C., 1992.

———. *Appearance teasing in childhood and adult body image.* Unpublished research. Old Dominion University, Norfolk, VA, 1993.

———, and T.A. Brown. "Body image in anorexia nervosa and bulimia nervosa: A review of the literature." *Behavior Modification,* vol. 11 (1987), pp. 487–521.

———, and T.A. Brown. "Gender and body images: Stereotypes and realities." *Sex Roles,* vol. 21 (1989), pp. 361–73.

———, B. Counts, and C.E. Huffine. "Current and vestigial effects of overweight among women: Fear of fat, attitudinal body image, and eating behaviors." *Journal of Psychopathology and Behavioral Assessment,* vol. 12 (1990), pp. 157–67.

———, and V.J. Derlega. "The matching hypothesis: Physical attractiveness among same-sexed friends." *Personality and Social Psychology Bulletin,* vol. 4 (1978), pp. 240–43.

———, and N.C. Duncan. "Physical attractiveness stereotyping among Black American college students." *Journal of Social Psychology,* vol. 122 (1984), pp. 71–77.

———, B. Gillen, and D.S. Burns. "Sexism and 'beautyism' in personnel consultant decision making." *Journal of Applied Psychology,* vol. 62 (1977), pp. 301–310.

———, and K.L. Hicks. "Being fat versus thinking fat: Relationships with body image, eating behaviors, and well-being." *Cognitive Therapy and Research,* vol. 14 (1990), pp. 327–41.

———, and L. Jacobi. "Looks aren't everything (to everybody): The strength of ideals of physical appearance." *Journal of Social Behavior and Personality,* vol. 7 (1992), pp. 621–30.

———, and L.H. Janda. "Eye of the beholder." *Psychology Today,* vol. 18, no. 12 (1984), pp. 46–52.

———, et al. "The psychosocial effects of androgenetic alopecia among women: Comparisons with balding men and female controls." *Journal of the American Academy of Dermatology,* vol. 29 (1993), pp. 568–75.

———, and T. Pruzinsky, eds. *Body Images: Development, Deviance, and Change.* New York: Guilford Publications, 1990.

———, and E. Smith. "Physical attractiveness and personality among American college students." *Journal of Psychology,* vol. 111 (1982), pp. 183–91.

———, and M. Szymanski. "The development and validation of the Body-Image Ideals Questionnaire." *Journal of Personality Assessment,* in press.

———, and C. Trimer. "Sexism and beautyism in women's evaluations of peer performance." *Sex Roles,* vol. 10 (1984), pp. 87–98.

———, B.A. Winstead, and L.H. Janda. "Your body, yourself: A *Psychology Today* reader survey." *Psychology Today,* vol. 19, no. 7 (1985), pp. 22–26.

———, "The great American shape-up: Body image survey report." *Psychology Today,* vol. 20, no. 4 (1986), pp. 30–37.

Dermer, M., and D.I. Thiel. "When beauty may fail." *Journal of Personality and Social Psychology,* vol. 31 (1975), pp. 1168–76.

Dion, K., et al. "What is beautiful is good." *Journal of Personality and Social Psychology,* vol. 24 (1972), pp. 285–90.

Drewnowski, A., and D.K. Yee. "Men and body image: Are males satisfied with their body weight?" *Psychosomatic Medicine,* vol. 49 (1987), pp. 626–34.

Eagly, A.H., et al. "What is beautiful is good, but . . . : A meta-analytic review of research on the physical attractiveness stereotype." *Psychological Bulletin,* vol. 110 (1991), pp. 226–35.

Fabian, L.J., and J.K. Thompson. "Body image and eating disturbances in young females." *International Journal of Eating Disorders,* vol. 8 (1989), pp. 63–74.

Fallon, A.E. "Culture in the mirror: Sociocultural determinants of body image." In T.F. Cash & T. Pruzinsky, eds. *Body images: Development, Deviance, and Change.* New York: Guilford, 1990.

———, and P. Rozin. "Sex differences in perceptions of body shape." *Journal of Abnormal Psychology,* vol. 94 (1985), pp. 102–5.

Feingold, A. "Matching for attractiveness in romantic partners and same-sex friends: A meta-analysis and theoretical critique. *Psychological Bulletin,* vol. 104 (1988), pp. 226–35.

———. "Good-looking people are not what we think." *Psychological Bulletin,* vol. 111 (1992), pp. 304–41.

Finch, C., and T.F. Cash. "Body-image experiences among heterosexual and gay/lesbian college students." Unpublished research, Old Dominion University, Norfolk, VA, 1991.

Freedman, R. *Beauty Bound.* Lexington, MA: Lexington Books, 1986.

Furnham, A., and N. Alibhai. "Cross-cultural differences in the perception of female body shapes." *Psychological Medicine,* vol. 13 (1983), pp. 829–37.

Garner, D.M., et al. "Cultural expectations of thinness in women." *Psychological Reports,* vol. 47 (1980), pp. 483–91.

Gillen, H.B. "Physical attractiveness: A determinant of two types of goodness." *Personality and Social Psychology Bulletin,* vol. 7 (1981), pp. 277–81.

Hangen, J.D., and T.F. Cash. "Body-image attitudes and sexual functioning in a college population." Paper presented at the annual meeting of the Association for Advancement of Behavior Therapy, N.Y., NY, 1991.

Hatfield, E., and S. Sprecher. *Mirror, mirror . . . The importance of looks in everyday life.* Albany, NY: SUNY Press, 1986.

Heilman, M.E., and L.R. Saruwatari. "When beauty is beastly: The effects of appearance and sex on evaluation of job applicants for managerial and nonmanagerial jobs." *Organizational Behavior and Human Performance,* vol. 23 (1979), pp. 360–72.

Heilman, M., and M. Stopeck. "Being attractive, advantage or disadvantage? Performance-based evaluations and recommended personnel actions as a function of appearance, sex, and job type." *Organizational Behaviors and Human Decision Processes,* vol. 35 (1985), pp. 202–15.

————. "Attractiveness and corporate success: Differential causal attribution for males and females." *Journal of Applied Psychology,* vol. 70 (1985), pp. 379–88.

Higgins, E.T. "Self-discrepancy: A theory relating self and affect." *Psychological Review,* vol. 94 (1987), pp. 319–40.

Jackson, L.A. *Physical Appearance and Gender: Sociobiological and Sociocultural Perspectives.* Albany, NY: SUNY Press, 1992.

Jacobi, L. and T.F. Cash. "In pursuit of the perfect appearance: Discrepancies among self- and ideal-percepts of multiple physical attributes." *Journal of Applied Social Psychology,* vol. 24 (1994), pp. 379–96.

Keeton, W.P., T.F. Cash, and T.A. Brown. "Body image or body images?: Comparative multidimensional assessment among college students." *Journal of Personality Assessment,* vol. 54 (1990), pp. 213–30.

Kleck, R.E., and A. Strenta. "Perceptions of the impact of negatively valued physical characteristics on social interaction." *Journal of Personality and Social Psychology,* vol. 39 (1980), pp. 861–73.

Krueger, D.W. *Body Self and Psychological Self: Developmental and Clinical Integration in Disorders of the Self.* New York: Brunner/Mazel, 1989.

———. "Developmental and psychodynamic perspectives on body-image change. In T.F. Cash and T. Pruzinsky, eds. *Body Images: Development, Deviance, and Change.* New York: Guilford, 1990.

Langlois, J.H. "From the eye of the beholder to behavioral reality: Development of social behavior and social relations as a function of physical attractiveness." In C.P. Herman, M.P. Zanna, and E.T. Higgins, eds. *Physical Appearance, Stigma, and Social Behavior: The Ontario Symposium, Vol. 3.* Hillsdale, NJ: Erlbaum, 1986.

Lazarus, R.S., and S. Folkman. *Stress, Appraisal, and Coping.* New York: Springer, 1984.

Lerner, R.M., and J. Jovanovic. "The role of body image in psychosocial development across the life span: A developmental contextual perspective. In T.F. Cash and T. Pruzinsky, eds. *Body Images: Development, Deviance, and Change.* New York: Guilford, 1990.

Major, B., et al. "Physical attractiveness and self-esteem: Attributions for praise from an other-sex evaluator." *Personality and Social Psychology Bulletin,* vol. 10 (1984), pp. 43–50.

Major, B., and K. Deaux. "Physical attractiveness and masculinity and femininity." *Personality and Social Psychology Bulletin,* vol. 7 (1981), pp. 24–28.

Mazur, A. "U.S. trends in feminine beauty and overadaptation." *Journal of Sex Research,* vol. 22 (1986), pp. 281–303.

Morris, D. *Bodywatching: A field guide to the human species.* New York: Crown, 1985.

Mueser, K.T., et al. "You're only as pretty as you feel: Facial expression as a determinant of physical attractiveness." *Journal of Personality and Social Psychology,* vol. 46 (1984), pp. 469–78.

Nakdimen, K.A. "The physiognomic basis of sexual stereotyping." *American Journal of Psychiatry,* vol. 141, no. 4 (1984), pp. 499–503.

Noles, S.W., T.F. Cash, and B.A. Winstead. "Body image, physical attractiveness, and depression." *Journal of Consulting and Clinical Psychology,* vol. 53 (1985), pp. 88–94.

Pertschuk, M.J. "Reconstructive surgery: Objective change of objective deformity." In T.F. Cash and T. Pruzinsky, eds. *Body Images: Development, Deviance, and Change.* New York: Guilford, 1990.

Petersen, A.C. "Adolescent development." *Annual Review of Psychology,* vol. 39 (1988), pp. 583–607.

Polivy, J., D.M. Garner, and P.E. Garfinkel. "Causes and consequences of the current preference for thin female physiques." In C.P. Herman, M.P. Zanna, and E.T. Higgins, eds. *Physical Appearance, Stigma, and Social Behavior: The Ontario symposium, vol. 3,* pp. 89–112. Hillsdale, NJ: Erlbaum, 1986.

Pruzinsky, T. "Psychopathology of body experience: Expanded perspectives." In T.F. Cash and T. Pruzinsky, eds. *Body Images: Development, Deviance, and Change.* New York: Guilford, 1990.

———, and T.F. Cash. "Medical interventions for the enhancement of adolescents' physical appearance: Implications for social competence." In T.P. Gullotta, ed. *The Promotion of Social Competence in Adolescence.* New York: Sage Publications, 1990.

———. "Integrative themes in body-image development, deviance, and change." In T.F. Cash, and T. Pruzinsky, eds. *Body Images: Development, Deviance, and Change.* New York: Guilford, 1990.

Rich, M.K., and T.F. Cash. "The American image of beauty: Media representations of hair color for four decades." *Sex Roles,* vol. 29 (1993), pp. 103–14.

Rodin, J., L. Silberstein, and R. Striegel-Moore. "Women and weight: A normative discontent." *Nebraska Symposium on Motivation,* vol. 32 (1984), pp. 267–307.

Rosen, G.M., and A.O. Ross. "Relationship of body image to self-concept." *Journal of Consulting and Clinical Psychology,* vol. 32 (1968), p. 100.

Rucker, C.E., and T.F. Cash. "Body images, body-size perceptions, and eating behaviors among African-American and White college women." *International Journal of Eating Disorders,* vol. 12 (1992), pp. 291–300.

Shontz, F.C. "Body image and physical disability." In T.F. Cash and T. Pruzinsky, eds. *Body Images: Development, Deviance, and Change.* New York: Guilford, 1990.

Sigall, H., and J. Michela. "I'll bet you say that to all the girls: Physical attractiveness and reactions to praise." *Journal of Personality,* vol. 44 (1976), pp. 611–26.

Silberstein, L.R., et al. "Behavioral and psychological implications of body dissatisfaction: Do men and women differ?" *Sex Roles,* vol. 19 (1988), pp. 219–32.

Silverstein, B., et al. "The role of the mass media in promoting a thin standard of bodily attractiveness for women." *Sex Roles,* vol. 14 (1986), pp. 519–23.

——, B. Peterson, and L. Perdue. "Some correlates of the thin standard of bodily attractiveness for women." *International Journal of Eating Disorders,* vol. 5 (1986), pp. 895–905.

Snyder, M., E. Berscheid, and P. Glick. "Focusing on the exterior and the interior: Two investigations of the initiation of personal relationships." *Journal of Personality and Social Psychology,* vol. 48 (1985), pp. 1427–39.

——, E.D. Tanke, and E. Berscheid. "Social perception and interpersonal behavior: On the self-fulfilling nature of social stereotypes." *Journal of Personality and Social Psychology,* vol. 43 (1977), pp. 656–66.

Sorell, G.T., and C.G. Nowak, "The role of physical attractiveness as a contributor to individual development." In R.M. Lerner and N.A. Bush-Rossnagel, eds. *Individuals as Producers of their Development: A Life-span Perspective.* New York: Academic Press, 1981.

Striegel-Moore, R.H., L.R. Silberstein, and J. Rodin. "Toward an understanding of risk factors for bulimia." *American Psychologist,* vol. 41 (1986), pp. 246–63.

Stunkard, A.J., and V. Burt. "Obesity and body image II. Age at onset of disturbances in the body image." *American Journal of Psychiatry,* vol. 123 (1967), pp. 1443–47.

Stunkard, A.J., and M. Mendelson. "Obesity and body image I. Characteristics of disturbances in the body image of some obese persons." *American Journal of Psychiatry,* vol. 123 (1967), pp. 1296–1300.

Thompson, J.K. *Body-Image Disturbance: Assessment and Treatment.* Elmsford, NY: Pergamon Press, 1990.

———, et al. "Development and validation of the physical appearance related teasing scale." *Journal of Personality Assessment,* vol. 56 (1991), pp. 513–21.

Wolf, N. *The Beauty Myth: How Images of Beauty Are Used Against Women.* New York: Morrow, 1991.

STEP TWO: WHERE DOES IT HURT?

Discovering Your Personal Body Image

Beck, A.T. *Cognitive Therapy and the Emotional Disorders.* New York: International Universities Press, 1976.

Brown, T.A., T.F. Cash, and P.J. Mikulka. "Attitudinal body image assessment: Factor analysis of the Body-Self Relations Questionnaire." *Journal of Personality Assessment,* vol. 55 (1990), pp. 135–44.

Butters, J.W., and T.F. Cash. "Cognitive-behavioral treatment of women's body-image dissatisfaction." *Journal of Consulting and Clinical Psychology,* vol. 55 (1987), pp. 889–97.

Cash, T.F. "Body-image affect: Gestalt versus summing the parts." *Perceptual and Motor Skills,* vol. 69 (1989), pp. 17–18.

———. *Body-Image Therapy: A Program for Self-Directed Change.* New York: Guilford Publications, 1991.

———. "The Situational Inventory of Body-Image Dysphoria." *The Behavior Therapist,* vol. 17 (1994), pp. 133–34.

———, and L. Jacobi. "Looks aren't everything (to everybody): The strength of ideals of physical appearance." *Journal of Social Behavior and Personality,* vol. 7 (1992), pp. 621–30.

———, R.J. Lewis, and P. Keeton. "Development and validation of the Body-Image Automatic Thoughts Questionnaire." Paper presented at the annual meeting of the Southeastern Psychological Association, Atlanta, GA, March, 1987.

———, and M. Szymanski. "The development and validation of the Body-Image Ideals Questionnaire." *Journal of Personality Assessment,* in press.

———, B.A. Winstead, and L.H. Janda. "Your body, yourself: A *Psychology Today* reader survey." *Psychology Today,* vol. 19, no. 7 (1985), pp. 22–26.

———, B.W. Winstead, and L.H. Janda. "The great American shape-up: Body image survey report." *Psychology Today,* vol. 20, no. 4 (1986), pp. 30–37.

Grant, J., and T.F. Cash. "Cognitive-behavioral body-image therapy: Comparative efficacy of group and modest-contact treatments." *Behavior Therapy,* in press.

Jacobi, L. and T.F. Cash. "In pursuit of the perfect appearance: Discrepancies among self- and ideal-percepts of multiple physical attributes." *Journal of Applied Social Psychology,* vol. 24 (1994), pp. 379–96.

Keeton, W.P., T.F. Cash, and T.A. Brown. "Body image or body images?: Comparative, multidimensional assessment among college students." *Journal of Personality Assessment,* vol. 54 (1990), pp. 213–30.

STEP THREE: WEIGHT, WARTS, AND ALL!

Getting Comfortable with Your Body

Benson, H. *The Relaxation Response.* New York: Morrow, 1975.

Butters, J.W., and T.F. Cash. "Cognitive-behavioral treatment of women's body-image dissatisfaction." *Journal of Consulting and Clinical Psychology,* vol. 55 (1987), pp. 889–97.

Cash, T.F. *Body-Image Therapy: A Program for Self-Directed Change.* New York: Guilford, 1991.

Kanfer, F., and A. Goldstein. *Helping People Change.* New York: Pergamon, 1980.

Lazarus, A.A. *Behavior Therapy and Beyond.* New York: McGraw-Hill, 1971.

———. *In the Mind's Eye: The Power of Imagery for Personal Enrichment.* New York: Rawson, 1977.

Mahoney, M.J., and C.E. Thoresen. *Self-Control: Power to the Person.* Monterey, CA: Brooks/Cole, 1974.

Wolpe, J. *The Practice of Behavior Therapy.* Oxford: Pergamon Press, 1969.

STEP FOUR: REASONABLE DOUBT

Questioning Your Appearance Assumptions

Beck, A.T. *Cognitive Therapy and the Emotional Disorders.* New York: International Universities Press, 1976.

Cash, T.F. *Body-Image Therapy: A Program for Self-Directed Change.* New York: Guilford, 1991.

———, and A. Labarge. "The development and validation of the Appearance Schemas Inventory." Unpublished manuscript, Old Dominion University, Norfolk, VA, 1993.

Ellis, A. *Techniques for Disputing Irrational Beliefs.* New York: Institute for Rational Living, Inc., 1977.

———, and R. Grieger, eds. *Handbook of Rational Emotive Therapy.* New York: Springer, 1977.

———, and R. Harper. *A New Guide to Rational Living,* 2nd ed., Hollywood, CA: Wilshire Books, 1975.

Guidano, V.F., and G. Liotti. *Cognitive Processes and Emotional Disorders.* New York: Guilford, 1983.

Langer, E.J. *Mindfulness.* Reading, MA: Addison-Wesley, 1989.

Lazarus, R.S., and S. Folkman. *Stress, Appraisal, and Coping.* New York: Springer, 1984.

Markus, H. "Self-schemata and processing information about the self." *Journal of Personality and Social Psychology,* vol. 35 (1977), pp. 63–78.

McMullin, R.E. *Handbook of Cognitive Therapy Techniques.* New York: Norton, 1986.

Segal, Z.V., and S.J. Blatt, eds. *The Self in Emotional Distress: Cognitive and Psychodynamic Perspectives.* New York: Guilford, 1993.

Young, J.E. *Cognitive Therapy for Personality Disorders: A Schema-Focused Approach.* Sarasota, FL: Professional Resource Exchange, Inc., 1990.

STEP FIVE: CRITICAL THINKING

Correcting Your Body-Image Errors

Beck, A.T. *Cognitive Therapy and the Emotional Disorders.* New York: International Universities Press, 1976.

Burns, D. *The Feeling Good Handbook: Using the New Mood Therapy in Everyday Life.* New York: Morrow, 1989.

Butters, J.W., and T.F. Cash. "Cognitive-behavioral treatment of women's body-image dissatisfaction." *Journal of Consulting and Clinical Psychology,* vol. 55 (1987), pp. 889–97.

Cash, T.F. *Body-Image Therapy: A Program for Self-Directed Change.* New York: Guilford, 1991.

———. "The development and validation of the Private Body Talk Questionnaire." Unpublished research, Old Dominion University, Norfolk, VA, 1992.

———, D.W. Cash, and J. Butters. " 'Mirror, mirror, on the wall . . . ?' Contrast effects and self-evaluations of physical attractiveness." *Personality and Social Psychology Bulletin,* vol. 9 (1983), pp. 351–58.

———, and M. Szymanski. "The development and validation of the

Body-Image Ideals Questionnaire." *Journal of Personality Assessment,* in press.

Ellis, A. *Techniques for Disputing Irrational Beliefs.* New York: Institute for Rational Living, Inc., 1977.

McMullin, R.E. *Handbook of Cognitive Therapy Techniques.* New York: Norton, 1986.

Rimm, D.C., and J.C. Masters. *Behavior Therapy: Techniques and Empirical Findings.* New York: Academic Press, 1974.

STEP SIX: YOUR OWN WORST ENEMY

Defeating Your Self-Defeating Behavior

Bandura, A. "Self-efficacy: Toward a unifying theory of behavior change." *Psychological Review,* vol. 84 (1977), pp. 191–215.

———. *Social Learning Theory.* Englewood Cliffs, NJ: Prentice-Hall, 1977.

Beck, A.T., and G. Emery. *Anxiety Disorders and Phobias: A Cognitive Perspective.* New York: Guilford, 1985.

Cash, T.F. *Body-Image Therapy: A Program for Self-Directed Change.* New York: Guilford, 1991.

———. "Understanding and changing body images: A cognitive-behavioral approach." Symposium presentation at the annual convention of the American Psychological Association, Washington, D.C., 1992.

Kanfer, F., and A. Goldstein. *Helping People Change.* New York: Pergamon, 1980.

Marks, I.M. *Fears, Phobias, and Rituals.* New York: Oxford University Press, 1987.

Meichenbaum, D. *Stress Inoculation Training.* Elmsford, New York: Pergamon, 1987.

Steketee, G., and K. White. *When Once Is Not Enough: Help for Obsessive-Compulsives.* Oakland, CA: New Harbinger, 1990.

STEP SEVEN: MORE THAN SKIN DEEP

Treating Your Body Right

Beck, A.T. *Cognitive Therapy and the Emotional Disorders.* New York: International Universities Press, 1976.

Cash, T.F. "The psychology of cosmetics: A review of the scientific literature." *Social and Behavioral Sciences Documents,* vol. 17, no. 1 (1987), MS# 2800.

————. "The psychology of cosmetics: A research bibliography." *Perceptual and Motor Skills,* vol. 66 (1988), pp. 455–60.

————. "The psychology of physical appearance: Aesthetics, attributes, and images." In T.F. Cash and T. Pruzinsky, eds. *Body Images: Development, Deviance, and Change.* New York: Guilford, 1990.

————. *Body-Image Therapy: A Program for Self-Directed Change.* New York: Guilford, 1991.

————, and D.W. Cash. "Women's use of cosmetics: Psychosocial correlates and consequences." *International Journal of Cosmetic Science,* vol. 4 (1982), pp. 1–14.

————, et al. "The effects of cosmetics use on the physical attractiveness and body image of college women." *Journal of Social Psychology,* vol. 129 (1989), pp. 349–56.

————, P. Novy, and J. Grant. "Why do women exercise?: Factor analysis and further validation of the Reasons for Exercise Inventory." *Perceptual and Motor Skills,* vol. 78 (1994), pp. 539–44.

————, J. Rissi, and R. Chapman. "Not just another pretty face: Sex roles, locus of control, and cosmetics use." *Personality and Social Psychology Bulletin,* vol. 11 (1985), pp. 246–57.

————, and J.M. Wunderle. "Self-monitoring and cosmetics use among college women." *Journal of Social Behavior and Personality,* vol. 4 (1987), pp. 563–66.

Fisher, E., and J.K. Thompson. "A comparison of cognitive-behavioral therapy versus exercise therapy for the treatment of body-image disturbance: Preliminary findings." *Behavior Modification,* vol. 18 (1994), pp. 171–85.

Hensley, S., and T.F. Cash. "Effects of aerobic exercise on state and trait body image." Unpublished research, Old Dominion University, Norfolk, VA, 1994.

Kanfer, F., and A. Goldstein. *Helping People Change.* New York: Pergamon, 1980.

Morgan, W.P. "Negative addiction in runners." *Physical Sports Medicine,* vol. 7 (1979), pp. 57–70.

———, et al. "Monitoring of overtraining and staleness." *British Journal of Sports Medicine,* vol. 21, no. 3 (1987), pp. 107–14.

Pruzinsky, T., and T.F. Cash. "Integrative themes in body-image development, deviance, and change." In T.F. Cash, and T. Pruzinsky, eds. *Body Images: Development, Deviance, and Change.* New York: Guilford, 1990.

Rodin, J. *Body Traps.* New York: Morrow, 1992.

Yates, A. *Compulsive Exercise and the Eating Disorders: Toward an Integrated Theory of Activity.* New York: Brunner/Mazel, 1991.

STEP EIGHT: HAPPILY EVER AFTER

Maintaining Your Positive Body Image for Life

Alberti, R.E., and M. Emmons. *Your Perfect Right,* rev. ed., San Luis Obispo, CA: Impact Press, 1974.

American Society for Plastic and Reconstructive Surgery. *Data on the frequency of various cosmetic procedures.* Arlington Heights, IL: Author, 1993.

Bernstein, N.R. "Objective bodily damage: Disfigurement and dignity." In T.F. Cash and T. Pruzinsky, eds. *Body Images: Development, Deviance, and Change.* New York: Guilford, 1990.

Bower, S.A., and G.H. Bower. *Asserting Your Self.* Reading, MA: Addison-Wesley, 1976.

Breslau, A. "The beauty of disfigurement." In R.E. Bochat, ed. *Special Faces: Understanding Facial Disfigurement.* New York: National Foundation for Facial Reconstruction, 1992.

Brownell, K.D. "Dieting and the search for the perfect body: Where physiology and culture collide." *Behavior Therapy,* vol. 22 (1991), pp. 1–12.

——, and T.A. Wadden. "Behavior therapy for obesity: Modern approaches and better results." In K.D. Brownell & J.P. Foreyt, eds. *Handbook of Eating Disorders.* New York: Basic Books, 1986.

——. "The heterogeneity of obesity: Fitting treatments to individuals." *Behavior Therapy,* vol. 22 (1991), pp. 153–77.

Bull, R., and N. Rumsey. *The Social Psychology of Facial Appearance.* New York: Springer-Verlag, 1988.

Butters, J.W., and T.F. Cash. "Cognitive-behavioral treatment of women's body-image dissatisfaction." *Journal of Consulting and Clinical Psychology,* vol. 55 (1987), pp. 889–97.

Cash, T.F. "Body image and weight changes in a multisite comprehensive very-low-calorie diet program." *Behavior Therapy,* vol. 25 (1994), pp. 239–54.

——. "Body-image attitudes among obese enrollees in a commercial weight-loss program." *Perceptual and Motor Skills,* vol. 77 (1993), pp. 1099–1103.

——. "Body-image therapy for persons with facial disfigurement: A cognitive-behavioral approach." In R.E. Bochat, ed. *Special Faces: Understanding Facial Disfigurement.* New York: National Foundation for Facial Reconstruction, 1992.

——. "Body images and body weight: What is there to gain or lose?" *Weight Control Digest,* vol. 2, no. 4 (1992), pp. 169ff.

——. *Body-Image Therapy: A Program for Self-Directed Change.* New York: Guilford, 1991.

——. "The psychology of physical appearance: Aesthetics, attributes, and images." In T.F. Cash and T. Pruzinsky, eds. *Body images: Development, Deviance, and Change.* New York: Guilford, 1990.

——, et al. "Current and vestigial effects of overweight among women: Fear of fat, attitudinal body image, and eating behaviors." *Journal of Psychopathology and Behavioral Assessment,* vol. 12 (1990), pp. 157–67.

——, and K.L. Hicks. "Being fat versus thinking fat: Relationships with body image, eating behaviors, and well-being." *Cognitive Therapy and Research,* vol. 14 (1990), pp. 327–41.

———, and C.E. Horton. "Aesthetic surgery: Effects of rhinoplasty on the social perception of patients by others." *Plastic and Reconstructive Surgery,* vol. 72 (1983), pp. 543–48.

———, et al. "Your body, yourself: A *Psychology Today* reader survey." *Psychology Today,* vol. 19, no. 7 (1985), pp. 22–26.

———. "The great American shape-up: Body image survey report." *Psychology Today,* vol. 20, no. 4 (1986), pp. 30–37.

Garner, D.M., and S.C. Wooley. "Confronting the failure of behavioral and dietary treatments for obesity. *Clinical Psychology Review,* vol. 11 (1991), pp. 729–80.

Goin, J.M., and M.K. Goin. *Changing the Body: Psychological Effects of Plastic Surgery.* Baltimore, MD: Williams & Wilkens, 1981.

Jeffery, R.W. "Behavioral treatment of obesity." *Annals of Behavioral Medicine,* vol. 9 (1987), pp. 20–24.

Kanfer, F., and A. Goldstein. *Helping People Change.* New York: Pergamon, 1980.

Kayman, S., et al. "Maintenance and relapse after weight loss in women: Behavioral aspects." *American Journal of Clinical Nutrition,* vol. 52 (1990), pp. 800–807.

Let's Face It. *Resources for People with Facial Difference.* Concord, MA: Author, 1994.

Marlatt, G.A., and J. Gordon. *Relapse Prevention: A Self-Control Strategy for the Maintenance of Behavior Change.* New York: Guilford, 1984.

Meichenbaum, D. *Stress Inoculation Training.* Elmsford, New York: Pergamon, 1985.

Pertschuk, M.J. "Reconstructive surgery: Objective change of objective deformity." In T.F. Cash and T. Pruzinsky, eds. *Body Images: Development, Deviance, and Change.* New York: Guilford, 1990.

Polivy, J., and P. Herman. *Breaking the Diet Habit.* New York: Basic Books, 1983.

Pruzinsky, T., and M. Edgerton. "Body-image change in cosmetic plastic surgery." In T.F. Cash and T. Pruzinsky, eds. *Body Images: Development, Deviance, and Change.* New York: Guilford, 1990.

Rodin, J. *Body Traps.* New York: Morrow, 1992.

——, L. Silberstein, and R. Striegel-Moore. "Women and weight: A normative discontent." *Nebraska Symposium on Motivation,* vol. 32 (1984), pp. 267–307.

Seligman, M.E.P. *Helplessness: On Depression, Development, and Death.* San Francisco, CA: Freeman, 1975.

Shontz, F.C. "Body image and physical disability." In T.F. Cash and T. Pruzinsky, eds. *Body Images: Development, Deviance, and Change.* New York: Guilford, 1990.

Steinem, G. *Revolution from Within: A Book of Self-Esteem.* Boston, MA: Little, Brown and Company, 1992.

Wadden, T.A., A.J. Stunkard, and J. Liebschutz. "Three-year follow-up of the treatment of obesity by very low calorie diet, behavior therapy, and their combination." *Journal of Consulting and Clinical Psychology,* vol. 56 (1988), pp. 925–28.

Wooley, W., and S. Wooley. "Feeling fat in a thin society." *Glamour,* (Feb. 1984), pp. 198–201.